"Today, car companies test electric and fuel cell cars by loaning them to real drivers. Who knew that in the 1950s and 'ŏus companies handed out futuristic jet cars? Steve Lehto's book tells the fascinating and compelling story of Chrysler's turbine cars in the jet age."

—PHIL PATTON, author of *Bug: The Strange Mutations of the World's Most Famous Automobile*

"This book is not for just the automotive minded; it is actually a nice little piece of America that will interest a wide audience. . . . Highly recommended."

—*CHOICE*

"Steve Lehto's lively history of Chrysler's turbine car program is a must-read for anyone interested in the history of the automobile in the jet age. . . . Lehto's engaging narrative offers a revealing glimpse into the world of automotive R&D at a time when the Big Three's power, influence, and creativity were at their zenith. . . . A story of bold engineering and bold predictions of a future that never was, *Chrysler's Turbine Car* is a valuable contribution that deserves a place on the shelves of historians and enthusiasts alike."

—DAVID N. LUCSKO, author of *The Business of Speed*

"Lehto covers every angle. . . . Should this book make it to your shelf? Absolutely." —*OLD CARS WEEKLY*

"Steve Lehto tirelessly researched Chrysler's turbine car to write a book that reads like an insider's account of the automaker's most ambitious design and engineering project. This is the tale of how Chrysler's attempt to merge the jet age with the automobile's century clashed with the automaker's chronic struggle as the rockiest among Detroit's Big Three. A relevant tale for our age."

—TODD LASSA, editor, *Motor Trend*

"This is a love letter to an automobile, but it's also an obituary of progress. The Chrysler Turbine Car embodied the elegant simplicity of progress. Steve Lehto gives a fascinating account of what kills elegant simplicity: cost, of course, and corporate muddle and, most lethal of all, government bureaucracy."

—P. J. O'ROURKE, author of *Driving Like Crazy*

Chrysler's Turbine Car

THE RISE AND FALL OF DETROIT'S COOLEST CREATION

STEVE LEHTO

CHICAGO
REVIEW
PRESS

First hardcover edition published 2010
First paperback edition published 2012
Published by Chicago Review Press, Incorporated
814 North Franklin Street
Chicago, Illinois 60610

ISBN 978-1-61374-345-4

The Library of Congress has cataloged the hardcover edition as follows:
Lehto, Steve.
Chrysler's turbine car : the rise and fall of Detroit's coolest creation / Steve Lehto.
p. cm.
Includes bibliographical references and index.
ISBN 978-1-56976-549-4
1. Chrysler automobile—History—20th century. 2. Experimental automobiles—
History—20th century. 3. Automobiles, Gas-turbine—History—20th century. I. Title.
TL215.C55L47 2010
629.222—dc22

Cover design: John Yates at Stealworks.com
Front cover photo: Bill Carry and the Ghia Turbine; Chrysler photo, courtesy of
Bill Carry
Interior design: Sarah Olson

Printed in the United States of America

For Jennifer,
and my brothers:
Ken, Bruce, Dave, Rick, and Tim

Contents

Foreword BY JAY LENO

In 1964, when I was fourteen years old, my family visited the World's Fair in New York. I wasn't old enough to drive yet, but I already loved cars, and I had heard about two that were going to be on display there. One was the new Ford Mustang, which, quite frankly, was the worst-kept secret in Detroit—there were plenty of pictures of that around. The second was the Chrysler Turbine Car, which was far more interesting. It had a totally new and different powerplant that had never been put in an automobile before: a jet engine. To be honest, I don't remember all that much about the Mustang from the World's Fair. But I remember *everything* about the Chrysler Turbine Car.

Chrysler had a huge display at the Fair, and the centerpiece was a small track where they were giving rides in the car. The lines to ride in the car were long, so I simply walked over to the edge of the area and looked at the car. Everything about the car was memorable. It had the lines of a space age car—not like the silly fins of cars from the 1950s—and even its turbine-bronze paint was unique. When the car started up and drove around the track, the sound it made was unlike anything I'd ever heard before. I watched it and was in awe. Would they be building and selling these cars by the time I got my driver's license? I hoped so.

Every magazine from *Popular Mechanics* to *Hot Rod* had articles about this car. "Will the Piston Engine Be Obsolete in Ten Years?" "Is This the Automobile of the Future?" At a time when the rest of the world was just getting piston-engine cars, America was moving on to jet-powered automobiles! Then, suddenly, the whole thing disappeared. Within a brief span of two or three years, all talk of turbine cars was gone. What happened? Where did they go? As the years passed, I learned that most had been destroyed by Chrysler. Why?

I finally achieved my dream of owning one of these cars in 2009. I found it to be a practical, quiet, and nice running automobile that could run on a number of different fuels. Tequila, diesel, perfume—anything that would burn with oxygen could fuel this car. What happened to this amazing automobile? In this book, Steve Lehto gives the most detailed and in-depth analysis of the engineers behind this program and their amazing auto. Here is the story of what happened to their dream of building a gas-turbine car.

Introduction

On a blustery December day in 1953, George Huebner Jr. and his fellow engineers at Chrysler rolled a top-secret car out of a garage in Highland Park, Michigan. No one outside Chrysler knew the car existed. In fact, it was hardly known *within* Chrysler. The 1954 Plymouth Belvedere didn't appear special until it was started. First a high-pitched whine, then a whooshing roar, split the cold air. It sounded like a jet. Powered by a jet turbine engine, the car roared without vibration.

———

Over the next two decades, Huebner and his engineers from the Chrysler Turbine Lab would build more than seventy "jet" cars, including a fleet of fifty that would be lent to the public in an unprecedented publicity campaign. The plan worked to perfection as the cars logged over a million trouble-free miles on five different continents.

The turbine engines required some unusual manufacturing processes, but the team hoped those issues, which would be quite expensive to resolve, could be addressed after they had proved the viability of the turbine cars. The cars also offered a solution to a problem that even Huebner and his colleagues could not have foreseen: the cars ran on any flammable liquid. Not just gasoline but diesel, kerosene, jet fuel, peanut oil, alcohol, tequila, perfume, and many other substances fueled Huebner's turbine cars at one time or another. Because this was pre-OPEC—and no one could have guessed that gasoline would ever cost more than a fraction of a dollar a gallon—the car's ability to burn a wide range of fuels was largely overlooked.

How different would America be now if we all drove turbine-powered cars? It could have happened. But government interference, shortsighted regulators, and indifferent corporate leaders each played a role in the demise of a program that could have lessened U.S. dependence on Middle East oil.

The Promise of the Jet Age

In the decades following World War II, the jet engine symbolized new technology that would propel the average American into the life of the future. After all, the cartoon "stone age family" was the Flintstones; the "space age family" was the Jetsons. Cars wore jetlike tailfins and other design touches to make them look as if they were designed by NASA and might wander off the planet one day. In 1962, John F. Kennedy announced to the world that America would lead the space race by sending a man to the moon and back. Science and technology were making promises that attracted attention and sparked imaginations. Soon, it seemed, we could all travel by rockets and jets.

The jet turbine, in its most basic form, is a relatively simple concept. Imagine a tube with a fan at the front—the "compressor" rotor—and a fan at the back—the "turbine" rotor. Run a shaft through them both, spray fuel between the rotors, inside the tube, and ignite it. When the air and fuel ignite, the combustion gives off hot gases, which expand and force their way past the turbine rotor. This causes the shaft connecting the rotors to turn, spinning the compressor at the front end of the tube. The compressor rotor will draw in fresh air and, as the blades gain speed, push more air into the combustion chamber. As more air gets forced into the chamber, the reaction becomes increasingly stronger; the rotors reach amazing speeds if everything is set up right. The exhaust from this contraption can put out enough thrust to push something as large as an airplane. Direct the exhaust at another set of fan blades that turn a gear set and the turbine can run a variety of devices: boats, trains, generators—even automobiles.

The jet turbine developed rapidly during World War II, largely driven by British and German research. Each country claimed an inventor with a patent on a jet turbine engine. Britain's Frank Whittle patented his design in 1930, while Germany's Hans von Ohain registered his with the German patent office in 1936. Both countries rushed to develop a turbine engine that could create enough thrust to power an airplane just as they went to war against each other. The later patent date of the German engine didn't reflect who flew first; the Luftwaffe put a jet aircraft into flight in 1939 and was using operational fighter jets in 1943. The British got theirs off the ground a couple of years after the Germans, and the jet race was on. Soon, inspired by the successes of the British and Germans, engineers around the globe were developing turbine technology.

Chrysler began researching turbines in the late 1930s, for both civilian and military use. Its leader in this field was a brilliant engineer named George Huebner Jr. Huebner had been born in Detroit in 1910 and seemed destined to work in the auto industry. His grandfather had sold parts to Henry Ford and, not believing in credit, had required Ford to pay "cash on the barrel head" for all parts delivered. His father was a stockbroker who published *Tooling and Production* magazine while Huebner was growing up. Huebner told interviewers he began tinkering with cars when he was ten, around the time he decided he wanted to be an engineer. A family legend told of how the ten-year-old Huebner came across a stranded motorist with his car in a ditch near the family cottage at Port Huron. Huebner asked the man if he needed help getting his car restarted. The motorist handed his keys to the confident young man, apparently not believing the car would be going anywhere before he returned with a tow truck. As the motorist walked away, Huebner popped the hood and soon had the car running again. He pulled it onto the road and drove it to the nearest driveway, where he left it for the motorist to find later.

Huebner did so well in school that he skipped a few grades and enrolled at the University of Michigan at the age of sixteen. At first he studied economics, thinking he might follow in his father's footsteps and become a broker. But he soon turned his attention to engineering. Before he obtained his degree, he began working for Chrysler. He eventually completed his mechanical engineering degree from Michigan by taking classes in his spare time.

Among the projects Huebner worked on at Chrysler was the A-86 aircraft turbine project. The A-86 was a turboprop aircraft—an airplane with propellers driven by jet engines. Although the fighter plane in which the engine was installed flew successfully, World War II ended shortly thereafter and further plans for its use were scrapped.

During the immediate postwar era, most engineers thought jet turbines, though fine for aircraft, would not be suitable for use in cars. Their main reasons were that the engines could never be made small enough to fit under a car's hood, that turbines burn too much fuel, and that the exotic materials needed for the intricate parts would be too expensive. But Huebner and some of the other engineers he worked with thought otherwise. Even as they worked on traditional automobile powerplants, Huebner and his colleagues would sit around, often after hours, discussing the possibilities of a turbine-powered car.

The British hadn't quit working on turbines after the war, and they were leading the way in placing one under the hood of a car. A 1950 *Motor Trend* article entitled "Will Gas Turbines Propel the Car of Tomorrow?" began with the sentence: "There's no reason why not. That's right . . . none." Lightness and simplicity were obvious advantages. The gas turbine weighed less than a piston engine of equivalent strength, and it had far fewer moving parts. It was also easier to work on and burned a wider range of fuels. The arguments laid out in the article were so compelling that a reader might have thought the piston engine was doomed.

And research was being conducted worldwide, according to the article. A company in Czechoslovakia was developing a turbine-powered car. The

French were said to have a working prototype. The British had several companies racing ahead on developing a turbine car, including the venerable Land Rover. In the United States, even Boeing was known to be working on an automotive gas turbine. *Motor Trend* noted that the firms working on the engines were "all airplane manufacturers . . . and they're the ones who are making no secret of their gas turbine research. But we can be sure that NO major auto manufacturer is ignoring the new power source in [its] plans for the future."

Motor Trend didn't know about the clandestine turbine research being conducted in Highland Park, Michigan, by George Huebner and company. Bud Mann, an engineer who worked on turbines at Chrysler for over thirty years, later said,

> The A-86 program [for military aircraft] fueled an idea that had been germinating in the minds of several Chrysler Research engineers for some time. Chief among them were Sam Williams, Dave Borden, and Bill Chapman, all dedicated engineers entranced with the notion that the smooth power surge of a turbine would provide an incredible experience in a passenger automobile. But the outstanding character and moving force of that program was George Huebner. He made this project his whole career, perhaps even to the detriment of others, which should have received a bigger share of the research pie. But, right or wrong, it is clear that the project could not have gone nearly as far as it did without a person of his dedication and personality.

At the time of the turbine program, Huebner was Chrysler's director of research, an office he had achieved by climbing steadily through the ranks at the automaker. In 1946 he had been named chief engineer of Chrysler, and he marked his tenure by placing more emphasis on the basics—chemistry, metallurgy, and physics. He was an early adopter of the electron microscope and the computer; he was even given an award by the Society of Automotive Engineers for his use of the computer in 1959.

Huebner also did not confine his work to automobiles. He spent time with Chrysler's missile program—in the 1950s and '60s Chrysler built guided missiles for the U.S. government—and he helped develop a turbo-prop engine for the military. The turboprop engine coupled a jet engine with a gearbox and a large propeller.

Huebner sat down with his engineers and laid out the project as he saw it. He led them methodically through the process of bringing the concept to a practical conclusion. The first step compared the characteristics of air-craft to the requirements of an automotive engine. The result was sober-ing, according to Mann. "Aircraft turbines consume six to eight times as much air as a piston engine; in the process, they devour fuel like sharks in a school of tuna; hot end materials are very exotic; cost is generally of little or no consequence." Worst of all, "There is no such thing as 'light load'—they don't idle worth a damn." The reference to cost referred to how, up until this point, turbines had been developed by the military, with its almost limitless budget. The same would not be true for Chrysler, whose engi-neers would have to find ways to design an economically feasible engine. Huebner divided the engineering hurdles they faced into categories of descending difficulty. The first category was a set of engineering problems that "looked impossible and which would require early solution before we could concede even to ourselves that we had a possibility" of success.

———

Huebner would become known as the father of Chrysler's turbine pro-gram, and almost all photographic evidence of the era contains images of Huebner standing near his turbines, grinning like a proud father. But while Huebner was the one who shepherded the program through Chrys-ler, it was an engineer named Sam B. Williams who overcame the techni-cal obstacles of making the automotive turbine viable.

Williams was born in Seattle in 1921. He attended Purdue University, where he obtained a doctorate in mechanical engineering. He came to Chrysler during the war. Everyone knew him as Doctor Williams, but his closest friends called him Sam. Although he worked closely with the flamboyant Huebner, Williams couldn't have been more different in his demeanor. Bad eyesight forced him to commit large quantities of data to memory, and he often spoke softly. In later years an interviewer, when he asked a colleague why Williams didn't speak more loudly, was told Williams didn't need to speak up. People listened to him; he was a "man used to being listened to." Visitors to his office in later years would ask about the rows of mini-cassette tapes he had lined up on his desk. Was he dictating letters faster than his secretary could type? No, his assistant would record himself reading technical journals and give the tapes to Dr. Williams. That way he could stay on top of the latest advances in the industry. On one occasion, a journalist insisted on an interview with Williams, and he finally relented. The writer hurried to town only to find Williams away on "last minute" business. He got a great tour of the facility where Williams manufactured jet engines and spoke to Williams on the phone, but he never knew if Williams had simply dodged him.

One of the first tasks Williams tackled was developing a turboprop engine for the U.S. Navy. Williams became fascinated by the concept of the turbine engine. He knew it was simpler than a piston engine and had fewer parts, and he believed it could be scaled up or down depending on the needs of the project. By 1946, Williams was submitting patent applications to Washington describing his improvements on the gas turbine powerplant; before he was done he held seventy-six patents on turbine engines.

Williams had no doubt that the turbine could be scaled smaller to fit into a car. Through innovation and invention, Williams and his engineers worked through all the problems others saw with the automotive turbine. After eight or nine years on the automotive project, Huebner and Williams rolled out a working turbine-powered automobile in 1953.

Was the end near for the piston-engine auto? *Motor Trend* thought so. In 1950 it had written:

> The competitive life-expectancy of the good old internal combustion engine is predictably short. As so often happens in history, first solutions to problems are complicated ones, steadily simplified in practice until, one day, the original solution has only historical interest. At any rate, prepare to welcome the greatest prime mover development since Watt harnessed the teakettle and un-harnessed the horse.

———

Bud Mann joined the team in 1950. Mann had been teaching mechanical engineering at Lawrence Institute of Technology in Southfield, Michigan, for three years when he decided to stop talking about engineering and go out and actually do some. He applied for a job at Chrysler because of its gas turbine program. The job didn't promise much career advancement, but the area of work was cutting edge. He found the assignment challenging, calling upon everything he had learned in school and as a professor.

One of Mann's first assignments was to spin turbine wheel discs to destruction in a lead-lined "spin pit" and study the resulting "garbage" for clues as to how to improve the design. "My reputation as 'chief trash picker' grew with each bursting wheel. Bill Chapman and I still carry mementos of one spectacular test when the lid of the spin chamber lifted, oh so briefly, at the instant of failure. We spent two rather painful hours in Chrysler's medical office while a nurse gingerly picked tiny bits of lead and high nickel alloy from our arms and bellies."

On another occasion, Mann ran a prototype turbine inside a test cell. The turbine's internal parts were those they were considering using, but the makeshift housing of the unit was sheet metal. If everything ran fine, they'd eventually make the housing sturdier. Mann ran the engine up to full speed and watched the gauges of his dynamometer. Suddenly there was an explosion as a piece of the power turbine blasted through the side of the sheet metal housing and punched a hole in a nearby wall. Mann duly noted there was a flaw in the turbine wheel, grateful that the piece of turbine wheel hadn't flown his way on its exit from the turbine.

———

Before 1950, the United States was self-sufficient with respect to energy. In other words, it was capable of manufacturing or producing as much energy as it needed. If it chose to buy oil from Saudi Arabia or some other faraway place, it was only because the price was right. Gasoline prices stayed low and petroleum was plentiful. Nobody gave much thought to fueling up the huge cars of the day while gasoline prices routinely hovered below twenty-five cents a gallon. The writing was on the wall, though. In 1947, the United States had exported more oil than it imported. By 1950, it was importing more oil than it was exporting. Once the situation tipped, there was no coming back.

Meanwhile, the turbine team at Chrysler forged ahead with their research and testing. One of the biggest problems they tackled was to find a way to recover a large part of the wasted exhaust heat from the engine, because that was a major drain on the engine's efficiency. One solution recycled the heat that ran through the turbine by way of a heat exchanger. Mann pointed out:

> Their selection of a rotating disc, a "regenerator," was about the last thing one would expect because of the complexity of building, sealing, and driving it. But their choice was prompted by the need to recover as much energy as possible, and the regenerator is potentially the best of all heat exchangers with effectiveness percentages in the mid-'90s. By heating the air entering the burner, it reduced the amount of fuel added to achieve the required turbine inlet temperature. At full power, this device saved about 50 percent of the fuel that would have been needed without it. And at idle and light load, where an automotive engine spends most of its life, it saved 70 to 80 percent of the fuel otherwise required. That's the plus side.

The downside was the complexity of building a working regenerator. The engineers took a piece of stainless steel 3 inches wide, only 0.004 inch thick, and 120 feet long, and wound it into a disk 2 feet in diameter. The material was relatively light, but it offered a huge surface area in a small space that could transfer a lot of heat. Sealing off the disk so that the hot air didn't just go around it was another problem the team had to—and would—solve through precision machining and the use of exotic metals Dr. Amedee Roy developed that could be finished so smoothly the parts did not need separate seals.

The "regenerator package was probably the most irritatingly persistent problem throughout the thirty-five-year life of Chrysler's gas turbine program," according to Mann, especially when the team was told they had to make it work and make it inexpensive. Having tackled other seemingly impossible tasks on this project, the team dealt with the regenerators and made them work.

Huebner spent most of his time shepherding the turbine project along, but others within the corporation called on his expertise from time to time. In the 1950s, the U.S. government rushed to get a satellite into orbit, developing the Redstone rocket program to launch it. Chrysler convinced the government that it could provide some of the best engineering minds and facilities for the project, and soon Huebner found himself visiting Huntsville, Alabama, the epicenter of the space program at the time. There he met and worked with the famous German rocket scientist Werner von Braun. Photos from the period show the two, attired similarly with ties and long-sleeved dress shirts, standing side by side examining rocket parts.

Never one to miss an opportunity to promote his work at Chrysler, Huebner wrote an article about his rocket adventures for *Boys' Life* magazine in which he explained what happened in "count-down land," starting with an early morning alarm clock and leading up to the thrill of watching the rocket launch, what he described as "the most dramatic, stirring event that man has ever seen." It was a rare article for Huebner in that he never mentioned the turbine engine.

Meanwhile, the turbine team finally developed an engine they felt confident enough about to actually place in a car. They dropped it into an otherwise stock 1954 Plymouth Belvedere. They marked the occasion by gathering around the car—thirty-five of the people who had worked on the car to this point—and pausing to have their picture taken. In this photo the turbine is frozen in the air, being lowered into the engine compartment of the car. Sam Williams stands next to the car; Huebner is standing nearby. At six feet tall, he is easy to spot among the group of men wearing suits and ties.

2

Chrysler's First "Jet" Car

On March 25, 1954, Chrysler—and Huebner—decided it was time to unveil its first automotive turbine–powered car to the public. Testing and research had accomplished much in the laboratory, but Huebner knew the truth lay in how the car performed on the open road. And despite the fact that the engine was stuffed into an otherwise stock 1954 Plymouth Belvedere, it would have been next to impossible to test the car on the road without people noticing the bizarre jetlike sounds it made. Huebner also saw a potential publicity bonanza: it was the first time in history that a production car was powered by a turbine engine.

Chrysler made the announcement in a press release "For Use in Afternoon Papers of Thursday, March 25, 1954." One paper that ran the release almost word for word was the *Detroit News*. The article explained how Chrysler's turbine car had comparable fuel economy to other, piston-engine cars, cooler exhaust, and better performance than cars with engines of similar horsepower. Among other highlights mentioned in the article was the fact that the Chrysler turbine had fewer than 20 percent of the parts of a conventional piston engine, and it weighed two hundred pounds less.

The photograph accompanying many of the first turbine car stories showed the Plymouth Belvedere next to a Chrysler garage in Highland Park, Michigan, surrounded by photographers and reporters. In most of the photos, Huebner either posed behind the wheel or stood next to the car—always grinning. In those days, even the reporters who appeared in the backgrounds of the photos wore suits, ties, overcoats, and hats. Huebner's was unquestionably the most expensive suit in any given photo. Still, the photos couldn't do justice to the scene; the real story was the car's engine whooshing like a quietly idling jetliner. Sam Williams can be seen sitting in the backseat of the car in some photos. No doubt he was smiling too.

Buried deep in the press release and article was a single sentence pointing out an odd feature of the engine, though not so interesting at a time when gasoline was twenty-five cents per gallon: "However, any of a wide range of petroleum fuels may be used, from gasoline to heavy fuel oil." It would be a year or two before someone thought of trying to run the turbine on other flammable novelty liquids such as tequila or perfume.

Chrysler recycled the language of the press release into a trifold pamphlet, boasting "Progress in Science." The text was reprinted almost verbatim, punctuated by a few photos of the turbine car and its engine. Huebner appears in a couple of the photos, although, inexplicably, he is not smiling. In one photograph where everyone else wears lab coats, though, Huebner is wearing his characteristic suit.

Not only was he a scientist—he eventually held forty patents—Huebner was also quite a promoter. He always managed to get journalists and photographers to events where the turbine car would make an appearance. He appeared in almost every photograph of the turbine cars—at least the ones with people in them—and some on the team noted that he certainly didn't "lack for ego." A natty dresser with overflowing charisma, Huebner came across almost as if he were royalty. Rumor within the department said he came from a moneyed background, but they didn't know for sure. Huebner may have even encouraged the speculation. But it didn't really matter; Huebner was great at his job, which was keeping the turbine project on the front burner at Chrysler.

Sam Williams left Chrysler at this time. Although Chrysler was continuing its turbine research for automobiles, Williams envisioned a broader range of applications for small turbines. He started his own company, Williams Research, which began developing turbine engines for boats, cars, aircraft, and cruise missiles. Williams and his company often developed or improved things others thought impossible. When Bell Aerospace built a rocket belt that a person could fly for twenty seconds, Williams built his own jet pack—turbine-powered, of course—that could fly for ten minutes.

Williams Research soon became a major supplier of engines to the jet aircraft industry and the military. In later years it would be renamed Williams International. Dr. Williams drew on his experience with the Chrysler automobile program, creating smaller, lighter, and more efficient jet engines than anyone thought possible. Williams eventually introduced an engine called the FJX-2; it weighed eighty-five pounds and produced seven hundred pounds of thrust.

On June 16, 1954, Chrysler brought the turbine car out for the dedication of the Chrysler proving grounds at Chelsea, Michigan. The proving grounds were huge—Chrysler bragged that it was the largest such facility in the world—and Chrysler invited anyone with press credentials to come out and see the huge track. The turbine was the showpiece of the day. Chrysler sat the press corps in a grandstand along one of the straightaways for a good view of the magnificent space age car. As cloudy skies drizzled on the reporters, and photographers fought to keep their camera lenses dry, the turbine car whooshed by.

The car ran fine, but Huebner and his crew had not yet worked out how to get it to start reliably. In fact, they needed to start it with an auxiliary air blower, so the mechanics started the car on the other side of the track—out of view of the reporters. "We kept it running, because if we shut it off we couldn't start it again in front of them," George Stecher, one of the turbine car's mechanics, admitted. The event was a success as reporters and photographers filled the following day's papers with details of the new vehicle. As always, Huebner had managed to create quite a buzz with his presentation; more than five hundred press representatives watched the day's activities.

A *Detroit News* article, "New Engines in Action," appeared the following day. "The public demonstration of the Chrysler gas turbine vehicle was one of the highlights of a full day of thrills and festivities held in connection with the dedication of the corporation's new 4,000-acre proving grounds near Chelsea." Somewhere among the thrills, Huebner spoke to the press about the future of the turbine car. "Within 10 years we should know definitely where we are going. Barring something unforeseen, we think the gas turbine is a feasible and practical powerplant. With continued development we should see it in passenger cars, but I cannot say definitely how long that will be."

The starting difficulty was avoided the next time the car made a public appearance. At New York's Waldorf-Astoria Hotel, the car was placed on a turntable for the public and the press to get a look. Indoors, no one expected them to fire up the jet engine.

There was a sense of urgency to get the Chrysler car in front of the public. Both General Motors and Ford were now said to be developing turbine cars. In fact, GM had already unveiled a working turbine-powered bus and launched a series of cars called Firebirds—show cars that were turbine-powered. General Motors had been designing and testing its own turbine engines, although it did not appear it had made as much progress as Chrysler had by this time. Although they got much publicity, the rocket ship–inspired cars were bizarre looking and impractical. One version had glass bubbles—one for each person in the car—giving it a twenty-first-century look but keeping occupants of the car from conversing. GM did not lend the cars to reporters or make them as widely available as Huebner had with the Chrysler turbines. GM shot film of the cars driving on a track, but this was no longer enough to feed the appetite of the public. The line was eventually discontinued, and the name Firebird was later given to a Pontiac muscle car. Likewise, the bus also disappeared from the public eye. It seems GM may have unveiled the vehicles too soon, before they were ready to be closely inspected by the automotive press.

Chrysler management knew there were very few believers in turbine technology within the auto industry of the time. There were still many nonbelievers within Chrysler. "Our primary purpose was to demonstrate to the corporation and to the rest of the automotive world that a passenger car driven by such an engine could compete with current production vehicles on the bases of fuel economy, emissions, and cost," Bud Mann said later. And it wasn't enough for the turbine car to operate. "It would have to do this while displaying its unique characteristics in terms of performance, smoothness, and the sheer excitement of driving a car. So from the very beginning our program was car oriented. Although we did a great deal of laboratory and dynamometer work, every concept, every idea, every improvement, was evaluated on the road."

Mann found the development years of the turbine program exciting, especially when they took the cars on the road. "This was to prove to ourselves that the system would work in real-world conditions but also, and not insignificantly, to drum up support among the car-buying public for this project. It certainly achieved that end—we received yards of press coverage, both lay and technical, and it was a very heady time for us."

Mann didn't get to go on any of the cross-country runs, but he did get to go on tour with the car on a few occasions. Chrysler sent the turbine cars out in hopes of getting the public interested in the car. On one such trip, Mann went with the car to Boston College and spoke to various audiences about the advantages of the new technology. Chrysler hoped people would demand the car be built once they had seen it. Mann then followed the car to Chicago and cities in Ohio.

It wasn't all fun and games, though. Mann remembers the

hard work, too, both in the lab and at the proving grounds, where we drove endurance on round-the-clock "soirees" for days on end. One of the more glaring deficiencies at that time was the battery-charging equipment. While it was being developed, there were times when the electrical system just did not have the energy to provide headlights for twenty-four-hour driving. So a standard car often accompanied a turbine car, aside and slightly up-track, for "driving lights." The novelty wore off after ten or twelve hours, but the sense of excitement and the team spirit never did.

To help with the difficult tasks they were facing, the turbine researchers were pleasantly surprised to find increased cooperation from other departments within Chrysler. Mann noticed other people were happy to drop what they were doing to help solve a problem with the turbine car program. Without question, the turbines were the high-profile darling of the company.

———

Other car companies could not keep up with Chrysler's efforts in the turbine arena, at least when it came to passenger cars. Ford experimented briefly with turbine-powered cars, primarily to see what the fuss was about. At one point Ford merely called up Boeing and ordered a few small aircraft engines. Once they were delivered to Dearborn, Ford shoehorned the engines into regular cars. One went into a 1954 Fairlane and another was put into a 1955 Thunderbird. Other than filling footnotes in books like this, nothing much came of Ford's brief trip into the turbine field. One story that made the rounds, and probably hindered others with their attempts to make turbines more palatable to the public, was how the Boeing-powered T-Bird set fire to grass and weeds at the side of the road as it roared by. The story might not have been true. Similar stories were told of the Ghia Turbine Cars, and those were untrue.

———

On Friday, March 23, 1956, newspapers ran photos of Huebner standing next to a turbine car—this one was a 1956 Plymouth. Huebner planned to drive the car cross-country to prove the reliability of the Chrysler turbine. At the press conference before the trip began, James C. Zeder, a vice president from Chrysler, explained that the trip was research-oriented. The drivers were engineers and would be examining how the car operated under real-world conditions. Although Zeder claimed they were seeking "data," Huebner appeared to be seeking publicity for his pet project.

As usual, the press ate it up. One photo documenting the "final hand-shake" before the engineers headed west shows Huebner leaning far enough out of the car so his face could be seen clearly by all the photographers present, saying good-bye to a New York City commissioner.

Before the trip, drivers for the turbine car flew to New York while the mechanics and support crew drove station wagons and a truck from Detroit to a rendezvous point in New York. From there, George Huebner and the rest drove the Chrysler Turbine Special across the United States. Among the drivers was a young engineer named Tom Golec and a few others from the Turbine Lab. The 3,020-mile trip took four days.

Typical of corporate America, planning for the road trip was more elaborate than the average drive in the country. An itinerary was laid out, and each member of the crew received detailed instructions on how the trip would work. A small caravan accompanied the turbine car, including a truck filled with tools and spare parts and three station wagons for support.

> On the highway, all cars will maintain a minimum distance of 500 feet from the preceding car. Upon entering and leaving large cities, the groups will close ranks. When refueling becomes necessary, it is requested that the station wagon and truck run ahead of the turbine car for 10 or 15 minutes at approximately 10 miles per hour more than the turbine car speed before stopping to refuel.

It is unclear whether the spacing of the vehicles was for safety reasons or to protect the image of the car. It might appear that Chrysler doubted the car's reliability if it looked like they were afraid to put the car on the road by itself.

From New York, the car would make stops in major cities: St. Louis, Tulsa, Amarillo, Albuquerque, San Bernardino, and Los Angeles. Each leg of the trip was detailed in advance: "New York to Harrisburg (167 miles)" began the first page of maps, with estimated departure time, elapsed time for the leg, and projected time of arrival. Golec kept notes in his logbook, observing discrepancies between the corporation's plans and what actually happened. He even kept odometer readings and average speed figures in the margins.

Keeping in tune with the space age times, the station wagons in the caravan were equipped with newfangled radio telephones. In fact, the driving crews even reported to the media with their radio telephones. An automotive writer in Detroit reported, for instance, that he'd heard an update from the turbine caravan that Monday night at 7:15 P.M. while the car was on the Pennsylvania Turnpike. The writer was more impressed by the phone call itself than by what the caravan reported. The only thing he wrote that wasn't in the previous press releases was that they were approaching the "Pittsburgh Interchange" at the time of the call.

Later Huebner wrote a first-person account of the trip for *Popular Mechanics*:

> Our turbine caravan was rolling along the Pennsylvania Turnpike at about 55 miles per hour. Dashboard gauges showed everything to be normal. Suddenly, a state-police car pulled up alongside and signaled us to a halt. I swung the Chrysler Turbine Special over to the side of the road.
>
> "What's wrong, Officer?" I asked.
>
> "Nothing," he answered with a grin. "We just wanted to see what's under the hood."

No doubt Huebner was also grinning when he popped the hood to show the officer the jet engine.

The trip was a success, although rumors preceded the car's arrival in Los Angeles. People said that the exhaust gases from the turbine could burn a person behind the car—or sear a woman's nylons!—and if the car sat at idle too long while running, it might scorch the asphalt. To dispel the rumors, Chrysler staged a press event in front of Los Angeles City Hall with an actor and actress from Chrysler's television commercials. "They stuck their hands right up to the tailpipe to show that it was not dangerous," George Stecher recalled.

———

Shortly after Huebner's successful cross-country jaunt in the 1956 Turbine Plymouth, Chrysler announced it would double the size of its turbine laboratory. Along with its announcement of the increase in the department, Chrysler told the press that it had recently leased a facility on Greenfield Road in Detroit that had formerly housed a company called Waters Manufacturing. The sixty-seven-thousand-square-foot facility would become the epicenter of Chrysler's turbine program. One article reporting the development also pointed out how General Motors and Ford each had "large-scale gas turbine development projects underway." Although the article suggested the companies were neck and neck in competition, Chrysler was well ahead of the other two car companies. In fact, GM and Ford would never achieve the success of Chrysler when it came to developing a practical automobile turbine.

Huebner told the press that the new space was needed for a variety of reasons. By adding the new building to the program, Chrysler could move equipment and personnel from Highland Park, freeing up more space for the metallurgical and chemical laboratories. It was clear that Chrysler was expanding the turbine program. The early prototypes showed the turbine's potential; now Huebner and his team would try to make the cars more practical and less costly to produce.

The Greenfield facility would house the assembly area for the turbine cars, but it was also the site of design and testing. Many engineers traveled back and forth from Highland Park so often that they ran regular shuttle cars several times a day. Mann spent many of his days at both locations.

People at the U.S. Patent Office began learning more about Huebner, Williams, and the rest of the turbine team around this time. Much of their groundbreaking work resulted in innovations and inventions worthy of patents. For example, Patent 2,795,928 was awarded to Huebner, Williams, and David Borden for their "Arrangement of component elements of a gas turbine powerplant" on June 18, 1957. That patent described ten unique features, including the heat regenerators, and many of the modifications that made the engine fit successfully under the hood of a car. For each new engine, a flurry of patent applications went to Washington, many bearing the names of Huebner and Williams.

Another name that appears on the patent applications is that of an Italian engineer named Giovanni Savonuzzi. Although Savonuzzi only spent a few years on the turbine program, he left an impression on quite a few people in the Detroit area. He went to Chrysler after working on the Karmann Ghia program in Europe, and he settled in the quiet village of Franklin, Michigan, a short drive from Highland Park. Franklin's police department consisted of just a few officers in those days, and they spent the better part of their time driving along quiet streets and waving to townsfolk. Shortly after Savonuzzi moved to town, they began to notice that the Italian engineer drove his car in an unusual fashion: according to another engineer at Chrysler, Savonuzzi's car was either "on or off." He didn't seem to know how to drive slowly. Speed limits were irrelevant. He didn't seem to notice that the pace of traffic in suburban Detroit was much less hectic than in his native Italy. Either way, when he moved back to Italy after working on the program for a few years, the Franklin police department was happy to see him go.

Another innovator at Chrysler was a metallurgist named Dr. Amedee Roy. Over six feet tall, with blue eyes and a heavy French accent, Dr. Roy spent his time looking for alloys suitable for use in the turbine engine. Roy was known for his controlling attitude; people in other departments knew they could not speak to anyone in Roy's department without speaking to Dr. Roy first. It was also well known that you did not want to argue with Dr. Roy unless you were ready to defend your position as if it were a matter of life and death. Dr. Roy was rarely wrong, which most who encountered him found out eventually. Most engineers who dealt with Roy also acknowledged—years later—that Roy was right so often that the arguments were probably pointless to begin with.

Dr. Roy and his team continuously developed new alloys within the metallurgical labs at Chrysler, focusing on durability but also searching for alloys that could be made cheaply. The ideal metals were often rare and expensive. After all, if the turbine were to ever be mass-produced, it would have to be affordable.

The next updated turbine engine went into a 1959 Plymouth. This new engine was designed for durability, with some of Dr. Roy's new alloys used in its construction. The new engine also included an inspired development: variable vanes that sat between the gas-generating first stage and the power-generating second stage. The vanes allowed the engine to burn fuel with less waste and to create more power when it was needed. This more efficient design also had better fuel economy, making almost twenty miles per gallon in its first jaunt, 576 miles from Detroit to New York. The *Detroit News* headlined, "19 Miles a Gallon Reported by Chrysler in Gas Turbine." Along with the high mileage, the turbine was reported to equal the performance of a contemporary V-8 piston engine.

After this successful run, Huebner jubilantly informed the press of the huge strides Chrysler was making. In the two years preceding this engine's launch, Chrysler's turbine development had accomplished more than it had in the entire decade before. This engine weighed less than earlier versions, but put out more horsepower. And for the first time it had been built without extensive use of exotic materials. Amedee Roy had led his department in reducing the amount of rare metal in the engine, and the automaker expected that future engines would use "no more critical or strategic materials than are being used in many consumer durable goods." Huebner insisted the goal was in sight: it was just a matter of time before Chrysler resolved all of the issues facing the development of a practical automobile turbine.

In May 1960, Huebner spoke to a meeting of the American Petroleum Institute held in Detroit at the Sheraton-Cadillac Hotel. He told them about the next-generation turbine from Chrysler. It would be comparable to a piston engine in acceleration and fuel economy and could be available for full-scale production within six years. Huebner held out high hopes for the new engine, which would be placed into test vehicles within the year. Along with finding cheaper metals and more efficient manufacturing processes to build the engine, Chrysler had also quieted the engine a bit. "The major problems have been solved. It remains only to consolidate gains so that the turbine can make available a low-cost, more convenient, and reliable power source than we have yet seen," Huebner explained. His presentation was widely reported, but the press did not mention what reaction—if any—the oil executives in the audience had to the idea that the engine could burn fuels other than gasoline.

In September 1960, on the other side of the world, a group of business leaders and government officials met in Baghdad, Iraq. They represented Iran, Iraq, Kuwait, Saudi Arabia, and Venezuela—all countries that produced oil. Rather than compete in the open market and see their oil prices fluctuate unpredictably, they decided to cooperate with one another and see if they couldn't bring some stability to their business. They named their enterprise the Organization of the Petroleum Exporting Countries. Westerners would later come to know it more commonly as OPEC.

———

In 1961, while the turbine program was making huge strides in bringing the jet engine to market, the Chrysler Corporation began experiencing a crisis in leadership—and finances. These problems had been looming for some time. In the late 1950s, Chrysler's auto lineup had been plagued with quality problems. It got so bad that the reputation of the company suffered and sales dropped dramatically. Three thousand dealers threw up their hands and simply stopped selling Chrysler vehicles altogether. Chrysler's products accounted for 25 percent of the American automobile market at one point in the early 1950s, but by 1959 the number had plunged to little more than 11 percent.

Panicked, Chrysler's board of directors searched for someone to try to steer the company out of its troubles. They chose a forty-two-year-old vice president named Lynn Townsend to take over. Townsend was a University of Michigan–trained accountant who had begun his career double-checking Chrysler's books while working for an outside accounting firm. He did such a good job that Chrysler brought him aboard, and soon he was doing more than just the books.

Perhaps as an indication of how undesirable the job appeared, Townsend was not the board's first choice; they had offered the job to a series of other people, all of whom turned it down. Among the people who wanted no part of taking the reins at Chrysler in 1961 were vice presidents of Ford and General Motors and the president of American Motors, George Romney. They even offered the job to Richard Nixon; the future president of the United States had recently lost the election to John F. Kennedy and was temporarily unemployed.

Once Townsend was in charge, he cut thousands of white-collar jobs, closed unprofitable plants, and stopped the company from spending money it did not have. With its leaner operating structure, Chrysler looked better poised to compete. With over two billion dollars in sales, the company turned a profit in 1961. Just two years earlier, it had lost five million dollars while making sales totaling 2.6 billion dollars.

To convince the buying public that Chrysler built better cars than in the 1950s, Townsend announced Chrysler's new warranty: in 1963, all Chrysler power trains would be warranted for five years or fifty thousand miles. Before this, the auto companies had only given twelve-month, twelve-thousand-mile warranties. Even those had been considered risky; the industry standard in the 1950s had been only ninety days or four thousand miles.

Townsend also recognized that Chrysler's lineup needed a makeover. He wooed designer Elwood Engel away from Ford Motor Company. Engel was responsible for some of the most beloved designs at Ford, including the Thunderbird and the recent Lincoln Continental. Townsend asked Engel to spiff up the lines of the Chrysler automobiles still on the drawing board. The first thing Engel did was chop off the tailfins that had become a staple of the American auto industry in the late 1950s, and he oversaw a reworking of the Chrysler Imperial.

Soon the company's market share shot back up to 20 percent.

——

On February 28, 1961, Chrysler unveiled its next turbine. The occasion was the Turbine Power Conference of the American Society of Mechanical Engineers in Washington, D.C. This third-generation engine was placed into three different Chrysler products, including a show car called the Turboflite. Unlike many show cars of its day, this car could be driven. At the time it was not uncommon for an automaker to build a car that looked interesting but could never run. For instance, around this time Studebaker was displaying its "Atomic" car. The car was said to be in the design stage, but when finished it would supposedly feature a nuclear-powered engine and a force field. Obviously, it was a pipe dream.

On the other hand, Chrysler's Turboflite was futuristic-looking, with huge tail fins, a wing in the back, and even air brakes like those used on aircraft. The Turboflite traveled the auto circuit and visited New York, Chicago, London, Paris, and Turin. Along with the Turboflite, the engine was installed into an otherwise ordinary 1960 Plymouth. And, to prove the engine's versatility, one was put into a 1960 Dodge two-and-a-half-ton truck.

After a few refinements, the third-generation engine was also installed into a 1962 Dodge and a similar Plymouth Fury. These were called the Turbo Dart and the Turbo Fury. Chrysler sent these cars on a cross-country publicity trip, which they accomplished without difficulty. The cars would have looked "normal" except that Chrysler painted a map of the United States on the doors of the cars and marked out the course the cars were taking. Anyone who saw the cars knew where they were coming from and where they were going.

The press also widely reported the cross-country ride. For instance, a *Detroit News* article described the trip in conjunction with rumors and speculation about what plans Chrysler was hatching for the turbines. "On the test will rest in part the decision whether Chrysler will build a limited number of gas turbine cars for use by a selected number of motorists." The *Pontiac Press*, named after a suburb of Detroit and not the car, led by writing, "The jet age for your car may be just around the corner. In fact, it is likely some selected motorists soon will be driving jet-powered cars."

Huebner saw to it that reporters would not miss the press conference where he unveiled the latest turbine cars. The event was held at the Tavern on the Green in New York's Central Park. Before heading west, Huebner and Chrysler vice president Robert Anderson told reporters that Chrysler planned a unique car into which they'd place the latest turbine. Perhaps as many as seventy-five would be built in this final evaluation of the turbine's viability. The *Detroit Free Press* reported: "Huebner left little doubt in his remarks that Chrysler's present intentions, at least, are to proceed into mass production of the engine. 'We would not be standing before you today if we did not believe that the trend which we have started already exists.'" Buried within the second page of the story was a sentence that pointed out how the turbine could be fueled with diesel fuel, peanut oil, gasoline, kerosene, alcohol, furnace oil, or jet fuel.

Huebner couldn't help taking a jab at the other car companies, which had chosen to watch, rather than participate in, the race for a viable turbine. "Our announcement will be greeted with feigned incredulity, but the fact remains that they have yet to do what we have done. We can only say that they aimed too low."

Chrysler also printed and distributed brochures entitled "America's First Gas Turbine Cars." The pamphlet is undated, but it features Huebner on the cover—of course—standing next to the Turbo Dart. It is filled with praise for the program, by Chrysler and others. "To quote the *Chicago Daily News*: 'Other major motor manufacturers are working on their own versions. Chrysler just seems to have a jump on its competitors.'" The document resembled a movie poster, with excerpted reviews from newspapers around the country. "The turbine engine is an automotive dream coming true," the *Syracuse Post-Standard* was quoted as writing. "Biggest news in the industry" was the blurb from the *Fort Wayne News-Sentinel*.

The pamphlet spoke of the turbine car as if it were a certainty. "When will they be available? Within a very few years. The TURBO CAR, as developed by Chrysler Corporation, is a practical car today. But since it is a completely new kind of car, time is needed to get it into mass production."

———

George Huebner took the wheel as the turbine car covered the 3,100-mile, four-day trip. He later said, "We embarked with a sense of high adventure. As the continent rolled smoothly past, our feeling of accomplishment grew and we, and those of our research group who could not make the trip with us, saw fulfilled our years of training, thought, and effort, of sometimes disappointment and of sometimes triumph."

Huebner made a point to drive the Turbo Dart through northern climates as well as warm ones; the car ran perfectly well in the snow and in the heat. Somewhere in Pennsylvania Huebner probably wished they had waited a few months before attempting the drive. Much of the Pennsylvania Turnpike "was driven in a blinding blizzard," and near Chicago, they "skated on glare ice." A short while later, the caravan cruised along with outside temperatures of eighteen degrees below zero. Through it all, the car performed flawlessly.

Chrysler sent along a few movie cameras to record the trip and later made a short film of the event called *Taming the Tornado*. The movie stressed the wide array of conditions encountered by the car without trouble. Across the Continental Divide, they hit altitudes over five thousand feet. The next day, they started in subzero temperatures in Arizona and drove into desert conditions approaching seventy-five degrees.

Later, Huebner's tales of the weather got a bit more dramatic. He told the Society of Automotive Engineers that he had driven "through snowstorms, freezing rain, subzero temperatures, and twenty-five- to forty-mile-per-hour headwinds." The car rolled uneventfully into Los Angeles on New Year's Eve, 1961. Huebner and the team checked into a local hotel and cleaned up the car and themselves. Huebner put on his best suit and presented the car to the local press, who showed up in droves to greet him. Chrysler's public relations representative counted 130 media people in the audience when Huebner spoke about the trip. Not wanting to let the crowd disperse without a bang, Huebner ended his remarks with an offer: did any of them want to have a ride in a turbine car? If so, there were two in the parking lot, and Chrysler was willing to let any member of the press have a ride in one of the cars that had just been driven across the continent. Huebner later said, "The meeting broke up with a mad rush to the sidewalk." It took two hours to give the members of the press rides, although Huebner felt certain he had seen several reporters sneak back into the line for a second turn.

When Huebner compared notes with the others who'd come along on the trip, he discovered that his Turbo Dart had achieved better gas mileage than a conventional car that had been traveling along with him, and the turbine engine showed no noticeable wear.

Taming the Tornado ended with a shot of the Turbo Dart driving along an airport runway with a large jetliner following close behind, drawing an obvious parallel as Chrysler announced that turbine technology for automobiles was no longer a theoretical possibility—it was here in practical form, thanks to Chrysler.

The public loved the short film. Chrysler made another, called *Riding the Whirlwind*, to explain how the new turbine engines worked. It opened with a shot of the Turbo Dart—the one Huebner had driven cross-country—racing along the beach at Daytona, then cut to a shot of the car running at high speed around a banked oval. This film even included an animated demonstration of how the turbine worked, in language a junior high school student could understand. Just in case viewers might think the engine would burn nearby cars, the film explained how Chrysler originated the regenerator and that the exhaust was now "safe and comfortable." "The gas turbine is simplicity itself," the narrator claimed. The film went so far as to insult piston engines with their carburetors that "squat" on top and the pistons going back and forth, as if the engines were ugly and silly. The accompanying animation depicted a piston engine, removing the unnecessary parts one at a time until nothing remained but a single spark plug and the engine fan. *Riding the Whirlwind* also hinted that Chrysler would build a small fleet of turbine cars soon, for the general public.

That turbine engines sounded different from piston engines was not lost on the Chrysler designers. Consumers associated the telltale sound of jet aircraft with what a turbine car should sound like. A problem lay in the little-known fact that much of the sound people equate with jets is actually gear noise from the various accessory drive gears people hear when an aircraft taxis. It is sometimes referred to as "gear singing," and some claimed that Chrysler engineers carefully left some of the jet sound in, making sure the accessory drive gears on the Turbine Car sounded adequately jetlike. At least early in the program, the engineers had worked to reduce the gear noise. They even tried a few with a set of composite (nonmetal) gears in the front gear box for the accessories. Although it was quieter, the gears couldn't withstand the high temperatures of the turbine environment, so the production models used metal gears.

Each successive version of the turbine engine incorporated innovations that Huebner, Tom Golec, Jerry Gross, and others developed during their testing and experimentation in Chrysler's Turbine Lab. For example, under the hood of the Turbo Fury sat two huge canisters right behind the grille. They were air intakes for the turbine, and their size testified to the need for clean air in the turbine. Their placement solved another problem, too: the intake of air into earlier turbines had made too much noise. By facing the dual intakes at each other, the engineers discovered that the sound from the two intakes canceled each other out. The issue of sound coming from the intake of the engine was always present during the development of the Chrysler turbines: internal documents from Chrysler even refer to the air filter as part of the "silencer assembly." Eventually, Chrysler's turbine engineers would reduce the sound of the intakes to an acceptable level.

———

In February 1962 the current lineup of Chrysler turbine cars was brought to Detroit as part of its tour around the country to visit Chrysler dealers. Chrysler held a luncheon on nearby Belle Isle and offered the press rides in the cars. During a presentation, Robert Anderson told the reporters about what had happened after the announcement of the upcoming program was made in New York. Chrysler had been flooded with letters from consumers who wanted a chance to ride in one of the next-generation turbine cars. He then invited the reporters outside to take a spin in a turbine car around the little island in the Detroit River.

Reporters who rode in the car that day were enthusiastic. One from the *Detroit News* wrote:

> A drive in the Dodge yesterday with Huebner revealed that the acceleration of the car is superior to a comparable piston engine with the same horsepower. The car had less vibration and also good handling characteristics.

Huebner said the high-pitched whine characteristics of the turbine power-plant can be eliminated through the same type of muffling developments as the piston engine. Chrysler promotion men said they had asked Huebner to keep the whine in the car to attract attention to it.

This last point was always a matter of contention; some who worked on the program insisted later there was no plan to keep any of the sound that could be eliminated. Be that as it may, the reporters focused on how the turbine compared to piston-engine cars in performance. No one seemed to care that the car could run on alternative fuels. It wasn't the fault of the press, however; even Chrysler didn't bother pushing the point.

One impressive aspect of Chrysler's turbine engine program at this time was the team Huebner had assembled to create the engine. Huebner knew the turbine team needed to enter new frontiers of research, so he sought out the best engineers, technicians, and machinists he could find. Some he found within Chrysler and some came from the U.S. Air Force, where they'd worked on military turbines. Jerry Gross joined Chrysler in 1963 to work on the turbines as a test cell engineer. He'd graduated from Southfield's Lawrence Technological Institute a few years earlier and worked at Ford on its turbine program. In a time of corporate austerity, Ford had let him go. Gross loved turbines. At Chrysler he ran all the testing to make sure the engines were durable enough for consumer use. "You name it, we ran it," he said later of the tests.

Once the team had assembled, it was a "creative bunch of people—in the whole program. Whether you worked in the lab or worked up in design or worked up in Amedee Roy's area, we were basically a 'Skunk Works' within Chrysler Corporation," Gross said, comparing the program to the top-secret department at Lockheed where the U-2 and SR-71 spy planes were developed for the U.S. government during the Cold War. He noted how Chrysler gave the group the best of everything, and the team became the envy of the other engineers at Chrysler. The machinists assigned to the program did such exceptional work that other departments within Chrysler often brought projects there rather than have regular machinists within Chrysler or an outside vendor attempt the job.

People in the automotive industry began taking notice of Chrysler's turbine progress, especially with the development of the third-generation engine. On March 7, 1962, the American Society of Mechanical Engineers gave Huebner an award "for his leadership in the development of the first automotive gas turbine suitable for mass-produced passenger automobiles." Chrysler proudly pointed out that this was the first time the organization had honored anyone in the automotive field this way.

Chrysler sent both the Turbo Dart and the Turbo Fury around the country to Chrysler dealers to test the waters. What would consumers think of the experimental engines? The curious public, receptive to space age thinking, responded enthusiastically. The cars traveled to ninety different major cities in North America, where they were shown first to the press and then to the public. The tour included Mexico and then extended to Europe. Spurred by the enthusiastic press—many journalists were allowed to drive the jet-powered autos—millions of people came out to see the cars. Chrysler tried to accommodate as many people as possible who wanted rides in the cars, and by the end of the tour nearly fourteen thousand people had ridden in one of the turbines.

Two of the people who took turns in the Turbo Fury were Alden L. Olson and his teenage son, Mark E. Olson, of Duluth, Minnesota. Alden had seen an ad promoting a weekend appearance of the turbine cars at a nearby dealer in Superior, Wisconsin. Father and son went out on the Friday night to the dealer, where they saw the Turbo Dart on the showroom floor surrounded by people; the Turbo Fury waited in the parking lot with its turbine running. Mark thought the engine sounded like a big vacuum cleaner. They soon got a chance to ride in the car. The Olsons were hooked.

Later, Huebner said that the purpose of the tour taken by the Turbo Dart and Turbo Fury was to "elicit and examine consumer reactions to the turbine." Chrysler asked people at these events if they were interested in the cars. If they answered in the affirmative, Chrysler sent them information on the program along with a questionnaire. Eighty-six percent of the people who received the package from Chrysler filled the questionnaire out and returned it. Chrysler had never seen enthusiasm or reaction on this scale before.

Huebner believed the turbine car struck a chord with the American people. Their reactions were overwhelmingly positive. Thirty percent of the people who saw these cars on display said they would have no problem buying a car with a turbine engine rather than a piston engine. Another 54 percent said they would seriously consider buying one.

The third-generation program ended on a high note during the Chicago Auto Show, which took place the week of February 17, 1962. Chrysler displayed three turbine vehicles there, including the truck, which had been driven 290 miles to the show from Detroit without difficulty. A few days before the show, Chrysler unveiled the vehicles to the press and officially announced the creation of the fourth-generation engine. This engine would be put into a limited run of fifty to seventy-five vehicles that would be made available to selected users toward the end of 1963. The cars were to be lent to members of the public at no cost.

The press was flabbergasted, and broadcast the idea as widely as possible.

3

The Fourth-Generation Engine: Chrysler's Viable Automotive Powerplant

The fourth-generation turbine was first placed in a Plymouth Fury in 1962. Chrysler issued a press release with a publicity photo to the media, showing the Fury with its hood raised. The photo emphasized the strange engine, and next to it stood George Huebner, smiling broadly and dressed as if he were posing for the cover of a men's fashion magazine. The jet engine looked nothing like an engine that a consumer might have seen on an aircraft. No one could have guessed it was a jet engine, even though it looked simpler and cleaner than a regular piston engine. For the most part it looked unremarkable.

But it was a thing of engineering beauty. The turbine weighed a mere 410 pounds and delivered 130 brake horsepower. It also generated a startling 425 foot-pounds of torque, putting it in the same league as Chrysler's legendary Hemi. The fourth-generation engine ran easily and impressively when demonstrated to the public. "It was totally different, and very, very smooth. In fact, one of the gimmicks we used to use at dealerships was that the engine ran so smooth, you could take a nickel—and stand the nickel on edge on top of the engine and the nickel would stay there," George Stecher said. "It was virtually vibration free, it was a different sound and was a different feel, and people were very excited about it."

Most remarkably, the engine was small and durable. Jerry Gross and his department ran one of the engines for five thousand hours on a test stand, in an era when a piston engine was not expected to last much longer than three thousand hours. During the five-thousand-hour run they periodically pulled the engine apart and examined the parts for wear or breakage. In the years leading up to the fourth-generation engine, they'd accomplished so much that the internal parts of the engine showed almost no wear during the tests.

Although the Chrysler turbine engine became more efficient with each generation, it did not get any less expensive to manufacture. The turbine required exotic materials, and many of the parts inside the engine had to be manufactured with remarkable precision. Tolerances inside the engine were critical, and, with the high speeds the internal parts reached during operation, it was imperative for the larger spinning components to be balanced to a degree not required in a typical piston engine. The turbine required the automotive engineers to achieve standards normally only found in the aerospace industry.

The internal parts of the turbine, therefore, required a different manufacturing method. While Chrysler manufactured most—if not all—of the parts for most of its cars, there were some parts inside the turbine engine that Chrysler was not equipped to create. Primarily, these were the parts of the engine exposed to the highest temperatures. The fan disks (there were two), the combustion nozzle, and the vanes, or blades, that controlled the output from the gas generator all had to be manufactured from exotic alloys capable of surviving an environment reaching 1,700 degrees Fahrenheit.

The ideal way to make such parts was a process called "investment casting." Engine blocks, connecting rods, differential housings, and other mundane parts on the average car could be cast using methods Chrysler and other auto manufacturers had employed for decades. This type of casting is what most people imagine when they think of molten metal being poured into a mold, or cast, to make metal parts. The molds vary in complexity, depending on what parts are being cast, but for the most part this simple method does not result in castings precise enough to perform in a turbine engine.

With investment casting, the manufacturer creates an exact model of the part to be cast. The model is made out of a special material, often wax. The wax model is then dipped into a "slurry"—think of it as plaster—and then removed. When the coating dries, it forms a mold of the wax model it encases. The wax model and its coating are then placed into an oven and heated. The wax inside the mold melts and drains out. After the mold has cooled, the manufacturer can then pour molten metal into the mold and make an exact replica of the wax model.

When the metal inside the mold cools—and the cooling process can take some time—the mold is then removed from around the part. The mold is destroyed in the removal process; it usually has to be broken into pieces to get at the part inside. The net result is a highly accurate casting of the part being made. The steps required to get to this point are time-consuming, require expertise, and must be repeated for each piece being cast.

In the early 1960s, Chrysler did not possess the facilities to do any of the investment casting; it hired a local company called Howmet, which specialized in it, to make the turbine disks, the ignition nozzle, and the nozzle blades for each of the turbine engines.

One of the reasons the fourth-generation turbine ran so well was that Gross and his department tested its components extensively. The turbine rotors, which turned no faster than 44,610 revolutions per minute in the engine, were tested up to 100,000 RPM in the lab. Special equipment was used for such tests, including the spin pit—the huge, lead-lined device in which the tests were run. The spin pit's inner walls were lined with oak and lead. The part being tested, such as a compressor or a turbine rotor, was placed near the top of the cylinder and attached to a turbine on the outside that would spin the part. A lid was placed on top of the pit to seal it, and the setup was turned on. Soon the part inside the pit would spin at speeds far in excess of what it needed to maintain to operate in a car. Inside the pit

small sensors monitored the part; the moment they sensed a slight difference in the dimensions of the part being spun—even metal stretches when
stressed enough—they fired a strobe flash in the pit and took a high-speed
photograph. (The camera was placed above the part being spun, placing it
out of danger if any parts might break loose.) A fraction of a second later,
the excessive speed would cause the part to fail. Pieces of the component
would slam into the lead-lined walls and the machine would shut itself off.

While technicians removed the parts from the pit, the film was developed. After studying the results, the engineers would either redesign the
part or, if it failed in the way they had expected, move on to test the next
component. Failures were common and sometimes spectacular. Even
though the lead lining muffled the noise, the engineers still had to wear
hearing protection while running the tests. Despite the lead lining and the
hearing protection, engineers could still hear the bang of the part slam-
ming into the lead wall when it broke.

On one occasion, Gross tested a fourth-generation turbine in a test cell,
with the gas generator and the power turbine together, hitched to a transmission and a dynamometer—a device that measures horsepower. He wit-
nessed a small flaw in the power turbine section with spectacular results.
He ran the engine up to full speed, where the gas generator of the turbine
spins at over 44,000 RPM. A small bearing in the rear failed, and in a fraction of a second, the shaft connecting the power turbine to the transmission broke. In that instant, the gas generator was blasting full force on
the power turbine rotor, which suddenly spun with no resistance. That
rotor became a "runaway," free-wheeling to an astronomical speed where
everything let loose. Before Gross or anyone else near the machine could
shut it off, they heard a muffled explosion. Then silence. The technicians
and engineers stared at the engine. Despite the incredible forces that had
just been unleashed inside the engine, no parts had broken through the
engine housing, which was formed out of very thick metal and designed
to contain any parts that might break loose during a failure. The engineers
carefully dismantled the engine, found the failure, and re-engineered the
part that failed so that it would never happen again.

It was a relief to the engineers that the shrapnel from the engine hadn't escaped the housing of the turbine. Some of the most spectacular accidents that have occurred with jet engines were caused by pieces spinning off turbines and not being contained within the housing; the Chrysler engineers now knew the engines were safe enough for consumer use.

It is noteworthy how powerful the forces were that Chrysler was harnessing. A turbine rotor spinning at 44,000 RPM might have a "tip speed"— the speed at which the tips of the blades move—approaching 1,700 feet per second. That's the equivalent of traveling a third of a mile in a second, or over a thousand miles an hour.

Not all the testing went smoothly, however. Dr. Amedee Roy's metallurgical wonders were sometimes tested by other departments, who did not always understand the miraculous characteristics of Roy's super alloys. In early 1963, Jerry Gross had recently joined the Chrysler team and was given the task of performing and observing the break-in process—how well the brand-new parts performed as they warmed up and cooled down the first few times they were used—for some new regenerator parts. The regenerators underwent immense changes in temperature, and Roy had developed various chemical coatings and alloys to allow them to gradually change shape and conform to the parts to which they were attached. During one test, Gross noticed that some of the coating between the regenerator and the "x-arm" it was attached to had flaked off. His task was to run the break-in process and report on whether it had succeeded.

At the next meeting with the heads of the various departments, Gross duly reported that the break-in process had gone well with the new configuration. He then made the mistake of casually volunteering that he had observed some of the coating between the two parts flaking off. Dr. Roy was not at the meeting, but some there undoubtedly raised their eyebrows, knowing word would get back to the sometimes fiery metallurgist.

Shortly afterward, Gross was sitting at his desk when he heard a "commotion" in the room, and someone with a French accent demanding to know "who this Gross fellow is."

"I turn around and hovering over me is this six-foot-plus, red-haired person with fire in his eyes, his mustache is standing on edge and undulating, very red-faced with the color slowly moving up toward his hairline and smoke, I swear, is coming out of his ears. The infamous Dr. Amedee Roy. I felt like a bird about to be attacked by the hawk!"

Gross stammered his response as Roy fired questions at him without waiting for complete answers. "Are you a metallurgist?" "How can you make such a statement?" Eventually Roy cooled down enough for Gross to apologize—he was not a metallurgist and had merely reported what he had seen. He hadn't meant any harm, and certainly wasn't trying to cast doubts on the performance of Roy's special metals.

As the temperature of the conversation dropped to normal, Roy suggested that Gross consult with him in the future before coming to conclusions involving metals. Gross agreed, and the two got along well after that. When Roy left the room, Gross's supervisor congratulated him. "You have just met and survived Dr. Amedee Roy."

———

In the early days of the turbine program, no one paid much attention to the versatility the engines displayed regarding fuel choice. Everyone knew turbines could burn a variety of fuels, but gasoline was the cheapest and most plentiful fuel available. Still, Chrysler finally started promoting the turbines' ability to run on many different fuels. The press release accompanying the photo of George Huebner smiling next to the Turbo Fury pointed out how the turbine "runs efficiently on various low-cost fuels including kerosene, fuel and diesel oil, low grade unleaded gasoline, and JP-4 (jet fuel)." Fuel oil was inexpensive, but few people thought of it as something to put in a car's gas tank. JP-4 sounded expensive—and where would you buy it? The ability of the engine to burn multiple fuels felt like little more than a parlor trick, akin to placing the nickel on top of the engine.

Perhaps the biggest advance made by the Chrysler Turbine Lab was developing the regenerators. In earlier turbines, much of the energy created by the combustion process was wasted because it went out the tailpipe of the turbine in the form of heat. Dr. Sam Williams and the rest of the team had sought ways to use those hot gases. They found that if they routed the exhaust gases over a metal wheel, they could make the wheel turn, and if they routed the intake air over the same wheel, it would transfer the heat from the exhaust to the incoming air stream. By raising the inlet temperature, the combustion process became more efficient. Transferring the heat from the exhaust back up to the combustion section of the engine lowered the temperature of the exhaust. This regenerator raised the efficiency of the turbine toward a level at which it might compete with the piston engine.

One more innovation in the later turbines was a set of blades that sat between the turbine on the gas generator and the power turbine. This assembly was a collection of vanes that moved like shutters. They could be set one way and the hot gas blasted out of the gas generator unimpeded. But turned the other way, the vanes blocked the gas flow so that very little of the turbine's output would flow out and over the turbine disk that drove the transmission.

The improvement was important enough to be featured in a Chrysler film. *Riding the Whirlwind* shows how the turbine's nozzle vanes worked. This ability to control the gas flow at this stage of the engine eliminated some of the weaknesses in simpler turbine setups. For instance, a jet airliner in flight runs at a constant throttle a majority of the time, so this sort of variability of its turbine output is less critical. The Chrysler turbine's variable nozzle blades allowed for better fuel economy at varying speeds, and even allowed for engine braking when the throttle was released.

Engine braking is the phenomenon drivers of piston engines feel when they are traveling at speed and then take their foot off the gas; compression in the engine cylinders of the car actually drags against the drive train and slows the vehicle a bit, even before the brakes are applied. The phenomenon is more noticeable in some cars and trucks than others. In a simple turbine, engine braking would not have existed because when the driver let off the throttle, the turbine would merely spool down, and since there was no direct connection between the gas generator turbine and the power turbine, the car would merely coast without having the turbine slow the car down. Although this was not a necessary function in an engine, average consumers were accustomed to it.

The fourth-generation turbine was now something much more than

the "tube with fans" described earlier. Its elaborate plumbing and duct-
work was a maze of precision craftsmanship and special metals developed
by Dr. Roy. Chrysler issued press materials to explain the process: Cold air
was drawn into the engine by the front set of blades. When the air passed
the first fan—the inlet air compressor—it gained temperature to over four
hundred degrees Fahrenheit merely from compression. It was then ducted
through the regenerator and, once the turbine was running, picked up
another eight hundred degrees before passing into the combustion chamber to be ignited. At the point of ignition, the process reached close to two
thousand degrees. Those gases then blasted through the turbine blades
and over the power turbine that drove the car, and then were ducted
through the regenerator wheel. There, the gases cooled and passed their
heat energy to the regenerator wheel. The final exhaust of this turbine
car was below two hundred degrees—cooler than a conventional piston
engine. Throughout the various stages, the air pressure within the turbine
hovered around four atmospheres—that is, four times the pressure of the
air before it became involved in the turbine process.

Most of the biggest innovations in the fourth-generation turbine were
not visible to those who saw the engine in a car, and the few nonengineers
who saw them probably did not know what they were looking at. Dr. Roy
and his metallurgical department had spent countless hours cooking various metals in ovens to see how well they transferred heat and withstood
punishment. Their focus was always on trying to find durable and appropriate metals that could be made inexpensively. Although some parts of
the engine could be made from aluminum, the turbine wheel, the diffuser,
and the diffuser cover caused a different problem: they were at the vortex
of the explosive process. Aluminum couldn't withstand the kind of temperature extremes the turbine generated. These parts of the engine were
often being baked at 1,800 degrees Fahrenheit, and were also the most
critical components in the engine; failure here would be catastrophic. Dr.
Roy created a blend of materials that met the turbine's needs and patented
some of the alloys.

Other materials remained closely guarded secrets. Everyone in the
industry knew what kinds of elements were being used, metals such as

nickel, chromium, and molybdenum. Roy figured out which combinations of these metals withstood the harsh environment inside the turbine. Company documents referred to the alloys simply as Chrysler Research Material, or CRM for short. Later variations of Dr. Roy's alloys were numbered: CR2A, for instance, was the vital material in one of the earliest turbines. Years later, engineers from Chrysler still referred to the materials by their CR numbers.

One other difference between the fourth-generation engine and the sort of turbine found in a jet was how the fuel was ignited. In a typical jet engine, the fuel is ignited by a spark plug to start the combustion process. Once the engine is firing, the electricity to the spark plug shuts off. The Chrysler turbine, on the other hand, would be running in a wider range of operations. The engineers had decided to allow the engine to idle down to speeds much lower than most turbines ever run, and then, of course, back up to full throttle (if necessary) without having to restart. The engine was designed to have the spark plug firing constantly, like a spark plug in a piston engine. That way the fire would never go out in the combustor when the fuel supply was choked off at idle—which was done to save fuel. In an interesting phenomenon, the turbine would continue to turn for a while, even with no fuel running into it. If the engine was warm, the regenerators continued to pass heat to the cold end of the system. That heat would expand air near the inlet and the various blades pointed it in the right direction. So long as air expanded at one end, the wheels kept turning. The system would slow down over time, though, because it lost heat while the combustor wasn't operating.

Sometimes there was a problem with the idle set-up of the turbine, however. After the idle, when fuel was sent to the engine upon acceleration, sometimes the fuel wouldn't light immediately. A moment later, when it did light, it would pop. The burner "relight" problem was considered to be aesthetic in nature—it didn't hurt anything, but it made the car sound as if it was not running as it should. Chrysler engineers addressed the issue by modifying the igniter and the problem went away.

4

The Ghia Turbine Car

"In the early 1960s we embarked on what turned out to be one of the greatest publicity stunts in automotive history, and I mean that in the most constructive sense. It was decided that we should get the driving public more deeply involved in the direction of the project, and thus began the Fifty-Car Program," Bud Mann reflected, years later.

Chrysler decided to launch a major program to test public interest in the turbine program, to see if people might actually consider buying a turbine-powered car. It designed a unique car in which to place the fourth-generation turbine powerplant and launched a publicity campaign that would dwarf previous public relations efforts.

Chrysler wanted a car whose appearance would be as unique as the powerplant under the hood. It had recently lured automotive designer Elwood Engel from Ford. He was now given the job of designing an appropriate vehicle for the turbine—"a car that would transport its driver a decade or two into the future the instant he sat down and closed the door. And that's exactly what it did," said Bud Mann. A few people jokingly called the turbine car the "Engelbird" because of a vague similarity to the Thunderbird he had left behind at Ford.

Some wondered why Chrysler didn't design a "far out" or space age design for the turbine car. After all, the show cars from Chrysler and GM had looked pretty futuristic. Chrysler opted to avoid the radical approach, so that when it asked for consumer opinions they would not be distracted by styling. Also, which is more impressive, a piston-engine car that looks space age, or one that looks normal but is actually powered by a jet engine?

The automaker sent Engel's drawings to the Ghia design studio in Italy, which specialized in custom, handmade auto bodies. Previously, Ghia had built many show cars for Chrysler, and even the limousine version of the Chrysler Imperial. One of those Ghia-built show cars wound up on the bottom of the ocean, strangely enough. A car called the Norseman, drawn in Detroit and built by Ghia in the mid-1950s, was finished and loaded onto an ocean liner for shipment to America. On July 25, 1956, the Norseman's slumber below decks on the *Andrea Doria* was shattered by the prow of the *Stockholm* as it sliced through the side of the ship. Forty-six passengers perished in the sinking, and the *Andrea Doria* took the Norseman to the ocean floor, 250 feet below.

The sinking of the ship with the show car on board led years later to the mistaken belief that there was a turbine car sitting on the bottom of the ocean. The Norseman was not turbine-powered, and the turbine cars that are often described as lying on the ocean floor were not created early enough to have been aboard the *Andrea Doria*.

Ghia was given great latitude in cleaning up Engel's drawings, and when they were finished the Ghia bodies were works of art. They were also not mass-produced; they were handmade. "You couldn't take the door off one and put it on another one. It wouldn't fit," George Stecher said later. But no one questioned Ghia's methods; its work was world renowned. Everyone, it seemed, used Ghia when a project called for the utmost in craftsmanship. Ghia not only made one-off show cars, it was equipped to build small runs of automobiles. If the cars from Ghia were acceptable to Chrysler, Ghia was in a position to build a few dozen of them if need be.

The completed bodies were shipped from Italy to Detroit in huge crates. Once ashore, most were brought to the Greenfield Road building. Ghia had already assembled and painted the bodies, and applied all of the exterior trim and interior upholstery. Chrysler installed the turbine engines, along with the chassis, at the rate of one per week. The Chrysler assemblers also did most of the electrical wiring, and installed the gauges, radios, and heaters. The first few turbines were assembled in Highland Park, but once they began assembling them faster, Chrysler moved the process to Greenfield. The Greenfield plant was better suited for assembly; it had once been used to build DeSoto taxis.

The first Ghia Turbine Cars were driven in Detroit in early 1962; the first five were considered prototypes as the assemblers worked out the bugs for installing the turbine engines into the custom-built cars. In fact, the first five were each slightly different, both from each other and from the fifty that followed. One Ghia prototype was bronze with a black vinyl top—the configuration Chrysler eventually chose for the bulk of the fleet. Another had no vinyl top and was solid bronze in color. One was white with a blue racing stripe. One had an all-leather interior, while another had leather and cloth upholstery. Another had an all-black interior, just in case the bronze color scheme got tiring on the eyes.

For aficionados who want to distinguish which cars were prototypes and which were "production" in photographs, the main observable difference is their rearview mirrors. The five prototypes were shipped from Ghia with their mirrors already installed. On the production cars, Chrysler installed its own mirrors, which looked like mirrors from any other car in the Chrysler line at the time. Another innovation of the time was how the interior rearview mirrors were attached to the windshields on these cars—they were glued. Although the practice is common today in the auto industry, it was an innovation for the industry in 1963.

———

The Chrysler turbine engineers were excited when the first of the cars came to the end of the assembly line and was started up. The bodies by

Ghia were perfect for the experiment. They looked like they were special. Bud Mann remembers:

> The styling, the trim, the instrument panel all contributed to this vehicle's unique aura, but mostly it was the *sound*. The high-pitched whine overlaid on a deep-throated "whoosh" gave a feeling of power unmatched by any vehicle short of a jet aircraft. We would later regard this as a serious noise problem, but to the two hundred or so people who got to drive these cars for three months, it was a real identity symbol. Driving through your neighborhood at midnight with that car let everyone know that you were *someone*.

The fifty cars assembled at the Greenfield plant were identical. They were painted the same "turbine bronze" and the interiors were all the same copper color. In case anyone wondered how alike the cars were, Chrysler's engineering staff report described the features and equipment of the Ghia cars and included a list of standard equipment. "All features and equipment are standard. There is only one body color and one interior trim combination. No options are available." In the forty-one-page report, that was the only sentence underlined.

At first the cars didn't perform quite as well as the engineers had expected. They noticed that the bodies from Ghia—so beautifully hand-crafted—weighed hundreds of pounds more than they should have. Tom Golec discovered that Ghia craftspeople had liberally applied lead to the bodywork to smooth out rough spots. Although it was a common practice at the finer body design studios of Europe, it added weight. Swinging a door open or closed felt like you were swinging a barn door, he said. Luckily, the trunk lid and hood were made from aluminum; otherwise the cars would have been even heavier. And, in another innovation, the aluminum body parts were reinforced with steel frames that were "glued" to the aluminum with structural adhesive. Again, this practice is common today, but the Ghia Turbine was among the first cars to appear in America built that way.

Chalking up slow throttle response to the added Italian weight, the engineers were also caught off guard by an unusual vibration when the cars got up to highway speed. Every other turbine car they'd tested had run smoothly, so why were the new cars vibrating? In fact, the first turbine cars had run so smoothly that the designers had to install extra rubber in the engine mounts to keep little bumps and unevenness in the roads from transmitting jolts into the passenger compartment. This was considered necessary because small bumps were not noticeable in a piston-engine car. The big V-8s of the day rumbled and vibrated so much on their own that none of the smaller road imperfections could be felt by the driver.

After ruling out everything else, the engineers pulled the tires off the cars and shaved the treads smooth. This solved the problem; the vibration they had felt was merely the tire treads on the pavement. This indicated how smoothly the car ran otherwise. In the average car with its recipro- cating piston engine, you could never hope to eliminate vibrations to the point where you could feel the tire treads bumping against the pavement.

Later, at the proving grounds, test driver Jerry Wenk remembered the car's lack of interior noise as its most memorable attribute. "At a hundred miles an hour inside that car, with the windows up, you didn't hear any- thing except road noise. It was a lot quieter than a conventional car at that time." Of course, the car sounded like a jet to anyone standing nearby when it was running, or to people in the car with the windows down. In many respects, the car mimicked that feature of a jetliner—it doesn't seem all that loud to passengers while in flight.

According to George Huebner, the cars cost in the range of fifty to fifty- five thousand dollars apiece to build, although the cost changed from time to time, depending on whom Huebner was telling about the price. At the time, most cars retailed at two to three thousand dollars. Part of the equa- tion was that everything on the turbine car was unique—nothing came from any other Chrysler platform. "Those 55 coupes were probably the most completely custom-built automobiles ever constructed at any time anywhere," Huebner said later.

The Ghia bodies probably cost around twenty thousand dollars or so, according to Virgil Exner Jr. Exner's father was a famous designer at Chrys- ler around this time. He had hired the Ghia studio to build many of the cars he designed (although the turbine car was an Elwood Engel design).

Later, Exner Jr. likewise worked as a car designer who contracted with Ghia to turn his drawings into reality. He said a show car his father had built in 1951 had cost twenty-five thousand dollars to build, and that the initial Ghia Turbine Car prototype probably cost around fifty thousand to build. Once the prototype was finished, however, Ghia made tooling from the car, which enabled it to make copies much more easily. Those copies probably cost about half or less than the prototype to make. But this does not address the cost of the engine. Chrysler never said how much each engine cost, but the point is moot. Even at twenty-five thousand dollars—without an engine—the car was far too expensive to market at the time.

Strangely, Chrysler never officially gave the turbine car a name. In an era when nameplates seemed to be more and more descriptive—Fury, Charger, Thunderbird—Chrysler placed only a single nameplate on the sides of this car. It read, simply, "Turbine." Many within Chrysler called the vehicle the Chrysler Corporation Turbine Car, while others called it the Ghia or Ghia Turbine to distinguish it from the other turbine cars Chrysler had already put on the road. The car was almost named the Typhoon, but you have to look closely at a film to see it. Chrysler had movie cameras rolling when the first Ghia Turbine bodies were uncrated after their trip from Italy. (Portions of the uncrating film can be seen in various Chrysler promotional films.) A close-up of one shows the scripted badge "Typhoon," where later all the cars bore a similarly scripted "Turbine."

The name Typhoon was later used on another Ghia-built car. Chrysler asked Ghia to make a two-seater version of the vehicle with a removable roof that Chrysler displayed on the auto show circuit. This prototype car was called the Typhoon and looked a lot like the turbine car, but it did not have an engine—turbine or otherwise. There had been discussion of officially naming the Ghia car the Typhoon, but Chrysler decided to name it simply the Turbine and leave it at that.

All of the Ghias except one were painted "turbine bronze," a metallic root beer color unlike any other paint commonly used on cars at that time. This distinctive styling carried through the entire car, making it a rolling work of art. The headlights were surrounded by bezels that contained fins, and the rear end had touches that also looked like they came from a rocket or airplane. Inside, the leather interior and deep pile carpet were also turbine bronze. Surfaces inside the car that were not turbine bronze in color were often brushed aluminum for a space age look.

The cars came equipped with all the basic comforts except air-conditioning. They had power steering and power brakes, demonstrating to people that the turbine engine could run the same accessories as a big V-8 piston engine. The dashboard featured three huge dials, including a speedometer and a tachometer. The tachometer was noticeable for its marking—rather than topping out at a pedestrian number like 8,000 or 9,000 RPM, this gauge was calibrated to peak at 60,000 RPM. Not far from the outlandish tachometer was a pyrometer that told the driver the temperature of the engine at its hottest point, the turbine inlet. It no doubt impressed consumers that the operating range was 1,800 degrees Fahrenheit, approaching ten times the engine temperature reading of a piston-engine car of the time. Of course, the gauges weren't there just to impress naive consumers; they were invaluable to troubleshoot problems later on, should the car start misbehaving mechanically.

An inspection of the car's interior revealed a few items of note. A decorative strip ran above the glove box with the phrase "Turbine Power by Chrysler Corporation." The glove box door, when opened, displayed a bright red circle that warned, "DO NOT USE LEADED GASOLINE." This warning was necessary because it had been discovered that even though the car ran on leaded gasoline, the lead additive damaged some of the internal parts of the turbine, and leaded gasoline was sometimes prone to a condition called "vapor lock." In the early 1960s, leaded gasoline was the most common fuel available at gas stations. It would take a little planning for some of the drivers of these cars to find the preferred fuels.

On the ceiling of the car, where the head liner met the windshield, directly above the rearview mirror, there was a small square stamped with a two-digit number. For example, a surviving Ghia at the Detroit Historical Museum is number 18, according to this ceiling tag. An obvious question is whether Ghia numbered the bodies as they built them, say from 1 to 55, but people who worked on the program at the time say they only recall using the last digits of the vehicle's identification number to describe each car. The vehicle number on the DHM car is 991225, stamped on an aluminum tag inside the driver's side doorjamb. The cars also had the last three digits of the vehicle number stamped on a brace in the engine compartment, and that was the number Ghia used when needing a shorthand method to refer to a particular car. The six-digit number was the entire identification number for the car—the car did not carry a full seventeen-digit VIN like cars do today.

The key that started the car was unusual, but users would never know by looking at it. Chrysler never made different keys for the cars—any Ghia Turbine key would start any of the fifty-five cars built. Bill Carry, who spent much of his time driving and working on the cars in the program, pointed out later how much easier it made things for the workers to not have to worry about which key went to which car. "We each had one key," he said. It also would not present a problem to users; since the cars were scattered all over the country they would never be confused with one another.

The power brakes on the Ghia Turbine were out of the ordinary—at least for a car. Most drivers would not notice, but the brakes were assisted by compressed air and designed and manufactured by Kelsey Hayes. Normally used for trucks, the air-over-oil brakes became necessary because the turbine did not generate engine vacuum like a piston engine. Here, the brakes were powered by compressed air from a small cylinder under the hood alongside the driver's side fender. The cylinder was filled by a small electric compressor. A warning light on the interior of the car warned the driver if the cylinder failed or lost air pressure; the cylinder was so small it took only a few seconds for the compressor to refill it under normal driving conditions. If the engine shut off while driving, the air in the cylinder would be more than enough to stop the car. If the air cylinder failed, the driver could still stop the car. It wouldn't have felt that different from stopping a typical car when the engine has shut down and the brakes lose their boost.

Another nice detail was a light the designers placed under the armrest on the driver's door. When the door was opened, the light came on. It served to make the door more visible to cars that might be driving by, and it also illuminated the ground next to the door so the driver could see where he or she was about to step. The only problem with the placement of the light was that if the door was regularly slammed, the lightbulb in the door needed replacement quite often.

Huebner tried to describe to the press what it was like to drive the Ghia. "The sensation of driving a turbine car can be described, but it is largely meaningless unless actually experienced. One can compare it to the difference in the sensation of a piston-powered aircraft takeoff and the takeoff of a jet. It is an impression of superb smoothness, of sleekness."

The turbine's power reached the rear wheels through a modified Chrysler Torqueflite automatic transmission. It resembled the automatic transmission that Chrysler placed in most of its cars, except that the Ghia car needed no torque converter. The gap between the power turbine and the gas generator picked up most of the slack in the system. Because some of the parts of the engine needed lubrication, the turbine team placed a larger fluid pan in the transmission and plumbed the engine as if it were merely an extension of the transmission. In doing so, Chrysler eliminated the need to perform oil changes. It also ran the power steering as part of this fluid circuit. The transmission fluid pump was powered by an accessory drive off the turbine engine.

Remembering the popularity of its previous films, Chrysler introduced the Ghia Turbine to the screen with a film showing it doing laps at the Chelsea Proving Grounds. This emphasized how thoroughly the car had been tested and how ready it was for general use. The car was then taken off the oval and driven on winding, twisting roads that were also part of the proving grounds. It was proclaimed an "engineering breakthrough." These films were distributed to anyone who might want to watch them, with more than a few being shown in high school science classes.

5

The User Program:
The Ultimate Public Relations Event

When the cars were ready, Chrysler launched one of the boldest experiments in the history of corporate America. On May 14, 1963, the Ghia Turbine was unveiled to the public for the first time. The press got to see it at the Essex House in New York City. Later that day, reporters were given the opportunity to ride in and drive the car on a two-and-a-half-mile course at the Roosevelt Raceway on Long Island. The next day, the car was brought to the Waldorf-Astoria Hotel for a viewing by Chrysler dealers.

The second day of the event was a bit livelier for Chrysler. To show how well the car performed in traffic, Robert Anderson, George Huebner, a public relations man, and one other passenger set out to cross Manhattan during rush hour. Although the cars had usually performed flawlessly with Huebner at the wheel, the car stalled at the intersection of 40th Street and Third Avenue. Despite repeated attempts, it would not restart. Traffic began to pile up on all sides. "Within minutes, other conventional piston-engine cars were tied up in all directions as the beatnik habitués of Third Avenue swarmed around the low, sleek, bronze-colored vehicle." The crosstown commute was abandoned, and Huebner later told the reporters the car was found to have a tank of contaminated fuel.

It was a rare piece of bad publicity for the turbine car. "Chrysler Turbine Car Stalls, Causes Manhattan Traffic Jam," read the *Detroit News*. Most readers who had been following the program assumed the fuel contamination consisted of water. Some skeptical readers—insiders who knew Huebner—wondered if the car hadn't suffered an actual breakdown. It was possible; after all, no cars are perfect. Those who knew Huebner best suspected that the car had broken down and Huebner made up the contaminant story as a cover, to protect his beloved turbine car.

A week earlier, Chrysler had announced that it would lend the fifty Turbine Cars to the public for a free test drive. Chrysler planned to lend consumers the car for a period of a few months to use as they wished. Then, when they turned the car in, Chrysler could get feedback on real-world use of the turbine. The news splash was huge. *Time* magazine ran an article on the upcoming program along with a description of the Ghia Turbine, even including a schematic diagram of how the car and its turbine operated. In a piece entitled "The Big Test," *Time* wrote: "Auto engineers who dream of finding a replacement for the complicated, churning piston engine have long looked wistfully at the gas-turbine engine that introduced the jet age." It explained how Chrysler had approached the various problems with the turbine. Then, "Next week it will introduce a smartly styled turbine-powered car that it considers reliable enough to turn loose, at least for testing's sake, on a segment of the general public." Coverage followed in the *Saturday Evening Post*, *Look*, *Newsweek*, and every major newspaper nationwide. Chrysler also said at the unveiling that if the reaction to the cars was positive, it was prepared to start mass-producing turbine-powered cars by 1965.

The immediate response from the public was overwhelming—thirty thousand people sent in requests to be involved in the program within six weeks of the announcement. Chrysler turned the requests over to the accounting firm of Touche, Ross, Bailey, and Smart. Chrysler told the firm to pick drivers at random using a few criteria: they had to either own a car or come from a household with a car, they had to be licensed, and they had to live in certain metropolitan centers chosen by Chrysler. All of the letters requesting vehicles were unsolicited; no one from Chrysler ever officially said how to apply for the cars, and Chrysler never printed entry forms. One letter came from a twelve-year-old boy who asked that his father be given a turbine car. Another came from an eighty-three-year-old retiree. From those thousands of letters, 203 were given the ride of a lifetime.

Look magazine ran a big feature on the car, with color photos of a pair of the cars and—of course—George Huebner standing nearby. "Run-of-the-road motorists will decide fate of radical new Chrysler engine," the sub-head noted. Interestingly, *Look* gave the value of the cars as half a million dollars each—ten times what Huebner had quoted elsewhere.

The *Look* writer loved the car. Chrysler let him drive it, and Huebner told the writer he had personally driven the car at speeds in excess of 120 miles per hour. It is unclear if Huebner was pulling the man's leg on the price and speed of the car, but it didn't matter. The story raved about the car and about how amazing the user program was going to be. The writer also asked General Motors and Ford what they thought of the turbine engine—especially the one in the Chrysler turbine car. The Ford spokes-person had good things to say about the notion, but the GM president stated that the turbine could not be economically produced "at the present time." When asked for his response, Huebner said, "They just haven't caught up with us."

In a taste of what would follow, Chrysler handed out beautiful bro-chures to the press. The four-page "Turbine Car Information" pamphlet featured expensive photos of the car surrounded by one of the best laid out press releases the auto industry had ever seen. Dated May 14, the lan-guage of the release was grand as well: "Chrysler Corporation today took a giant step into the future with its introduction of the world's first family-size passenger car specifically engineered and designed for turbine power." Among the descriptions of the car were quotes from various Chrysler exec-utives and spokespeople—many of which would appear verbatim in the next day's papers—and praise for the car. "New styling for new power is embodied in the limited production Chrysler Corporation Turbine Car. Smooth, sculpted lines of the new turbine car give it a contemporary per-sonality all its own."

One typical rave review ran in the September 1963 issue of *Mechanix Illustrated*: "If some fuzzy cat had invented the turbine engine before the piston engine and if all our cars today were turbine-driven, what would the inventer [sic] of the piston engine do? In my opinion, he would cry his eyes out while slowly starving to death."

The review continued: "Let's take this bucket of steam on a test run. The first thing you notice is a brand-new sound. Those of us accustomed to the muffled explosions of old Nellie will have to get used to that jet-like swish of the turbine. If there were a lot of them on the road it would be more like spending an afternoon at the airport than on a turnpike." The driver took his for a spin to see how fast it would go. "I drove this car about 40 miles flat-out on Chrysler's high-speed track. Top speed was 108 to 108.5 and at (hold your hat) 44,000 RPM. As I recall, I did 110 MPH at 46,000 with the old model." Later he wrote, "What do I think of this turbine rig? I like it. It's quite possible that the gas-turbine-powered car may have the entire market in ten years or less. The piston engine could well be on its way out."

One man who responded to the call of the turbine was a field service engineer for General Electric named Bill Carry. Carry was familiar with turbines—GE was one of the main manufacturers of them and supplied its engines to Sikorsky and other helicopter manufacturers. Carry routinely worked on these turbines and had begun to wonder what kind of power-plant a turbine would make for a car. When he heard about Chrysler's experiment of lending the cars, he wrote and asked for a job on the pro-gram. He was quickly granted an interview, hired, and given the task of overseeing the service on the fleet of Ghia cars. Apparently his mechani-cal engineering degree from Notre Dame and his experience working on the helicopters that ferried the president to and from the White House impressed someone at Chrysler enough to take a chance on the techni-cian with no automotive experience. Carry later suspected that no one else within Chrysler wanted the job.

Carry reported for work just as the first Ghia rolled off the assembly line. He familiarized himself with the specifics of the Chrysler turbine and the Ghia car, and began planning how the cars would be serviced over the next few years. At the point of assembly, a couple of engineers joined the process to make sure that everything went smoothly. Later Carry said, "The two engineers in Service spent about three months familiarizing themselves with the engine and vehicle. They did this during the spring, about seven or eight months before the delivery program commenced, by making a general nuisance of themselves in the turbine laboratory, the experimental road test garage, and the proving grounds. They spent many hours observing assembly and disassembly, test cell operations, vehicle installations, and other development test operations."

Because Chrysler wanted the downtime on these cars to be minimized, it made sense to assign the task to the best mechanics Chrysler had. At the time, Chrysler trained dealership mechanics at six centers across the country. Each center had a service training manager who oversaw the instruction of the mechanics. Carry decided to make those managers the experts on the turbine cars for each region. It was a great idea for a couple reasons: If the cars went into production, these individuals would need to train the rest of the mechanics how to repair the cars. And these individuals were clearly the best mechanics in Chrysler's fold—they were already the ones who taught the rest how to repair cars.

Al Bradshaw served as a Turbine Service Representative who handled one of the regions. Before he came to Chrysler, he'd worked on some jet cars for racers trying to break land speed records at the Bonneville Salt Flats. Like Bill Carry, his previous experience with turbines brought him to the front of the program.

Everyone who wrote to Chrysler regarding the program received correspondence thanking them for their interest and telling them to wait. A second letter, dated October 1963, recapped the development of the turbine car and described how the cars were going to be lent to the public for the next two years. Chrysler also apologized for not being able to accommodate all requests.

As we wrote you before, while 50 turbine cars can be effective in producing significant results in our market testing program, such a small number of cars, unfortunately, is not nearly enough to satisfy the 20,000 requests that we have received. We, of course, would like nothing better than to be able to supply all of the people who have written us asking for turbine cars. I believe you will understand, however, why the user selection system is based on the over-all needs of the market test, and not on any personal considerations.

The letter was signed by John F. Bunnell from Chrysler Marketing. It included a press release that explained how the accounting firm of Touche, Ross, Bailey, and Smart would select the users for the experiment. If nothing else, the third-party accounting firm deflected blame from Chrysler, from those who might be upset they didn't get a car as part of the program.

Chicagoan Richard Vlaha was the first consumer to take delivery of a turbine Ghia, on October 29, 1963. The handover took place at Chicago's Water Tower Inn in front of a huge press contingent. Chrysler president Lynn Townsend spoke to the press. "We've now reached the time when the first motorist selected to test and use the turbine car under normal conditions is about to receive his car. He and his family will be participating in a kind of market evaluation which, as far as we've been able to determine, is entirely new to the automobile industry." Someone asked why Chrysler was doing this—lending out experimental cars to the public. He told them, "It is a necessary piece of research concerning the size and characteristics of the market for this new kind of automobile. And, since it is a test, an experimental market research project, it has no pre-ordained outcome." After his presentation, Townsend asked if any of the press in attendance might like a ride. The rest of the day was spent giving rides in the car to everyone at the event.

A twenty-five-year-old systems engineer for IBM, Vlaha soon found himself being filmed by news cameras as he waved good-bye to his wife and climbed into his borrowed turbine car. Just to make sure the reporters present and those who couldn't attend got the details of the story correct, Chrysler handed out press releases that contained every imaginable detail of the Vlaha delivery. His wife's name was Patricia, and they had three children: Theresa, Kathleen, and Richard, aged three years, two years, and eight months. Vlaha was born November 8, 1938, and had attended St. Mel High School before going to DePaul, where he got his B.A. in mathematics. Many newspapers parroted the press releases in their next issues, and added little. For instance, the *Detroit News* article "Public Test of Turbine Cars Starts" recounted the details of Vlaha's personal history but did not quote Mr. or Mrs. Vlaha.

What the press did not know was that the Vlahas had already driven the turbine car. Richard had written to Chrysler asking for a turbine car when he saw a brief mention of the upcoming program in the *Chicago Sun-Times*. A short time later, his wife called Richard at work to tell him that Chrysler had called and asked if they could buy the Vlahas dinner—and interview them for the program. The Vlahas enjoyed a nice meal with some people from Chrysler and, as the waiters cleared the table, got the go-ahead.

A few weeks later, Chrysler called and asked the Vlahas to come out one evening to Soldier Field's parking lot. There they found the men they'd met at dinner standing by an eighteen-wheel semi-tractor trailer truck. After exchanging pleasantries, the representatives from Chrysler rolled a turbine car out of the truck. The Chrysler reps wanted the Vlahas to familiarize themselves with the car so that when they got in the car and drove away—in front of the media—there wouldn't be any hitches. After driving the car around the big parking lot in the dark for a while, they felt comfortable driving the jet car. Chrysler had decided to not take any chances with this, the first time the car was being lent to a user. Practice runs, the nights before delivery, became routine in delivering the cars to users.

The press treatment the Vlahas received became the norm, as Chrysler went full force in publicity mode for each user period. After the user was selected, the public relations department hired a local "Kelly Girl" and gave her the task of contacting every local media outlet near the user's home. Newspapers and radio and television stations received press releases and information about the car and the local user. The packets included the promise of a test drive to any media person who showed up to cover the delivery. The events were well attended by the press, largely from the effort Chrysler invested in promoting them. In the era of the afternoon newspaper, the events were held in the morning to ensure the coverage would appear the same day.

A highlight of the press event was always the moment that Chrysler turned the keys over and let the reporters ask the user questions. Although it was usually a simple give-and-take with the media lobbing softball questions—"What do you think of the turbine car?"—once in a while there were fireworks. A sixty-seven-year-old gentleman from Oklahoma City who bore a striking resemblance to Colonel Sanders of KFC fame went into a tirade about the state's governor. The "thieves" in the capital were taxing the state out of existence! His favorite thing about the turbine car was that he could use fuels that weren't taxed. A flustered Chrysler public relations expert named Dave Jolivette took the stand when the man stopped and pointed out that the opinions they had just heard "do not reflect the opinions of the Chrysler Corporation."

————

Like the 202 other consumers who would take delivery of a Ghia Turbine in the next two years, Vlaha received an hour-long orientation on how the car operated and what to expect. More often than not, the person delivering the car was Jolivette. Once in a while, Huebner showed up to hand over the keys, saying a few words to the press and posing with the consumers for photos.

Chrysler even developed a checklist to be reviewed with the consumer at the time of delivery. Quite a few times when Jolivette wasn't available, Bill Carry acted as the Chrysler representative who delivered the consumer's car and gave the instructions to the users. The checklist was similar to those used nowadays when a buyer takes delivery of a new automobile at a dealership, although salespeople often abbreviate or skip the process when they think the buyer knows how to drive a car. The Ghia Turbines were different; they required a thorough understanding by the consumer to avoid problems later. After the "walk around," the consumers were shown how to operate everything in the interior. Although much of it was similar to a typical car, many of the switches were tucked away nicely. It's not that the switches had anything to do with the turbine; the designers in Italy had simply outdone themselves in making this car unique. The heart of the presentation was the "user maintenance and responsibilities," where the rules on fuel types were discussed, and the "driving" section, which covered the strange series of operations required to start the car.

Merely starting the car was described in eight steps, although an experienced driver would soon learn that these steps weren't all that complicated. There was no need to pump the gas pedal while starting the car, a habit many drivers would have to fight considering that many other contemporary cars required a driver to pump the pedal once or twice on cold starting. The consumer was told simply to "Turn key to start and release." At that point, the engine would fire itself up and soon reach operating temperature and speed. Consumers were warned to watch the appropriate gauges: the temperature would quickly rise to between 1,100 and 1,400 degrees Fahrenheit. The engine idle speed would rise to 18,000 RPM. Once the gauges showed the correct numbers, the driver was told to check the oil pressure and the ammeter to make sure the battery was charging, and the car was ready to drive. As simple as the startup procedure sounds now, many drivers managed to get it wrong, and some damaged the engines in the process.

The last "general" section was a potpourri of advice. Drivers were told to keep a lookout for appropriate fuel sources. Although the turbine could burn a variety of fuels, diesel was preferred. "If appropriate, instruct chauffeur or garage attendant in vehicle operation and maintenance." The Chrysler rep was also prodded to teach other members of the family how to operate the car and even to explain the function and operation of turbines in general, if the consumer showed an interest and wanted to know more. At that point, the rep handed the consumers a copy of the Driver's Guide and they were ready to enter the turbine age.

———

The Vlahas drove the car for three months, putting 3,635 miles on it. There was a two-week period when they didn't have the car, after Patricia Vlaha was rear-ended at a red light in Cicero. Chrysler maintained the insurance on the cars as part of the program, and Patricia wasn't at fault, so Chrysler quickly set about getting the car repaired.

Who was qualified to repair the hand-built, Italian-crafted work of art? Carry shopped around and found the Chicago area's best body shop to do the repairs. Once the car was there, they called Carry. Did Chrysler have any spare body parts for the cars? The trunk lid was so badly damaged that on a typical car it would have needed replacement. Fortunately, when Ghia manufactured the fifty-five cars, they had also sent over a few extras of each body panel for just such occasions.

Carry shipped a spare trunk lid to Chicago; the body shop wouldn't have to paint the piece, though. All of the body panels had been painted in Italy. A puzzled body shop manager called him a few days later. The trunk lid didn't fit. It wasn't even close, being almost half an inch too short. Carry had worried that this might happen; each Ghia car was unique due to the Italian handcrafting. A part from one wouldn't necessarily swap with the same part from another Ghia car. Carry asked the body shop if it was possible to pound the old trunk lid straight and refit it to the car. It was, and the car was soon back on the road. Overall, the cars in the program were lucky with respect to auto accidents. This was the worst accident any of the cars suffered.

That is not to say that the cars remained pristine throughout the program. Quite often they were returned to Chrysler with small dings and dents. The problem was most pronounced on the aluminum hood and trunk. Al Bradshaw recalled seeing quite a few cars dented on those two surfaces, quite possibly by people simply placing heavy objects on the car and not knowing how prone the aluminum was to damage.

The Vlahas were impressed with how smoothly the car ran. Richard found it "relaxing" to drive because of how quiet it was compared to his regular car. They fueled it with diesel, which was readily available in the Chicago area, and soon became the center of attention everywhere they went. Reporters wanted to go for drives. Patricia found the car surrounded by strangers when she returned to it in the grocery store parking lot. People stopped their cars in traffic and got out to walk over and look at the car while the Vlahas waited for traffic lights to change. For the young couple, the attention was fun and exciting.

Although the Vlahas loved the car, they did notice it got horrible mileage during their city driving. While the turbine could get over ten miles to the gallon on the highway, the Vlahas spent much of their time driving in the city, where the mileage was much lower. Years later, Richard remembered that there was only one thing Chrysler told him never to discuss with anyone: the gas mileage. Whenever he was asked—and he often was—he feigned ignorance and deflected the topic to something else about the car. The Vlahas also believed that the press was inclined to bash the car. When they weren't asking about the fuel economy, they seemed to ask a lot of pointed questions aimed at the car's limitations. One reporter commented, "It's not much of a family car, is it?"

In a stunt that would have made Huebner proud, Richard and a co-worker at IBM decided to impress some of their friends at nearby Motorola, a customer of IBM's. They put the Ghia into the back of an eighteen-wheeler truck, with Vlaha still in it, and drove over to Motorola's loading dock. There, they backed up the truck, pulled the car onto the loading dock, and then Richard and his co-worker drove the car into the Motorola building. People came running to hear what was making the whooshing noise. Richard carefully drove the car down the wide hallways to the cafeteria, where he pulled it around and shut it off for inspection by the Motorola workers.

On another occasion, Richard drove the car to downtown Chicago and couldn't find a legal parking spot. He pulled into a no-parking zone and got out. A few minutes later, a crowd began to gather and ask Richard questions about the car. Before too long, a police car pulled up and an officer approached Richard. Richard apologized and offered to move the car. The officer waved him off. "Leave it where it is," he said with a smile.

After three months, the Vlahas turned the car back in to Chrysler. Richard asked if they might get credit for the two weeks that the car was in the collision shop, but Chrysler had already scheduled the car for its next delivery. After a week of inspection, cleaning, and double-checking, the car was then turned over to a forty-eight-year-old president of a "metal products company." He drove it for 6,775 miles and then returned it to Chrysler in May. The Ghia Turbines went like that, from one driver to another, crossing the spectrum of careers and demographics of the early 1960s. The Vlaha Ghia Turbine spent most of the test period in and around the Chicago area, while the others spent their time traveling around various metropolitan centers in the lower forty-eight states.

Users were required to sign a legal document entitled "User/Chrysler Corporation Turbine Car AGREEMENT." In a near-impossible feat, Chrysler's legal department managed to condense the lending contract to a single page, albeit a long and fancy-sounding document. Chrysler made the users affirm that they had a "good and safe driving record," they would not allow unlicensed people to drive the car, and the car would not be used for anything but normal, personal transportation. The users were also forbidden to attempt to repair the cars or to take them out of the country. In exchange for that promise, the users got use of the cars for a three-month period, with Chrysler picking up the tab on all costs, maintenance, and insurance. All the users had to give was the promise to cooperate with Chrysler during and after the program by giving Chrysler feedback and allowing Chrysler to use the users' pictures, likenesses, and statements in advertising or other forms. The only real cost to the consumers was the fuel, something they would have had to pay for any car they drove.

Consumers soon noticed the advantages of the turbine car. It started instantly, regardless of outside temperature. Test drivers in frozen climates were pleasantly surprised to find that the car would not only start instantly but would also have heat for the passenger compartment upon starting up. In piston engines, heaters draw their warmth from the engine coolant, but not until the engine reaches operating temperature. In the Ghia Turbine, the heater got its warmth from air ducted out of the turbine itself. This allowed for heat the moment the car began to run. It also furnished instant heat to the defrosters.

Added to that, the car ran quietly, with virtually no vibration. Chrysler engineers even noticed—even if the consumers didn't—that the engines didn't wear and lose power over time the way piston engines do. After all, there were no parts scraping against each other as in a piston engine.

Initially Chrysler hoped to run the Ghia with a typical twelve-volt electrical system like that on a regular car. This would have allowed Chrysler to use the same lights, motors, and other electrical components as the other cars it sold at the time. During testing, however, Chrysler discovered that the twelve-volt starter could not always turn the turbine fast enough to start it reliably. The only solution was to use a twenty-four-volt starter. This required two batteries and a starter unlike anything that Chrysler used in any of its cars at the time.

Rather than rewire the entire system of the turbine car, the designers struck an innovative solution: they put two batteries in its trunk to crank the starter. When the car was being started, both batteries were used. Once the car started, it automatically switched over to a single-battery system. The electronics of the time were primitive by today's standards, and the dual system required a huge switch that weighed "almost twenty pounds," according to Carry. It worked, and the problem was solved.

Carry also trained others to work on the cars, and he set up mechanics at various Chrysler Service Training schools from around the country to retrain mechanics as necessary to work on the turbines. The heads of the schools came to Chrysler's facility in Centerline, Michigan, where Carry gave them hands-on training on various aspects of Ghia repair. They came from New York, Atlanta, Chicago, Kansas City, Los Angeles, and Detroit. The white Ghia was the car used in many of these sessions and can be seen in photos of the training sessions. In one, Carry showed mechanics how a turbine engine was replaced, with the white Ghia up on a hoist. As one of the first five turbine cars built, the white Ghia was considered a prototype and would not be involved directly in the user program. The cars were "easy to take care of, [and] pretty simple to understand. It was not difficult for these guys to become competent in taking care of them," Carry said. Even so, once the program started, Carry often flew out and supervised repairs on the turbine cars so that he could compile information Chrysler could use in the future. The goal of the program was to "keep any down-time on vehicles in the field to an absolute minimum."

In fact, many of the regional managers found themselves running around at odd hours, repairing the vehicles. Not all of the repairs were catastrophic. If a user ran the car out of fuel, it often would not restart unless the engine was primed. It was something that Chrysler didn't want an amateur trying, so such technicians as Al Bradshaw, Bill Hamer, and Carry often found themselves getting cars started that had merely run out of fuel. They discovered a few other peculiarities of the car during the program. The brakes were probably too small for how much the car weighed, and needed servicing a bit more often than expected. When they had the chance, they would update the cars, fixing problems the program had helped identify before they became apparent to the users.

Some of the repairs, of course, were more involved. The technicians in the field never opened the engines up, however. If the turbine had an internal problem, the entire assembly was replaced and the defective engine sent back to Detroit for study. Bradshaw thought it was possible that the engine was replaced at least once in every car in the user program. On one occasion, Hamer replaced the engine in a car at a dealership without using a hoist. He jacked the car up in the air and placed it on fifty-five-gallon oil drums to work on it. It was a precarious arrangement, but it worked. He may have known it would work from earlier conversations with Bradshaw; Bradshaw had used the same technique to replace an engine in a turbine car in Colorado.

Another time, Bradshaw and a few others from Chrysler had to get two turbine cars across Nebraska before morning. The cars flew across the plains through the night at a hundred miles an hour, with the only excitement being a wayward pig the cars had to dodge. Bradshaw said later that he felt the cars could have run like that for days.

At the end of 1963, Chrysler dealers from across America converged on Detroit for a meeting hosted by the company, to be updated on what they could look forward to. Huebner spoke to them about a single concept: the Chrysler Turbine Car. Those in attendance certainly knew about the cars, and most had probably seen one of the cars in the fleet on the road at that time. Huebner gave them a quick history of the car that was part pep talk, part inside look for those who would be working closely with the company in the future, perhaps even selling these cars.

Huebner told the audience about how the two cars used in the cross-country drive contained the only two engines of that generation turbine Chrysler had at the time. "There were no spare engines and had an accident occurred, we could not have replaced either of these cars. The turbine was strictly on its own. It had to stand or fall on these two embodiments of nine years of research." He outlined the story of the car, how the program had progressed, and how there was a strong likelihood the cars would be eventually sold to the public. He ended on a high note: "This is a revolution and we at Chrysler are the revolutionaries."

———

In the second week of January 1964, the Society of Automotive Engineers met, as they usually do each winter, at Cobo Hall in Detroit, Michigan. Representatives of the industry spent four days listening to speeches and presentations from others in the industry, as well as walking among exhibits of vendors seeking business. Chrysler had quite a presentation for the rest of the automotive world to see: they lined up four presentations on the turbine car program, headlined by George Huebner. Huebner delivered his overview paper on "The Chrysler Regenerative Turbine-Powered Passenger Car," and was soon followed by more specific papers on the details of the engine itself, a paper by Dr. Roy on the metallurgy of the engine, and a final paper on the laboratory work done on the program.

Some wondered how Huebner had time to write the extensive paper he delivered, considering how busy he stayed promoting the project. Although Huebner's name appears as the paper's author, Huebner had major portions of the paper written by engineers in his program, including Bud Mann. Copies of his final speech were printed and distributed at the convention, but the draft Huebner read from showed his handwritten corrections to an earlier version. The changes he made between drafts are quite telling. A section that spoke of the shortfalls in the first turbine engine is simply crossed out. Huebner was willing to tell the rest of the industry all about the latest Chrysler turbines, he just wasn't prepared to tell them anything that seemed negative about the project. He may also have left out solutions to problems the other engineers wondered about. Why give away the answers for free?

———

One perk of working on the program was having access to the cars. Dave Jolivette handled much of the public relations for Chrysler on the Ghia turbine program, and he often took a Ghia home on the weekends. His son Bruce—who would grow up to work at Williams International, the company founded by turbine pioneer Sam Williams—remembered fondly tooling around Detroit and the suburbs in a Ghia Turbine that his father had borrowed for the weekend. Bruce was just a teenager at the time, and he loved the attention the car received. People often stopped at their house to get out and look at the Ghia parked in their driveway. Bruce and his dad would go out and talk to anyone with questions. On one occasion, they found themselves caught in traffic in nearby Ann Arbor when they noticed that the driver in a convertible behind them was yelling to get their attention. "Where can I buy one of those?" he shouted. Dave waved and told the man the cars weren't for sale—at least at the time. "I don't care how much it costs—I want one!" the man yelled back.

Another thing Bruce remembered well was the sound the Ghia Turbine made after it was parked and turned off. Years later, after microwave ovens were invented, he equated the sound of the engine cooling to the popping of microwave popcorn. The crackling sound came from the cooling of various metals in the engine.

Bud Mann took a Ghia car home a few times as well, and remembered the car as being simply "fun" to drive. He remembered talking with a fellow engineer named Peter Angell, who had taken his dog for a ride in the vehicle. During the entire ride, Angell's dog howled and whined, reacting to the unusual sound of the turbine engine, and possibly to supersonic frequencies humans couldn't hear.

———

Every Ghia Turbine Car came with a Driver's Guide in the glove box. Keeping with the turbine bronze theme, the book had a very expensive-looking metal-flake, bronze-colored cover. Not missing an opportunity to sell the uniqueness of the car, the guide started out: "The Chrysler Corporation Turbine Car introduces a pioneering concept in automotive powerplant design and function. Evaluation of turbine power by the motoring public is the purpose of the Turbine Car. The Driver's Guide was prepared for you . . . the person selected by the Chrysler Corporation to evaluate this revolutionary new vehicle." The introduction ended with a cautionary note: "News of the introduction of this car has aroused great public interest. It can be expected that many people who see it will be interested in examining the turbine car inside and out. Such public interest and inspection is most desirable with supervision. On occasions where the car will be parked in public places, it is suggested that you lock the vehicle rather than leave it open or unattended."

To keep unwanted visitors from gaining access to the car's trunk or engine compartment, the turbine car had uncommon features for the time: neither the trunk nor the hood could be opened without access to the interior of the car. In the early 1960s, most automobile hoods could be raised simply by finding a latch at the front of the car, usually right inside the grille. The trunks of most cars did—and still do—have locks that can be accessed from the outside of the car. The Chrysler Ghia Turbine Car had a release lever for the trunk behind the driver's seat and a release lever for the hood under the dash. There was no way to access either, with or without the key, without getting inside the car first.

———

The third Ghia car to roll off the Greenfield Road assembly line in Detroit—the eighth Ghia built overall—was delivered locally to a banker from Royal Oak, Michigan. The delivery took place at the Sheraton-Cadillac Hotel in Detroit, where Chrysler vice president Paul Ackerman handed a set of keys to Charles Goebel. The press attended in force. They loved it when Goebel's wife, Jeannine, swiped the keys from her husband and hopped behind the wheel first.

In what would become the norm for a user of the turbine car, Goebel found himself the center of attention everywhere he went, and it spilled into the local media. The *Detroit News* wrote a follow-up piece on him a week after he took delivery. "It's been quite a week," he told the paper.

I've been leaving the car in the bank parking lot and practically every customer sees it and wants to know about it. They ask the tellers or any bank employee they can buttonhole what type of fuel it uses, if it's easy to drive. Some ask to sit inside. As a result, we've had to brief all employees on the car. We're closed on Wednesday afternoons and I've made up a list of employees who want rides during that period.

People gawked in traffic too. "People lower their car windows on the freeways to try and hear what the turbine sounds like. The car attracted a crowd at church and has been a big hit at the local car wash." His seven-year-old son even gave tours of the car to neighborhood children, who then ran home and brought back their parents for rides. "The car has performed flawlessly so far, in bad weather and good. The whine from the turbine seems no more noticeable than the noise made by a conventional engine."

Some consumers took advantage of Chrysler's generous offer more than anyone expected. One man took his turbine car from New York to Florida and back. His fifteen thousand miles were possibly the most anyone put on during possession of a car, but another family put twelve thousand miles on their car in three months.

———

The cars stayed in the public eye—and press—for two years, even if they weren't for sale. Chrysler shot another film, a fifteen-minute piece aimed at its dealers. The movie explained the program and how dealers might benefit from the Ghia Turbine Cars even if they weren't for sale yet. As dealers watched cars being built and then driven at the proving grounds, a narrator extolled the virtues of the turbine. They also saw their brave leaders on screen, watching the cars roll down the world's only turbine car production line. For once, George Huebner Jr. wasn't the only well-dressed executive on screen. He was joined by Lynn Townsend, president of Chrysler; Robert Anderson, vice president of product planning; and Paul Ackerman, vice president of engineering—though the narrator credits Huebner as the driving force behind the turbine.

The film explained to dealers the next step of the turbine marketing program: the shopping center tour. Chrysler would arrange with local shopping centers to put up a display, the centerpiece of which would be the Ghia Turbine. It would be joined by a few other products from Chrysler and its divisions. The display would also feature explanations of how the turbine worked and how Chrysler was on the leading edge of automotive technology. Salespeople from local dealers would meet and greet shoppers as turbine technicians from Chrysler explained the Ghia to visitors.

Chrysler also expected the local press to participate, in essence giving the entire project free publicity. Before the exhibit hit town, the local press would find press kits on the turbine cars in their mailboxes. Why would the press bite? The film's narrator explained how the local press would be invited to the deliveries of the turbine cars to the users in the program. In case that wasn't enough, the press would also be invited to the shopping market exhibits before they opened to the public, and, after getting the rundown from the Chrysler reps there, they'd all receive rides in the turbine car. Huebner had not forgotten how the Los Angeles press corps had stampeded to the curb of his hotel when he offered them rides in a turbine car at the end of his cross-country trip.

The film explained how the tour would also introduce Chrysler's radical new five-year, fifty-thousand-mile warranty on its new cars. No other car company backed its products so well. The turbines might draw in shoppers, but the public relations and the new warranty would entice them to buy. These promotional steps paid off. Chrysler had only 9.6 percent of the U.S. market share in 1962, its lowest figure ever. The following year, its share jumped to 12.4 percent, and the number continued to rise. This change in direction occurred during the turbine car's shopping center campaign.

The campaign described in the film was known as the "Turbine Car Exhibition Round-Up." Chrysler also issued a press release describing the program to news outlets. Its stated goal was to show the car and Chrysler's expertise to two million people in nineteen "key markets" in thirteen states. The exhibition coincided with the launch of the user program, and for a while they would run at the same time. Shoppers would even be encouraged to enter their names at the displays to get themselves into the user program. Buttressing the display were four "pentastar-shaped pagodas, featuring some of Chrysler's contributions to automobile design; a fifth pagoda serves as an information center for the entire show."

Another highlight of the campaign was the Hemi, the 426-cubic-inch engine that Chrysler began selling to the public and racing in the NASCAR circuit. The press release again emphasized the industry's first five-year or fifty-thousand-mile warranty. The release ended with a list of the cities to be visited. No doubt the media in those cities and their neighbors received the press release first. The shopping center campaign was also supported by newspaper ads, paid for by Chrysler.

As part of the national campaign, dealers received posters for their display windows that promoted the upcoming turbine appearances. The dealers were also given little models of the Ghia Turbines to give to people who took test drives in any Chrysler product during the period. In anticipation of the public's love of free stuff, the narrator warned that the miniature Ghia models might be put to better use if given only to targeted prospects.

Robert Anderson, vice president of product planning, wrapped up the film with a statement: the campaign would generate two years of public relations that showed Chrysler on the cutting edge of technology. Even if the Ghias never made it to the buying public, the "free" advertising would be priceless. Anderson then brought out Bob McCurry, assistant general manager of Chrysler's Dodge division, and John Norton, McCurry's counterpart at Chrysler-Plymouth. McCurry liked the shopping center idea and thought it would reach a huge number of people. Norton hoped people would leave the exhibit and get into their own cars, compare them to the new Chryslers they had just seen, and be lured into a nearby Chrysler dealer.

———

In the spring of 1964, Alden and Mark Olson, the father and son who'd ridden in the Turbo Fury at the dealership in Superior, Wisconsin, were told by relatives they were visiting in Minneapolis that a Chrysler Turbine was on display at the nearby Har Mar shopping mall. The Olsons headed out to the mall, and as they pulled into the parking lot, a bronze Ghia Turbine Car whooshed by them.

Alden and Mark "stood in awe"—the car was so much more beautiful than the 1962 model they'd seen before. It had just been delivered to locals to use for a three-month period, and the delivery had been coordinated with the Round-Up display at the mall. Although they were too late to witness the presentation of the keys, the Olsons were able to see another Ghia on display inside the mall. They spent two hours at the display, as Mark pestered Chrysler reps with questions about the turbine car. Before they left, Mark asked how users were picked for the program. A rep gave him a brochure and told him that anyone who wanted to be considered needed to write to Chrysler in Michigan and ask for a questionnaire.

When they received it, Mark and his father spent two nights preparing their answers to the questions Chrysler asked, trying to second-guess what the Chrysler reps would look for in potential users. The form asked for a variety of information, such as where the applicant's children went to school, what clubs the applicant belonged to, and what hobbies he or she had. While many of the questions were clearly geared toward finding out who would see the car if the applicant was chosen, some were aimed to fit the driving style of the customer with the better characteristics of the turbine engine. Question 5 asked applicants to break down, by percentage, how much of their driving was done "at low speeds (under 50 m.p.h.)" and how much "at highway speeds (over 50 m.p.h.)" Happy with their responses, the Olsons sent the completed questionnaire off and waited.

———

In May 1964, Chrysler delivered a car to the Emmett family of Cleveland at the Westgate Shopping Center. George Huebner made the trip and gave a short presentation to the press before turning the keys over to the lucky users. He noted that the Emmetts were getting the thirtieth car of the program, and that the previous twenty-nine had already logged over ninety thousand miles. He also carefully noted that Betty Emmett was officially the "user" of this car; her husband, Dick, was simply along for the ride.

It also appeared that Huebner and Chrysler may have been fielding complaints from consumers who wanted turbine cars but didn't like their odds with the random selection process employed by Chrysler. Twice in his short talk at the Emmett delivery event, Huebner mentioned Touche, Ross, Bailey, and Smart, the accounting firm Chrysler had hired to select the drivers for the program. His message was very clear: don't blame us—blame them!

———

Meanwhile, back in Detroit, the Ghia team continued assembling a car a week until all the Ghia bodies were on the road. The fiftieth car was delivered to a driver in Des Moines, Iowa, at the end of July 1964. In the time since they'd delivered the first car to Richard Vlaha in Chicago, the engineers had already discovered some issues with the cars. Although the problems were minor, they would often be solved by incorporating small changes into the cars that had not yet been built. Other modifications were made to the cars during their week-long layovers between drivers.

While the users were driving their cars all over the country, Chrysler continued testing the vehicles. One long-running test taking place at the Chelsea Proving Grounds racked up miles on one of the Ghia prototypes to see what kinds of problems extreme mileage might cause. The Ghia Turbine logged over a hundred thousand miles without any major problems.

In another test at Chelsea, the turbine wheel broke loose from its shaft. At a speed near 44,000 RPM, the failure was spectacular—and catastrophic. As engineers and service technicians tore the engine apart for an autopsy, they discovered a problem in the turbine construction. The weld that held the turbine disc to the shaft was inadequate for the stresses the parts were subjected to. While wondering if the problem might be isolated, they got a call from Bill Carry, in the field.

Earlier, Carry had found himself taking a Ghia Turbine Car in for its between-user inspection and predelivery check-up not far from his hometown of Norwich, New York. He picked it up in Buffalo, and the next driver lived in Syracuse. Carry figured he'd take a week-long vacation while he was there. He decided to take a spin by the old homestead and show the Ghia to his brother-in-law. After the typical walk around, they got into the Ghia and Carry gunned the engine. Suddenly there was an explosion, like someone firing a shotgun in the passenger compartment. Then everything went quiet. The gauges went dead. In a fraction of a second, the weld between the turbine shaft and the turbine disc had failed. The explosion sound was most likely the result of the iron disk, spinning at over 40,000 RPM, hitting something and then ricocheting into something else—all within the confines of the engine housing. Carry spent the week replacing the engine and performing detail work on the car.

Although he felt mildly embarrassed about being behind the wheel of the car when it suffered such a catastrophic failure—especially in front of his brother-in-law!—Carry soon found that the failure wasn't his fault. He shipped the engine that had died back to Highland Park for an inspection, and the weld was soon identified as the cause—the same thing that caused the turbine failure at Chelsea. Soon thereafter, a few other Ghia Turbine engines failed in the exact same way, all at roughly the same mileage.

The welding issue was the kind of problem the user program was good for: discovering weaknesses in the car that only real-world use could identify. In the past, the turbine parts had been welded together by inertia welding—one part was held in place and the other was spun at a high speed. The two parts were forced together, and where they met, the friction was so intense that the two parts melted together and became a single piece.

Dr. Roy—the metallurgist—was in charge of not only the materials that went into the engines but also the manufacturing processes of the parts for the turbines. When he studied the failed parts he discovered the problem: microscopic cracks formed in the disk near the weld. Roy suspected the cracks resulted from the fact that portions of the disk farther from the weld did not get as hot as the spot being welded. The difference in temperature caused the disk to expand and contract just enough to form microscopic cracks, which over time became larger cracks that caused the failures.

Roy knew of a recent development in manufacturing that could solve this problem. A German physicist had discovered a way to weld pieces of metal together by using a beam of electrons. This electron beam welding had only been invented a few years earlier, and electron beam welders were still very expensive. Roy traveled to Maryland and bought one of the machines for Chrysler's turbine program. His bosses were unhappy with the amount of money the device cost, but he explained to them that this was the only way to solve the problem.

Soon the turbine technicians were electron beam welding the shafts and replacing the units inside the engines as quickly as they could. From that point on, all engines that were shipped out contained the updated weld. Three quarters of the way through the program, every single engine had been updated, and none of the updated discs ever failed.

The turbine techs became adept at troubleshooting and repairing all manner of engine failures, often without calling for help from other departments or—heaven forbid—from people outside Chrysler. More than once, regional representatives found themselves fabricating parts just to get the cars home. Bill Hamer got a call to diagnose a dead turbine car in Connecticut one evening. When he got there, he found the car's distributor had failed. The cars used a regular distributor to fire the turbine's single spark plug, and, like any other automotive distributor of the time, they were prone to periodic failure. Hamer called Detroit and found that it would take some time for a new distributor to be flown out to him, so he decided to get the car back to his base in New Jersey and work on it there. He scrounged some electrical parts from an old car radio to rig up a system that would work. Old radios used a vibrator coil in their power supplies, and Hamer was familiar with the old-style ignitions in Model T Fords. Those primitive ignition systems merely needed something to generate an intermittent spark, and since the timing of the spark would not matter in the turbine, the parts from the radio did the trick. Hamer got the turbine home with the makeshift ignition in place. "It didn't go any farther, but it got me to where I had to be," he said.

———

Automakers have always struggled with the issue of engine wear. Everyone knows that piston engines age and lose power over time. Many of the reciprocating parts in a piston engine, including the pistons themselves, scrape against other parts of the engine, wear out over time, and become less efficient.

To minimize wear, the turbine engines were specially tuned at Chrysler before they were shipped to the field or installed in cars. The tuning process, called "matching," was repeated when the engine was put into a car. Technicians measured engine speed and the temperature inside the engine and made small adjustments to the vane actuators inside the turbine to get the turbine to its optimal performance. It required a fine balance; running the engine hotter produced more power, but it also put more stress on the internal parts of the engine. Running cooler was easier on the engine but created less horsepower.

———

Around this time—still quite early in the user program—Chrysler realized that it could have sold Ghia Turbine Cars to the public if it wanted to. Dave Jolivette, in public relations, also handled the mail that came in to Chrysler inquiring about how to get into the user program. Now, mixed in with that mail, he began seeing requests from consumers who wanted to buy one. Some wanted a turbine car so badly they sent in blank checks made out to Chrysler—all Chrysler had to do was name its own price and deliver a car. Jolivette sent the checks back with a kind note, thanking them for their interest. These prototype cars, no matter how well they ran, were not for sale.

A service representative from Chrysler stayed in touch with the Ghia users during their three-month test periods, and scheduled one or two inspections during that time as well. Carry saw to it that the inspections were thorough. Even the slightest flaw in the car's performance or appearance was immediately corrected. Carry also stayed on call whenever a car broke down—anywhere in the nation. How fast were the cars repaired? "Right now," he explained. "I mean, I got out of my bed at two o'clock in the morning and got on an airplane on a number of occasions."

Carry would get himself to the stricken Ghia and repair it as quickly as possible. If necessary, he'd have Chrysler ship parts—even whole engines—to wherever he might be working on the car, in an effort to get the car back on the road fast. The user agreement stipulated that nobody other than a Chrysler representative should work on the cars. This point was underscored in the Driver's Guide. Under "Emergency Starting Procedures" drivers were told that push-starting the car was impossible, and if a jump-start wouldn't start the car it would be best to call Chrysler. "Do not permit the emergency man to attempt to diagnose the trouble. Instead contact your Turbine Service Representative."

One Chrysler mechanic later said that if a major engine failure occurred, they were very careful about how they handled the repair. They'd tow the car to a local dealer and then work on it after everyone else had gone home. More often than not, they'd merely swap the old engine out and put a new one in, an operation that could easily be accomplished before the dealer mechanics showed up the next morning. As far as anyone knew, the failures and repairs were nothing more than minor. Al Bradshaw later said that the after-hour repair of the cars was merely so that the mechanic could have some peace and quiet while working on the car at a strange dealership. Otherwise, mechanics, salespeople, and even customers would be tempted to stand around, gawk, and get in the way.

Still, the Turbine service reps knew that part of their job was to protect the images of Chrysler and its turbine car. "When we were out there, we did everything we could to try and keep the image of the corporation in a positive light. Once in a while we were asked what happened and we'd say, 'Oh, nothing,'" Bradshaw admitted.

In an inspired design, the engines and transmissions were matched and paired at Chrysler so they could be shipped as a single unit. If an engine needed too much work, the entire unit would be replaced. Anticipating that this might be the case—whole engines being replaced rather than repaired—the chassis of the car was designed to allow the engine and front suspension to be dropped out of the car as a single piece.

Chrysler sometimes decided to pull out and examine an engine that had nothing wrong with it. Once, Bradshaw removed an engine in Texas that ran perfectly; it had achieved high mileage without failure, and engineers in Detroit wanted to tear it down and examine it.

To replace an engine, Carry or a regional training manager would first receive a huge crate from Detroit—the turbine, the transmission, and all the packing. Shipping the crated engines even caused a slight hitch in the program: the crates were so large and heavy that only the larger airlines could handle them. Carry, Bradshaw, and Hamer often found themselves making arrangements for the crates to be trucked from some faraway airport to the dealership they were using for the repair.

The rest was relatively simple. First, the mechanics disconnected the various parts of the engine from the body and then lifted the car up in the air. The old turbine-transmission setup would be pushed away and the new one rolled into its place. Finally, the Ghia would be lowered onto the new unit and the bolts replaced. The total replacement of an engine and transmission was simple compared to a similar job with a piston-engine vehicle. Carry and Bradshaw noted that it could be performed by two mechanics in half a day.

———

Although various users drove the cars, Chrysler tracked the program by the car, not the driver. A typical example was car number 28. The Chrysler technicians and mechanics referred to each car by the last two digits of its serial number, and "28" bore the number 991228 on the aluminum tag inside the driver's side doorjamb.

This car was delivered to the service department on May 14, 1964, with 1,470 miles on its odometer. After performing some engine repairs—the turbine seemed to be running hot—they delivered the car to its first user in Cleveland, Betty Emmett. She was a thirty-four-year-old junior high school teacher who incorporated the car into her class lessons. She got it with 1,964 miles on May 28. About a month later, Chrysler called the car in for an inspection—Emmett had driven it about two thousand miles—and replaced the fuel filter. On August 26, the user period was over and the service technicians got the car back. It had 10,402 miles on its odometer and the igniter plug needed replacing.

The car sat around for a few weeks while a new user was lined up. The technicians reconditioned the car and updated all of the systems. The lubrication was replaced along with the air filter. While they were working on it, the bearing failed in the gas generator. The replacement parts were updated to prevent a repeat of the failure.

On September 17, the car was delivered to a user in Providence, Rhode Island. William Grunden, a thirty-seven-year-old minister, parked his regular transportation—a 1960 Dodge—and began driving the Ghia. He received it at 10,748 miles and brought it in for inspection at 11,611 miles. Technicians replaced a faulty voltage regulator—many of them needed replacement, so an update was coming anyway—and they also repaired a quarter panel that had been damaged somehow. Fault was irrelevant on the body damage, with Chrysler owning and insuring the car. On November 16, the car was inspected again. There was no new body damage, but the car needed an oil leak fixed and some fine-tuning on its brakes. Grunden turned the car back in on December 16, with 16,697 miles.

The car sat for a week or two while the technicians replaced and updated some of the ignition parts and refinished a body panel. It is unclear if this was the same body panel that had been damaged before, or if this had been merely a careless driver. On January 7, 1965, the car was delivered to its next user in Manchester, New Hampshire, Dr. Ethan Howard. He got it with 17,487 miles and drove it for a little over a month before its first inspection. At 19,812 miles, the air pump was replaced. Otherwise, it was an uneventful user period and he turned the car in on April 7, with 21,605 miles.

Chrysler kept the car for a week, reconditioning and updating a variety of ignition parts. The tires were replaced and the transmission needed to be rebuilt—possibly due to user abuse. Bill Carry had noticed that a good number of the vehicles needed transmission overhauls when they were returned by the users. The transmission in the car had been specially adapted for the turbine. The bands inside the transmission were modified because of the high torque characteristics of the engine at low speeds. If they hadn't been, the car would have shifted much more harshly because a piston engine—such as the ones the transmission had been originally designed for—didn't create as much torque at low speeds. Still, the mechanics on the program suspected some users were manually shifting the car. That is, they were putting the car into "Low" gear instead of "Drive," then waiting too long to shift the car into the next gear. Doing that would have stressed the internal bands of the transmission as well. Chrysler would have to test the cars to see if the problem lay with the cars or the drivers.

Car number 28 was then delivered to Raymond Baldwin, a "petroleum distributor" in Burlington, Vermont, with 22,213 miles. Baldwin was fifty-eight at the time, and he may have wondered about his future selling petroleum as he drove a car that didn't necessarily need gasoline to run. About two months later, the car was returned for an inspection. The only thing they found to fix was body damage; this car somehow seemed to absorb a lot of bumps and bruises. After bodywork, Baldwin took it back out and finished his tour with it. He turned it in on July 15, with 25,327 miles.

Chrysler refurbished the ignition system again—the starter/generator brushes caused a bit of a problem with all the cars during these tests—and did some minor maintenance. On August 24 the car was delivered to a user in Brockton, Massachusetts, with a mileage of 26,855. This user was Joyce Young, a "housewife." She was thirty-seven at the time and drove it for a couple of months. At 29,071 miles, car number 28 had its only inspection at which nothing needed to be done to it. A slight oil leak developed later on that required it to be returned for a fix. On November 24, the car was turned in for the last time. With 31,467 miles accumulated between May 14, 1964, and November 24, 1965, the car was shipped back to Detroit.

Car number 28 was unique in at least one respect: two of its five drivers were women. Only 23 of the 203 drivers—just over ten percent—were women. Otherwise, the car was typical in that it had five different drivers for three months each. The drivers were numbers 29, 63, 105, 147, and 186, respectively (from the list of users numbered 1 through 203).

———

In February 1965, sixteen-year-old Mark Olson was watching television one evening, waiting for his parents to return home, when the phone rang.

A man named "Mr. Brown from Chrysler" asked him to tell his parents that he'd be stopping by to visit in the morning. Before Mark could ask whether this had to do with the turbine program, the man hung up. When his parents got home, Mark told them the news. He had to go to school the next morning before the man arrived, so Mark ran home at lunchtime to find out if the man's call involved the family getting a turbine car. "I ran— now I do mean 'ran'—home, and when I came in the door, my dad [Alden], with a huge grin, handed me a large brown envelope. Inside was a driver's manual, history book, engineering manual, sample user agreement, and a few other things."

Mark then learned that they had to keep the impending delivery of the car a secret. It would be delivered in May, but until then, they couldn't tell anyone. Chrysler intended to maximize the publicity of the event, and didn't want any early word of it to spoil the surprise.

Like the other users, Alden Olson met with Chrysler representatives the day before his scheduled delivery. They gave him the detailed walk around the car and even let him drive it a bit to get accustomed to it. The next day—delivery—the Olsons had breakfast with several representatives from Chrysler at a local restaurant, where the program was explained to all of them in detail. The reps even related stories they'd gathered from other users. They told the Olsons how the Vlaha car had been rear-ended, and how much trouble they had getting the body repaired.

At the nearby Edgewater Motel, the Olsons were presented to the press as the newest users in the Chrysler turbine program. Mark remembers it as a "room full of cameras," and during the next few months he found out "what being a celebrity was like." After a few more words from the Chrysler reps, the show moved out into the parking lot for the delivery. Photos were taken, and it wasn't until after noon that the Olsons finally got to drive off in the car.

Mark later discovered that the car his family got to drive—serial numbered 991232—was the same car he and his father had seen in the parking lot at the mall when they had visited the Chrysler display the previous spring.

Mark's experience with the car was unique. His father let the sixteen-year-old drive the car quite a bit. The Olsons put thirteen thousand miles on the car while they had it, and Mark drove five thousand of them himself. Mark remembers well the attention the car drew wherever it went—whether while driving or merely parked in his family's driveway. Buying diesel at truck stops always caused a commotion as truckers and other travelers crowded around the car. Likewise, the Olsons were often interrupted at dinnertime by knocks at the front door. "Is that a turbine car? Can we hear it run?" The Olsons put down their silverware and answered questions. Once, they gave an impromptu demonstration of the car to a busload of high school band members when the bus driver decided to stop and ask about the car. Although they usually enjoyed the attention, the Olsons once or twice parked the car in the garage just to get it out of sight—and let them get some peace.

One time, Mr. Olson drove the car to his job, where his boss saw it and liked the looks of it. Strangely, his boss did not want a ride when Alden offered him one. Rumors later swirled around the shipyard where he worked that the boss had called Chrysler and inquired about buying one of the turbine cars, and that he'd been turned down. It made little sense to him—they'd lend one for free to his employee, but not sell him one?

The Olsons encountered a few problems with their car, but none were related to the turbine. On one occasion the speedometer assembly quit working. After a bit, they called Chrysler, and Al Bradshaw came out and repaired it. The time the odometer did not work accounts for a difference in the mileage the Olsons say they drove and the 12,242 miles that Chrysler says they did.

Another problem was a brake failure that happened while Mark was at the wheel. Luckily, no one was hurt—and neither was the car—and a quick repair took care of it. The last problem was a bit more dramatic: the engine quit while the family was driving across Nebraska. It turned out to be more difficult to get the car to a dealership than it was to repair. Once there, a local mechanic found that the problem was nothing more than a broken wire in the fuel system, and the car was running again.

The Olsons were there when the mechanic started the car for the first time after the fix. A crowd had gathered to see the car run. When it got near idle speed, there was a large "Boom!" A cloud of white smoke came from the exhaust, and Mark saw "a very old lady with white hair and a cane start jumping up and down, saying, 'I want one of those cars! I want one!'" The mechanic explained that an explosion could happen on occasion after this kind of repair and that it would not harm anything. Mark had no idea why the woman decided she wanted one of these cars at that moment. Did she just want a car that started with a bang?

On August 13, 1965, the Olsons went to the airport and picked up a man from Chrysler who would take the car back from them. The whole family felt sad to see the car go, especially sixteen-year-old Mark. He had taken pictures of the car with an Instamatic camera, but years later he wished he'd taken more. He also kept a few souvenirs from the car, including the user guide, the jacking instructions, and a "few other little things." At the time he worried it might have been inappropriate to do that, but years later he spoke with the men who refurbished the cars between users. They told him virtually anything could have been pried off the car without raising eyebrows at Chrysler. Looking back on it years later, Mark wished he'd thought to grab the "Turbine" emblem off the air cleaner, or perhaps even the hood ornament.

———

While the Olsons were using their turbine car, Arthur Forrester of Oklahoma City had an adventure of his own with one. Al Bradshaw delivered the car to Forrester on April 14, 1965, and the sixty-seven-year-old cabinetmaker decided to immediately take it to Slippery Rock, Pennsylvania, to show it off to his relatives. The next Saturday morning, Forrester called Bradshaw. "It's Arthur Forrester and I've wrecked the car." He was calling from Chesterfield, Missouri, and the car had been involved in a collision at an intersection where someone—it was unclear who—had missed a red light or a stop sign. The car was still drivable, so Bradshaw told Forrester to continue on to Slippery Rock. There, a local body shop straightened out the hood, the grille, and the fender and replaced a broken headlamp. It turned out that Forrester had overestimated the damage. He was probably more concerned about getting the car into an accident so early in his user term.

Bradshaw found himself arranging for body repairs on the turbine cars more than once, and it wasn't easy to find qualified facilities. In particular, many body shops wouldn't touch the aluminum hood and trunk lid. In Los Angeles, Bradshaw found a place that advertised low-price paint jobs ($39.95). The manager of the company had experience with aluminum, though, and whenever a turbine car in California needed body repairs, it was sent there. Customers getting their cheap paint jobs were probably shocked to see the Chrysler turbine cars in the shop alongside their clunkers.

6

The Globe-Trotting Ghia

Chrysler held onto five of the Turbine Cars and used them for a variety of promotional and test purposes. A few weeks before the Vlahas got their car, a Ghia was shipped abroad for another prong of the publicity assault. The car toured around the world and made headlines in unusual ways almost everywhere it went.

On August 25, 1963, this Ghia was carefully loaded onto a Pan Am DC-7C and flown to Geneva, Switzerland. To load the Ghia on and off the plane, special lifts were used and extra care was needed. The plane's cargo doors left only an inch of clearance on each side as the car's handlers carefully slid the car into the plane. Pan Am provided a special crew for the trip to do nothing but load and unload the car. They had to be careful; Chrysler sent only one car on this trip, and it couldn't afford to have the car damaged while it traveled on the other side of the world.

Chrysler documented the tour with another one of its films, *Passport to Five Continents*. It featured a dashing young mechanic who accompanied the car everywhere it went and served as the film's narrator as well. They said his name was Demetrius and he was the son of a Greek immigrant who also worked at Chrysler. Although the film touted the Ghia as a huge step forward for automobiles, it also emphasized Chrysler's cutting-edge leadership in the field and its growing global presence.

The trip—and movie—started in Geneva at Chrysler's international headquarters. The car traveled to twenty-four foreign cities in twenty-one countries on five continents over the next four months. Everywhere the car went, the press showed up in droves. Headlines proclaimed its arrival, and it was met by dignitaries and VIPs of remarkable stature. In Geneva, the car was examined by the Aga Khan and by Hank Ketcham, the creator of *Dennis the Menace*.

From Geneva, the car traveled to London, where Demetrius struggled—as most Americans do—with driving the Ghia on the "wrong side" of the road. Luckily, he didn't "pile it up," as he feared he might. The camera caught the Ghia as it whooshed by Big Ben, the sound of the turbine mixing in with the chiming of the bells from the clock tower.

Demetrius raved about visiting Paris, and newsreel-style footage showed the Ghia negotiating traffic near the Eiffel Tower and the Arc de Triomphe. "I'll never forget my first look at the Eiffel Tower. I couldn't believe I was really in Paris. Yet, there it was in front of me and my turbine," he said. "I thought traffic was bad in Detroit. Ha! Paris tops them all." Chrysler timed the Ghia's arrival in Paris to coincide with the Paris Auto Show, then the largest in the world. Huge crowds showed up to see the Ghia on display. Among the car's VIP visitors was French president Charles de Gaulle. Members of the press delegation at the show were shocked when the president knelt on the ground to get a closer look at the car. Some considered it undignified for the president to kneel in public, but the Chrysler contingent at the show loved it.

Occasionally, Demetrius went a bit over the top when he praised the car. "Sometimes I couldn't believe it was really me in Europe—and with this automobile! I had in my hands the steering wheel of the world's most exciting car. It seemed like the whole world was at my feet," he gushed. Footage showed people lining up to see the car in the rain, and marquees in front of businesses announced the dates the car would arrive.

Newspaper reporters loved the vehicle and ran photos of it along with their stories. The turbine Ghia appeared in many newspapers in languages other than English; Demetrius brought home clippings from Japanese, Turkish, and Chinese newspapers. The *Sun* of Australia screamed in a headline that took up the tabloid's entire front page: "FIRST JET CAR IN SYDNEY." The article promised photos of the car inside the paper. In a move that George Huebner could appreciate, Demetrius even managed to get himself into a few of the photos.

Even royalty showed up to pay homage to the Ghia. Prince Bertil of Sweden came out to see the car. President Roberto Chiari of Panama asked to look under the hood. To impress the president and the onlooking press, Demetrius placed a glass of water on the running engine to show the absence of vibration. In the Philippines, he swung by the president's mansion and woke him from his siesta. Upon seeing the car, he asked for a ride, which he was given. The premier of South Australia praised the car and asked Demetrius when Chrysler would start building them locally. Demetrius diplomatically told him the decision was up to those at the company. Stockholm was on the itinerary, as was Puerto Rico. A fueling stop for the airplane on the Cocos Islands was perhaps the most remote place the Ghia found itself on the adventure.

While in Mexico, the film documented the car driving past some of the older buildings of the culture. In front of one, a small crowd thronged the car, including a couple of pretty girls who talked to Demetrius. The film doesn't record what words were exchanged, although Demetrius claims that he "even learned a few words of Spanish" while he was there.

The president of Mexico, Adolfo Mateos, asked if he could take a spin in the turbine car—fueled by a tank of tequila. Demetrius called Huebner, who quickly had the engineers in Detroit run a few gallons of locally purchased tequila through a turbine to see how it would burn. When the engine ran flawlessly, Huebner gave word to the Mexican contingent that tequila wouldn't be a problem. It was rumored at the time that someone else drove the car fueled by the perfume Chanel No. 5.

In all, the Ghia traveled forty-seven thousand miles in the Pan Am jet. Along with the places mentioned earlier, the Ghia saw Turin, Bombay,

Singapore, Cape Town, and Buenos Aires. The touring Ghia was also accompanied by an English Chrysler employee who loved to drink alcohol. When he traveled to countries with restrictions on alcohol, such as India, he brought a doctor's note that stated his health was threatened if he wasn't allowed to drink. Presumably he was mortified by the demonstration where they poured cognac in the tank to show South Africans the broad range of useable fuels.

The Ghia tour abroad also served as a goodwill gesture for Chrysler's international plants. While in Australia, the car visited a large facility where Demetrius shook hands with his Australian counterparts. He even drove the car through the plant as the workers cheered. On film, he raved about the high caliber of workers on the lines in other countries. He watched assembly in Rotterdam and visited a plant in England. He saw Chrysler plants being built "like crazy" in the Philippines and Turkey.

From the language Demetrius used, it seems as if the film was aimed at a much younger audience than the car would have been sold to. "Then of course, there were the girls. Pretty girls," Demetrius said. He pointed out how you have to be "very careful" how you speak to a girl in the Middle East. "I can tell you one thing: there isn't one girl in the world—in the whole wide world—that wouldn't go for a guy in a Chrysler turbine. I just happen to know. Naturally, every girl we met wanted a ride in the turbine. The only ones who could were reporters." Clearly Demetrius hoped for female reporters by the end of the trip.

7

Other Ghias in America

Two Ghia Turbine Cars were also featured at the World's Fair in New York, 1964–65. These two cars were probably responsible for more publicity than all of the other cars in the program combined. Technically, the fair was not an official World's Fair—due to squabbling between the U.S. organizers and the international organization that sponsors World's Fairs—but, in typical American fashion, the organizers just went ahead and did it.

Symptomatic of the Fair's troubled organization, it had at least two themes, maybe three. "Peace Through Understanding," was the official theme, but others, such as "Man's Achievements on a Shrinking Globe in an Expanding Universe" and the "Olympics of Progress," were commonly used. Which you chose to call it probably depended on whether you were for or against the Vietnam War, involved in the new ecology movement, or swept up in the fever of the 1964 Tokyo Olympics. The centerpiece of the fair was a twelve-story-tall stainless steel globe donated by U.S. Steel.

One criticism of the Fair was that it was too commercial, and Chrysler's six-acre display helped fuel the criticism. Chrysler showed its full lineup of cars as well as two turbines in the shadows of a fifty-five-foot-tall engine and a car eighty feet long with twenty-foot wheels. The Ghia Turbine Cars were the highlight of the display, once visitors saw past the oversized fluff. Chrysler gave visitors turbine rides around a small test track that had been set up just for this purpose. The second Ghia was also there as backup, just in case the one giving rides broke down. The last thing Chrysler wanted was a very public breakdown. Local dealers in the region gave car shoppers who came to their dealerships tickets good for a ride in the Ghia at the Fair.

Chrysler's display was in part a response to the General Motors display of a futuristic-looking show car at the previous World's Fair in Seattle in 1962. There, the GM Firebird turbine car had spent the entire show parked. At the New York World's Fair, Chrysler gave rides to a staggering number of people—more than 350,000. Even more wanted rides but were turned away. Many people saw the lines and decided to just watch the cars zoom past. People without tickets were chosen at random for the rides. Chrysler also logged 18,500,000 spectators who stopped by to see the Ghia Turbines. Meanwhile, over at the GM exhibit entitled "Futurama," visitors were shown the cities of the future—on the moon and the bottom of the ocean—where they would while away the hours watching nuclear-powered robots mine the ocean floor for minerals.

Right before the Fair opened, Chrysler told Bill Hamer, the East Coast technician who oversaw the cars at the Fair, to take one of the cars over to the local television station. There, he was interviewed on camera and filmed while driving the car around the station's parking lot. The entire piece ran the next Sunday morning on a children's show hosted by Sonny Fox, *Wonderama*, on New York's WNEW. Sadly, Hamer attended a church service that ran long the morning it aired, so he had to rely on his neighbors' reviews of it when he got home after it ended.

The two Ghias at the Fair were modified slightly, based upon knowledge gleaned from the user program. The track where Chrysler let people ride in the turbine car was set a few feet below ground level and, during the summer months of the Fair, ambient temperatures at the turbine's air intake often hit 120 degrees Fahrenheit. Making matters worse, the Ghia was driven slowly around the small track, creating a situation ripe for overheating the engine.

To prevent this, the turbine technicians installed a small fan in front of the oil cooler—normally, air passed over it as the car was being driven, hopefully at higher speeds than these—and the drivers of the car at the Fair were told to always let the air circulate through the system for at least twenty minutes after the engine was shut off. These two simple steps allowed the Ghia cars at the Fair to operate for six months, thirteen hours a day, with no mechanical problems. The main complaint heard at the Fair was the length of the lines to ride in the Ghia Turbines. Many were turned away, and even more decided it wasn't worth the wait in the long lines.

The cars were driven around the display track by college students hired by Chrysler for the job. Hamer recalled later that brushes with the wall were the primary problem he had to deal with on these cars. The track was surrounded by a short stone wall, which the drivers scraped a few times. The cars also wore out tires at an alarming rate, because the small course seemed to consist of nothing but hard, sharp turns.

———

Other Ghia Turbines were lent out to reporters and automotive writers during the user program. A strange dichotomy emerged: most general news reporters and writers raved about the cars, but the automotive press hated them. Familiar with driving sports cars—exotic foreign cars with sexy curves—and American muscle cars with huge engines, the automotive writers had no idea what to make of the little car with the strange-sounding engine. They quickly jumped on the fact that the engines didn't respond to the throttle the way the other cars they tested did. A contemporary muscle car might run a quarter-mile from a dead stop in thirteen or fourteen seconds; the figures reported by the press for the Ghia were far from that. In fact, the press reported a zero-to-sixty figure of over twelve seconds. Editorials called the entire turbine project a dead end because of this performance "problem." What most journalists, and many others who drove the car, missed was that the Ghia really was fast by the standards of the day. Chrysler just didn't want anyone to know about it for fear they'd damage the cars.

The Ghia's engine produced maximum torque at 0 MPH. That is, while standing still, a driver could hold both the accelerator and the brake firmly to the floor and the car would not move. When it came time to move, releasing the brake launched the car like a rocket. This is sometimes called a "brake torque" and is relatively abusive when performed on a typical piston-engine car with an automatic transmission. However, the Ghias were set up without a traditional torque converter. This allowed a brake torque to be performed without harming anything in the drive train. Driven this way, the Ghia could run a standing quarter mile in a much faster time, much closer to the times of other cars then on the road.

In response to criticism from the press about the car's performance, George Huebner made a trip to California to show how fast a Ghia could be. He staged a race between himself—driving the Ghia—and another driver behind the wheel of a big-block Dodge. Launching the Ghia from a high-revving brake torque, Huebner blew away the Dodge. Reporters— who seemed to follow Huebner whenever he left his house—duly reported the story, but the automotive journalists dismissed it as a stunt.

Sadly, these same writers also downplayed the other major advantage of the turbine car: its ability to burn a variety of fuels. The only time they wrote about the car's versatility with fuel was almost always as a novelty: hey, it sounds funny and it will run on tequila!

———

Chrysler manufactured ¹⁄₂₅-scale plastic models of the Ghia Turbine Car, and it seemed like everyone affiliated with the company had a case of them to present to anyone who might help spread the word. The service representatives who delivered the turbine cars to users often left a dozen or so with the user's family as a sort of parting gift. While the supplies lasted, Chrysler dealers gave away thousands of models to anyone who asked for one. The box they came in bore the title "The Experimental Chrysler Corporation Turbine Car" and included photos of the car from a variety of angles as well as a photo of the powerplant. The description on the box was detailed: "This is the dual-generator automotive gas turbine engine that powers the Chrysler Corporation Turbine Car."

The back of the box told "The Story of a Principle, a Promise, a Challenge, and an Engine." It explained the Ghia car and how it worked quite well:

> The turbine principle of power is one of the oldest in the world. The windmill was one of the earliest turbines—driven by the air around it, turning the grinding mill attached to it. A turbine engine is more sophisticated, of course, and it must make its own wind. It does this by drawing in the air through a compressor, heating the air to form a hot rushing gas then directing the gas against turbine wheels. The spinning turbines transmit power through drive shafts to the vehicle itself as well as to all accessories. An automotive gas turbine engine—to be functional—has to be made from low-cost readily available materials, by mass production techniques.

Descriptions of the various functions followed, with a few final paragraphs to sum up:

> Its fuel economy is comparable to that of a piston engine, but it operates on a wide variety of fuels, including white gas, diesel oil, kerosene, [and] JP-4 aircraft turbine engine fuel. Now that Chrysler Corporation has perfected the principle, which holds the promise of a truly great powerplant for automobiles, and overcame the challenge it presented, the Turbine Car now has the mission to determine how car owners will like driving a turbine-powered car. Watch for it! The exciting new Chrysler Corporation Turbine Car will soon be on the streets and highways of America.

White gas was the name given to fuel that did not include lead. Due to the ways gasoline was marketed in America in the 1950s and '60s, many people today do not realize that unleaded gasoline was actually purer than "regular" gasoline. Back then, lead was added to gasoline to raise its octane, and this leaded gasoline was called regular. In later years when the lead was no longer added, the fuel was referred to as "unleaded." The distinction arose because the addition of the lead to the gasoline caused major problems in some engines.

In the turbine cars, gasoline was not preferred to diesel or fuel oil because it was more prone to "vapor lock," a condition where the liquid fuel turns to vapor while still running through the fuel lines. The underhood environment of the Ghia car was quite hot, which made the potential for vapor lock high. Although it was harder to find, the Chrysler technicians preferred kerosene as a fuel for the car; it burned cleaner and smoked less than diesel.

The lack of easily available fuels for the car—white gas and diesel were not as easy to find back then—was probably the biggest problem with the program, according to Al Bradshaw. Many of the service calls he went on were the result of users running out of fuel or from users burning contaminated fuel.

Meanwhile, the turbine's fuel economy may not have been as wonderful as Chrysler had hoped, but it wasn't bad either. The Ghia could easily get mileage in the "high teens," sixteen or seventeen miles per gallon, Bill Carry said later, comparable to a contemporary V-8–powered car. In light of the variety of fuels it could burn, one could forgive the Ghia for the low figure.

Tom Golec recalled that part of a typical press demonstration involved setting up a turbine engine with a series of different fuels on a stand that could be selected by flipping levers. One fuel they often used was peanut oil, which made the exhaust smell like someone was baking cookies. Jerry Gross knew the Ghia could burn peanut oil—he'd accompanied the car to the Dothan, Alabama, Peanut Festival, where as part of the car's appearance, he ran it on the oil. He likened it to the smell of a good Chinese restaurant. Test drivers at the Chelsea Proving Grounds recall filling the tank with perfume for a demonstration; the area stank of perfume, even from a distance, but the car ran fine on the strange fuel.

———

Another Ghia spent its entire life in testing at the Chelsea Proving Grounds, where a test driver named Jerry Wenk was one of a privileged few who got to operate the car. To make sure that nothing happened to the expensive car, Chrysler allowed only a few select people to drive it. If the vehicle needed to be moved because it was blocking someone else's car, they'd call Wenk over to move it. This was partly based on the knowledge the turbine engineers were gaining about how important it was for the cars to be operated carefully.

The tests Wenk ran focused on performance. Other groups at the facility tested other aspects of the car, such as endurance. Wenk spent his time working on acceleration and fuel economy. He remembered that the car's acceleration wasn't "all that great" when compared to a piston-engine car. It didn't take him long to figure out, however, how the car could be made to run fast—as a professional test driver, he knew to try the brake torque trick. Later he said that the car, when driven that way, could run the quarter mile in the low thirteen-second range, a rather quick trip for a car from any era.

When not employing the brake-and-accelerator trick, the car didn't accelerate all that well from a dead stop, but from a roll it ran much better. For example, the turbine did remarkably well pulling out and passing at highway speeds. The car could quickly hit 100 MPH if the driver wasn't careful, Wenk recalled.

As for the car's durability, the car never broke down or failed while Wenk was working on or driving it, and he and his crew put thousands of miles on it to simulate consumer use. Wenk would take the car out and drive it for a while at a certain speed, bring it to a stop, back it up, and then take off and do it all again. The cycles he ran put the engine and transmission through all of the various phases they'd go through in the real world. They drove the car this way for days on end, stopping only for shift changes and for drivers to take short coffee breaks. An interesting point was how Wenk was instructed to cool the transmission in the car. The best way to cool the transmission fluid was to get the car moving fast so air would move through the fluid cooler; Wenk and his crew would do laps at a hundred miles an hour to cool the car down.

Much of the work was done on a straightaway—two miles straight with a turnaround pad at each end—next to Chelsea's monstrous oval. Wenk would launch the car from a dead stop and go flying down to the other end of the stretch. He'd bring it to a stop, turn it around, and do it again. All along, he was timing the runs and watching the gauges to make sure the turbine was healthy. The car ran perfectly for Wenk the whole time. That said a lot; during Wenk's tenure at the proving grounds, he "scattered" quite a few engines. Still, he never saw a turbine he was driving explode— or fail, for that matter—despite running the car through every possible condition a consumer would.

Not long afterward, Wenk received permission to put the Ghia in Chelsea's 1964 annual parade. He brought the car home but wound up driving another car in the parade, while a co-worker from the proving grounds drove the turbine.

Wenk continued running tests on the car from 1964 through 1967. While driving the car, Wenk noticed how much better the car was assembled than a typical car from 1964. The hand-built work of the Ghia shop "was very noticeable. Particularly the interior, which was beautiful." Sadly, he thought the car's biggest problem was that it was just ahead of its time. "It was a fabulous car and a once-in-a-lifetime chance to drive one."

———

Another Turbine Car—one of the first few assembled—was painted white in Italy and later received blue racing stripes. It was the only car in the fleet not painted bronze. Chrysler shipped the car to California, where it costarred in a movie called *The Lively Set* with James Darren. The film actually credited "Chrysler Corporation's New Gas Turbine Car" as if it were an actor, announcing that it was "seen in action for the first time in a motion picture." Perhaps Universal thought the car had a future in Hollywood.

Onscreen, the car raced on a road course with plenty of high-speed action and thrills typical of the era. The only Hollywood trickery in the film came from the fact that Chrysler refused to let any actors or stunt people drive the car; it could only be driven by a Chrysler employee. George

Stecher—the turbine mechanic—can be seen behind the wheel of the screen shots that aren't close-ups.

Al Bradshaw, the regional manager, also accompanied the car on the set and maintained it as necessary. The turbine ran flawlessly, but the car went through several sets of brakes, which Bradshaw had to replace.

One more piece of Hollywood deception came from a fake hood the filmmakers put on the car. They made another hood out of fiberglass and rigged it to come off during the race. They hoped to add a bit of excitement to the story—but also to allow the camera a close-up of the engine compartment, revealing a turbine engine instead of a piston engine. Without that shot, moviegoers might have wondered if the car was actually turbine-powered.

The film was a throwaway otherwise. "Youth in action—they live with zest, excitement, and romance. They're equally at home at the drag races, in the long-distance endurance runs, with jet-propelled cars, the Bonneville speed trials. They look to the future and they're especially intrigued by the car of tomorrow—the gas turbine car," the announcer said. Darren races and wins in his gas turbine car, although the audience probably suspected he would since he was the good guy of the film. He even gives a few strangers a speech on the virtues of turbine cars, including their low exhaust emissions.

Some film historians with a revisionist bent have suggested that *The Lively Set* had good race scenes if not a good plot, but they are clearly mistaken. Although the appearance of the car onscreen seems magical to watch, the race scenes were obviously filmed at low speed and sped up, while the close-ups were shot in front of ridiculous fake backgrounds.

8

The User Experiment

Meanwhile, across America, lucky users were getting to drive the turbine cars. One such user was Dr. Stuart Bicknell, a forty-five-year-old dentist from San Diego. At the Mission Valley Shopping Center, he visited the Chrysler shopping mall display with his son, who, as they walked away, prodded him into entering his name for the user program. Dr. Bicknell was surprised by a phone call a few days later when a Chrysler rep asked if he could come down for an interview. The rep asked a series of questions about what the doctor drove (a late-model Cadillac) and where the Ghia would be parked if he were chosen. Dr. Bicknell noticed the rep's eyes light up when he mentioned that the car would be parked in front of his dental practice most days, right on one of the busiest streets in town. The rep also asked about how many people the dentist interacted with, probably to estimate word of mouth. Dr. Bicknell had children, an eleven-year-old daughter and a fifteen-year-old son, and said that he thought it might have hurt his chances if his children had been teenagers with licenses.

On September 10, 1964, Chrysler delivered the Ghia to Bicknell's dental office to begin his three-month tour with the car. The first thing the doctor did was drive it by a friend's custom auto body shop, knowing that his friend might have heard of the car but had not seen it yet, and let him drive it. Dr. Bicknell noted the strange noise the engine made; he never quite got used to the whine. He did learn to deal with the slow throttle response—at least, slower than a piston engine.

The interior of the car, on the other hand, he really liked. The Italian craftsmanship seemed to impress everyone. The Bicknells eventually brought the car around and showed it to their friends and relatives, just as they would with any new car they bought. No doubt Chrysler hoped users would do this, to boost publicity for the cars and expose them to as many people as possible.

Chrysler gave Bicknell a number to call in case he had any mechanical problems, although he never used it. The only maintenance or repair the car received while in Bicknell's possession was when Chrysler updated the starter, as they did on every Ghia car. Chrysler took the car for a day and then returned it. Later, Chrysler took the car for two weeks—to act as a stand-in on *The Lively Set*. Bicknell noticed whitewash in the doorjambs upon its return. Bill Carry later said he didn't think the white Ghia had been damaged during filming, but they might have wanted another car merely for different angles and shots to save shooting time.

For fuel, Bicknell mentioned to his local Texaco station—"Trust your car to the man who wears the star"—that he needed special fuel for three months. Although the Chrysler rep who dropped the car off had listed exotic and novelty fuels such as paint thinner, Dr. Bicknell asked for kerosene. The station ordered a fifty-five-gallon drum of kerosene, which he used whenever he refueled in town. Otherwise he ran diesel or white gas in it, and he never had much trouble finding fuel.

Bicknell ran up to Los Angeles from San Diego a couple of times, and on one occasion he dropped by to visit the kids' uncle. The uncle asked to take it for a drive and took the Ghia to a service station, where he called an attendant over. He told the attendant that the car was making a funny noise and asked him to look under the hood to see if the radiator was boiling over. The attendant opened the hood and saw the turbine—and no radiator, of course—and was stunned until the uncle explained it to him.

If this story was true—it may have just been family legend—the attendant was the only person in North America who had never heard of the turbine car by this time.

Bicknell's son, Charlie, got to drive the car, too. Years later, he recalled that his mother pointed out to her husband that the Ghia Turbine was a once-in-a-lifetime opportunity, and that Charlie really ought to be allowed to drive the car. Technically, letting an unlicensed driver get behind the wheel of the Ghia was a violation of the user agreement Dr. Bicknell had signed, although such transgressions probably took place more commonly than anyone cared to admit. Charlie's mom drove them over to an abandoned navy housing complex where buildings were being demolished. The roads were still there, so Charlie's mom switched seats with him and let him drive around the deserted streets for fifteen minutes or so. Forty years later he still recalled how thrilling it was. He also vividly remembered the smell of the car's exhaust—the burning kerosene reminded him of being at the airport, near the big jets. At the time, he thought the odor was one of the coolest things about the car.

The Bicknell children also had occasion to be dropped off and picked up from school in the Ghia Turbine during their user period. Charlie described the distinctive sound of the turbine as similar to a loud vacuum cleaner. He noticed the stares and comments it got from the other children being dropped off or picked up. One day, his dad shut the engine off for a few minutes and then fired it up as he was about to leave. The turbine suffered an ignition pop, the "aesthetic" problem where the fuel exploded before the turbine started running smoothly. A puff of smoke came from the tailpipe of the car as Dr. Bicknell whooshed away. Charlie remembered how his friends "oohed and ahhed."

Charlie's little sister, Camilla, was not lucky enough to be able to drive the car. Only eleven when the car was given to the family, she remembered the vehicle's bronze color brightly contrasting with her father's more conservative Cadillac. From the backseat, where she often rode, she remembered running her hands over the finned aluminum tube that ran the length of the car's interior from between the front seats of the car into the trunk. She also remembered that it was never possible to take just a quick trip in the car because they always spent so much time explaining and showing the car to people. Her father joked with her that if they ran out of gas, he'd pull over and buy some Vitalis hair tonic. She also remembered that her mother might have wished on more than one occasion they hadn't driven the car to church. Once in a while, the Bicknells would sneak out of church early. The car's distinctive turbine sound meant they had to wait until the rest of the congregation was leaving before they could head to their car. Like her brother, she remembered being picked up and dropped off at school in the Ghia. "Parents picked their kids up in an alley next to the school, and everyone could hear her coming for at least a block away," she recalled.

Before they turned the car back in, the Bicknells decided to memorialize their turbine adventure on film. They took the car to Shelter Island, near San Diego Bay, and Uncle Gordon shot a hundred feet of movie film of the car driving around. Charlie snapped pictures of the car as well, which he treasured decades later.

On December 10, 1964, Dr. Bicknell turned the car back in, with 2,342 more miles than it had when he'd gotten it. A Chrysler representative debriefed him, asking him questions for about half an hour. The rep asked him—hypothetically—if he'd consider buying a turbine car if it were being sold for twenty thousand dollars. He replied that he might consider buying the car if the price was right, but that he was leaning toward the Cadillac; the price quoted for the turbine car was much more than the Caddy had cost him. He mentioned his concerns about the engine noise as well.

One thing Bicknell wondered about was why Chrysler never marketed the Ghia car with a regular piston engine. He thought the looks of the car were good enough that it shouldn't have been tied to the availability of the turbine engine. Before the Chrysler rep left, he gave the family three of the Ghia Turbine models, one for the parents and one for each child. Charlie carefully saved his in the original box, and over forty years later he still had it.

———

One of the last Ghia Turbine Cars built for the fifty-car test program was delivered to Ray and Doris Fenstermacher in Allentown, Pennsylvania. Ray had read in the local paper about Chrysler's user program and wrote asking for a car. He said later that he merely got a phone call asking if he was available to take delivery of the car in September 1964. The event was set to take place at a local Holiday Inn, and Chrysler had invited a huge press contingent. The Fenstermachers remember the next few days as a flurry of publicity and excitement as the local press turned them into minor celebrities. While he had the car, Ray worked as a machinist for Mack Trucks, although at times he felt like he was doing public relations for Chrysler. Neither Ray nor Doris minded in the least—they loved it!

The entire experience felt a bit surreal. The man from Chrysler who delivered the car was named, just coincidentally, George Fenstermacher. After the walk-around and demonstration of how the various systems worked, George broke the bad news to Ray and Doris: due to a paperwork mix-up, the license plates for this car hadn't arrived yet. It would be a heart-breaking day's wait before Ray and Doris could legally take the car out for a spin. "It was eating my heart out. It was parked there in front of my house and I couldn't use this thing!" Part of the problem was that Ray and Doris were the first users of this particular Ghia car— it had never been plated before.

One issue the Fenstermachers remembered later—something that was universally repeated by other users—was how it was impossible to take the car out for a short trip. Even a quick run to the store for a loaf of bread, normally a ten-minute jaunt, might turn into an hour-long discussion about the car with a group of strangers in the store parking lot.

"The car attracted attention like you wouldn't believe," said Ray. Its distinctive jet engine turned heads and attracted crowds everywhere it went. Ray was generous with the car—anyone who asked for a ride got one, and most who asked to drive it were likewise given the key. The only stipulation was that one of the Fenstermachers had to be in the car, as called for in the agreement with Chrysler. Ray kept a diary and logged eighty drivers of the car besides himself and Doris, and more than 190 who rode in the car during his three-month user tour.

Ray had to improvise a bit to fit his four children into the car's two rear bucket seats. He put a piece of plywood across the seats and fabricated a bench that would sit on top to accommodate his youngsters. Ray and Doris took their family on trips to Maine and Washington, D.C., while racking up over nine thousand miles in the car.

Doris drove the car quite a bit as well. "If [Ray] wasn't driving it, I was." She remembered an interesting incident with Ray behind the wheel. In Washington, D.C., a police officer flagged them down and said that he'd been speeding. Without pausing, he then asked what kind of car they were riding in. Ray suspected the officer's curiosity was piqued by the whining sound the engine made even at idle. Rather than write a ticket, the officer then escorted the family to Arlington National Cemetery, where they had been headed to see John F. Kennedy's grave.

The Fenstermachers' phone began ringing on a regular basis. Complete strangers called, seeking rides in the car. Many belonged to organizations such as local schools or 4-H clubs that wanted a demonstration for educational purposes. Ray and Doris accommodated as many of them as they could. Another reason Ray used every occasion possible to drive the car was that it was the first brand-new car he ever had.

When Ray took the car to the local gas station to refuel, he pulled up to the kerosene pump. Attendants came running. "What the hell are you doing? It ain't gonna work!" they yelled. Ray smiled and explained how it would, and filled his tank. The kerosene cost twenty or thirty cents per gallon less than the pump gasoline.

Chrysler called Ray periodically to check on the car, but he never encountered any problems with it. The only time someone had to come look at the car while it was in his possession was the time the emergency brake handle broke. A mechanic came out and fixed it the next day.

At the end of the user period, Chrysler sent some people out to the Fenstermachers' home to interview them and retrieve the car. The conversation lasted about an hour and was tape-recorded. "They asked me how I enjoyed it and I told them, 'Tremendously,'" Ray recalled years later. The only drawback he could think of was the lack of pickup—the sluggish acceleration issue raised by most of the users. He spent more time telling them about the things they liked about the car, including the instant heat and the ease of starting. Again, these sentiments were almost universal in the user program.

The Chrysler reps asked if Ray or Doris might be interested in buying such a car if one were for sale. Ray said he would, depending on the price. Someone floated the figure of twenty thousand dollars and Ray and Doris balked—the house they lived in at the time cost less than half that! The Fenstermachers were adamant that they loved the car and would have bought one if it were priced lower. The Chrysler reps suggested that the car would last much longer than a regular automobile because of its turbine engine, but even that wasn't enough to convince Ray and Doris.

Before they left, the men gave Ray and Doris a couple dozen of the miniature Ghia Turbine Car models, which they passed on to their kids, friends, and family. With how many people Ray and Doris had let into the car, it wasn't easy for them hang onto any of the models. Ray said later that as they watched the car being taken away, he felt "like crying, broken-hearted. Like they were taking some part of me with them. I enjoyed it for ninety days and it was a wonderful experience." The Fenstermachers were sixty-sixth on the list of 203 users, and turned their car back in right before Christmas, on December 23, 1964.

———

While the Bicknells jetted around Southern California and the Fenstermachers gave rides to everyone in Allentown, another turbine car was delivered to Edwin Fox of Fort Wayne, Indiana. Fox had seen the story of the turbine car on television and sent a letter to Chrysler asking to be included in the program. Not many of the twenty-four-year-old's friends thought he had a chance—many thought he was crazy—until he received an application from Chrysler in the mail. The form asked for basic information—so that Chrysler could look into his driving record—and also information about his family. Fox was married with two small children. He was surprised the form didn't ask what kind of car he was driving at the time. Later, he was told that Chrysler intended to distribute the cars without regard to whether a user was already a Chrysler customer. Representatives from the automaker told him that they had liked his application because he was a young family man. Fox was only a year older than the youngest person in the user program, a twenty-three-year-old dental student.

In early October 1964, when Fox had all but forgotten about the application, he received a call from Chrysler. The caller wanted to know if he'd be available in two weeks to take delivery of the car. Fox was shocked. He made arrangements to be present at a hotel near Fort Wayne where the car would be delivered. The night before, two men from Chrysler took the Fox family out for dinner and explained the whole program to them. They made it clear that Chrysler expected Fox to be an ambassador for Chrysler for the next few months and answer questions people might ask about the car.

The next morning, in front of a group of reporters and photographers, the Chrysler reps handed the key to the car over to Fox, then waved and left. Fox and his wife spent the next hour or so posing for photos and doing their best to answer questions—some of which they'd only learned the answers to the night before.

Once he got to drive the car, he really liked it. It was different from other cars he'd driven, and he noticed it was a bit "sluggish" from a dead stop. Once it was going, however, "it really went," he said later. "It was kind of funny. You couldn't go too far with the thing because everyone would bug you. Whenever you stopped, a ten-minute refueling stop would always end up being forty-five minutes or more. You'd go to the grocery store to pick up something—if I was in a hurry I took my regular car. I didn't want to drive [the turbine car] because it had a whistle to it. And made everyone want to look at it. They were always questioning what it was."

Fox solved the fuel problem quite simply: he had the man who delivered heating oil to his house drop off a fifty-gallon drum of heating oil for the car. Fox would pull the turbine car into his garage and refill the tank with the oil—another of the acceptable fuels—which cost only fifteen cents a gallon, rather than fifty cents a gallon for gasoline at the local gas station.

One possible side effect of driving the car for Fox was a job promotion. At the time he worked for S. S. Kresge (later renamed K-Mart) as a part-time receiving clerk. After he got the car, he became a permanent full-time employee. "They thought if Chrysler thought I was good enough to have something like that, I would be a good employee."

During the fall and winter that Fox had the car, it experienced no mechanical problems. Every week, Fox picked up a Chrysler technician from the airport, took him to the local dealer to look the car over, and then later took the tech back to the airport. The visits were just for routine maintenance and observation, though.

Fox gave quite a few rides to friends and neighbors, and he answered as many questions as he could. He also had the opportunity to drive the turbine car in the snow and cold. He noticed it had several advantages. The most impressive thing for the Fox family was how fast the car had heat. The "sluggish" starts also kept the rear wheels from spinning in the snow, and, of course, the engine started right away, regardless of the temperature outside. For people in northern climates, these would all be big selling points.

On one occasion, Fox managed to show off a bit to some local hoodlums. At the gas station, during one of the ten-minute refueling stops that had been dragged out by bystanders, some teenagers in a souped-up hot rod approached him. "They wanted to know if that thing there would really 'go.'" Fox said it would, and they laughed. He suggested they go out on the highway and see. From a forty-mile-an-hour roll—both cars side by side— the driver of the other car signaled to Fox that the race was on. Fox pushed the pedal to the floor and watched the teenagers' V-8-powered Ford drop away in his rearview mirror. "They didn't know what happened."

Like every other user of the program, Fox had to give the car back after his three months were up. Fox hated to give up the car. He was debriefed for an hour or so and told the Chrysler reps he'd love to buy one of the cars if they ever went up for sale. They asked if Fox had any ideas to improve it. The Fox family could think of none. His wife, Mary Lou, liked it as well. "We loved the car. If they'd put it into production, I would have bought one," he emphasized later.

In Pikesville, a suburb of Baltimore, a Ghia Turbine was delivered to the family of Gerald Herman on May 11, 1965. The Hermans were listed as the 157th users on the list of 203. They spent the summer of 1965 jetting around the area. Earlier that year, Gerald had read an article in the *Wall Street Journal* about the ongoing program, and, with encouragement from a friend who owned a Chrysler dealership, he wrote to Chrysler and asked about getting a car.

His daughter, Bonnie, then twelve years old, remembers being shooed from the house one afternoon as a top-secret meeting took place at the house; the Chrysler reps were coming to interview the Hermans and determine their suitability for the program. Shirley Herman remembered that the Chrysler reps were very interested in whom they interacted with on a daily basis and who would see the car if they had it. That they traveled by car quite a bit, and belonged to a country club, seemed to help with the rep. She also thought Chrysler had picked them because of their location and because their family of four was a good cross-section of America, for marketing purposes.

A few weeks later, young Bonnie was temporarily traumatized as her parents missed her graduation from sixth grade. The school she attended held an annual event where the outgoing class "danced the maypole," yet her parents had to take delivery of the turbine car at the same time. They tried to make it to school in time for the ceremony but just missed it. When they pulled up in the jet car, however, the other children stopped asking where her parents were and started asking what they were driving. The children, as well as the teachers and other parents in attendance, were awestruck by the wild car.

At one point that summer, the Hermans visited the New York World's Fair and saw the Chrysler exhibit with the Ghia Turbine on display. Seeing the long lines to ride the car, the Hermans could only chuckle; they had one of the cars at home in the driveway they could drive any time they wanted until August. On other occasions, they drove the car to Philadelphia and Washington, D.C. Bonnie remembers well going for after-dinner rides with her parents and brother many nights that summer. Often they would drive to a local ice cream parlor, where they parked the car and answered questions from the people who gathered around it. On the drive home, they passed the local fire station, where the firefighters would wave and yell nice things as they drove by.

On one occasion, Bonnie's father let a friend drive the car on a winding country road while Bonnie was in the backseat. She couldn't see the speedometer, but years later she remembered being terrified that her mother might find out how fast her father had let his friend drive the car with the children in it. She might not have minded as much as Bonnie feared; on another occasion, the Herman parents let their fifteen-year-old son drive it. They figured it was a minor infraction—Dennis already had his learner's permit and would turn sixteen the week after they returned the car. Up to that point, it was "torture" for Dennis, who feared the car would be turned back in before he got a chance to drive it.

The *Baltimore Sun* ran a story on the Hermans, which even featured a photo of Gerald standing near the car. For many years Gerald kept a framed copy of the photo on his office wall and told anyone who asked how much he loved the car when he had it.

There was only one occasion when Mr. Herman called Chrysler to come and take care of a problem with the car, but no one in the family remembers why. Years later, Bonnie and Shirley both recalled that it may have been as simple as running out of fuel in a place where appropriate fuel could not be easily obtained. Regardless, Chrysler sent a tech promptly, and the turbine car was soon back on the road.

The only drawback to the car, according to Shirley, was trying to find diesel for it. In 1965, the Hermans could only find diesel locally at truck stops, so they had to plan their trips accordingly. On the other hand, both Shirley and Bonnie vividly recall the luxurious leather interior. Of course, it had nothing to do with the turbine powerplant, but it was something they both remember. Shirley enjoyed the attention the car received, even if it meant having questions yelled at them in traffic by strangers. She even remembered how the car "confused" many of the young men who considered themselves car buffs. "What year is that? What kind of car is that?" they asked. "They didn't know what in the world it was."

Forty years later, Shirley still has the model of the car the rep gave her when they returned the car to Chrysler.

———

Back in Highland Park, Michigan, Bill Carry had devoted a wall of his office to tracking each of the fifty loaner cars. On the left he listed the cars from top to bottom, and a time line ran from left to right. Carry followed the progress of each car—who had it, where it was, what work was done on it—and watched as the chart crept across the wall. In the week between users, the car would be cleaned up—they didn't call it "detailing" yet— any needed maintenance was performed, and the paperwork for the next driver was prepared. Most often, the work was performed at the nearest regional Chrysler facility or a local dealer.

The cars required very little routine maintenance. They did not need oil changes, because the lubricant in the system lasted much longer than oil in a piston engine. Most of the time was spent cleaning the cars and performing updates, upgrading parts on the car based upon the knowledge base Chrysler was gaining from the big experiment. The huge air filters also required very little maintenance. Although they were paper-based, they had aluminum wire frames that allowed the mechanics to remove them and merely slap them on a hard surface to shake loose most of the accumulated dirt. If that didn't work, they could wash the filters with water and then replace them. They only had to swap them out if they were damaged or clogged beyond cleaning. Actually, most of the air filters in these cars survived two washings before they needed to be discarded.

Several months into the program, some of the Ghia cars' engines began suffering problems that startled the technicians and engineers: users complained that they lost power. After the engines were torn down and examined, they found destroyed air seals between the engine housing and the regenerators and between the gas generator and the housing. After countless hours of examination and testing, however, the techs were convinced there was nothing wrong with the seals. They then decided to interview the users. Nothing obvious surfaced, but after a few users spoke of starting the car a particular way in cold weather, the technicians realized the users weren't following the instructions in the User's Guide.

The guide specifically told drivers to wait until the tachometer hit 20,000 RPM before placing the transmission in gear. It was an amazing lack of patience that led to this problem; the engines normally hit operating speed within seconds of starting, but under cold weather conditions it might take as long as eight or ten seconds. Placing the car in gear before the turbine was spinning fast enough had caused the problem. Fuel was pumped into the combustor at too high a rate for how slow the turbine was spinning. The result was a severe overheating condition within the engine that damaged the seals. Unburned fuel also found its way to the regenerators, which would then clog.

The engineers realized the solution was simple: they prevented it in later cars "by modifying the automatic starting system so that the driver could not override it." In fact, the corrected cars would shut themselves off if a driver tried to start driving impatiently. Carry pointed out years later that many of these problems would be simple to resolve in today's cars, with their modern sensors and onboard computers.

The Chrysler turbine engineers felt that this kind of problem could only have been discovered in a user program such as this. Bill Carry later commented, "This situation is one of those unforeseen things that glares fiercely when it is discovered because it is such an obvious shortcoming. But, prior to the User Program, only people familiar with the gas turbine operated them, and they (because of their familiarity) would never allow this to happen." Carry said that this experience converted him from being a believer in gauges to a proponent of warning lights for "general use" automobiles.

Another mechanical problem that surfaced during the program was a "soak back" condition with the bearings. In a device with parts that move as fast as a turbine, bearings are vital to allow the moving parts to move as fast as possible. The Ghia engine did not have a traditional oil system because jet engines don't need them—so few parts rub against one another that they need very little lubrication. The one place lubrication was necessary was in the highly stressed bearings on the turbine shaft. They held a shaft that turned forty-four thousand times a minute—a shaft that could get very hot because of the environment it sat in. With the engine running but the car not moving, very little cooling took place under the hood. There was no traditional radiator in the car either, as the engine had no cooling system. Under extreme conditions, the oil in the system could become damaged by the severe heat, and once that happened, the bearings could be damaged and the shaft would sometimes seize. One place this phenomenon was observed was at the World's Fair, where the cars were driven slowly around an asphalt track that got very hot in the summertime. Later engines included some parts made out of different materials that helped dissipate the heat and avoid the problem.

One of the stranger setups found inside the turbine was its use of air bearings. At some places inside the engines, where the engineers wanted to eliminate drag, they designed the turbine in such a way that air rather than oil was pumped through the clearances. These air bearings produced virtually no friction and hence ran cooler and lasted longer than traditional oil bearings. The clearances in question—between the two surfaces held apart by the air—measured only a few ten-thousandths of an inch.

———

By about the halfway point of the program—the end of 1964 or so—Carry and his service technicians had figured out how to repair any Ghia failure that occurred in the field short of a "destructive-type failure." Obviously, cars that failed like that merely had their engines replaced rather than repaired, and that operation could be performed in the field as well. Even so, the service techs often found themselves hopscotching around the country, fixing cars in different states on the same day.

Al Bradshaw was called to repair a car in Texas. Its user had run over some train tracks without realizing the car didn't have the clearance. The bottom of the engine scraped on the train tracks, and the car quit running a little way further down the road. While he was replacing the part that had been knocked off the engine, Bradshaw got a call to repair a car in Topeka. He finished the repair in Texas, drove the car to San Antonio, and caught a plane to Kansas. The car in Topeka was an easier fix. The user had merely run it out of fuel and couldn't get it restarted.

During the user program, Chrysler managed to keep attention focused on the cars. Delivering the turbine cars to users still managed to get good press coverage well into the second year of the trial. Bill Carry had to put a lot of thought into it sometimes. He still has photos showing one of the cars being delivered in Indiana in the parking lot of—what else?—the Indianapolis Motor Speedway. In other photos, he stands in front of a Ghia Turbine with the hood raised, pointing at something while a young couple of future drivers look on. That photo was snapped in the parking lot of a hotel in Ohio, with an impressive crowd surrounding the young couple and the car.

Carry not only delivered many of the cars, he also picked them up at the end of a user's program run. Carry noticed consumers occasionally became evasive or uncooperative when it came time to explain failures or breakdowns in the Ghias. In fact, Carry and his techs found the principal obstacle to their job was obtaining reliable information from the users. If a car broke down, it was not uncommon for the users to tap dance around what had happened, to try and deflect the blame, even if no one was at fault. Vagueness and ignorance were often encountered by the service technicians. The service techs and interviewers from Chrysler found they had to develop interviewing skills that often meant approaching a subject indirectly or making small talk to loosen up a user. Carry found it odd, though, how some users were "unable to answer the simplest inquiry about any aspect of the vehicle's operation."

This lack of cooperation was offset by something else Carry observed: he was often impressed by how clean the cars were when they were returned. Users often vacuumed them out and washed them before returning them. Carry attributed this to the fact that many of the users felt special for having been selected for the program in the first place.

Along the way, Chrysler engineers worked the bugs out of any problems they encountered as best they could. One perplexing issue was a loss of power as the engines aged. The engineers knew that as the various nozzles and blades aged they might accumulate dirt and become less efficient. The service techs tried everything to clean the turbines in the field short of tearing them apart. Toward the end of the program, someone at Chrysler discovered a "magic powder"—an inexpensive material that was simply run through the system like a cleaner. It left behind no residue as it cleaned the turbine's vital parts. The magic powder was proprietary; although some people within Chrysler knew what it was, they never told anyone.

In fact, one day Al Bradshaw was working on a car that needed to be cleaned and discovered that he had no magic powder with him. He remembered that the can it came in was labeled "Thompson Hayward Chemical," so he gave the company a call. Could they deliver to him some of the "Chrysler Research 107"? They told him that they knew of someone near him who would give him some and sent him to a local bakery with instructions to ask for "baker's ammonia." The bakery gave it to Bradshaw, who noticed that the cooking ingredient looked just like the stuff Chrysler called CR-107. He used it. It worked.

Bradshaw's bosses panicked when he told them he'd obtained the magic powder locally. Chrysler thought it had a monopoly on the supply, believing no one else knew what it was. Bradshaw never told anyone else, and his bosses later forgave him. After all, he'd gotten the job done fast, which was the primary goal. Years later, he laughed about it. The bakery told him they used the powder to make animal crackers.

Carry wrote later that if the turbine car were ever put into full-scale production, a small port could be placed near the front end of the turbine for cleaning purposes. "The entire cleaning procedure will consist of opening the port, slowly pouring the material in while the engine idles, and closing the port—truly an 'instant tune-up.'"

The magic tune-up was more than simply the imagination of the Chrysler technicians. Several engines were removed from high-mileage Ghias and placed on test stands back in the Highland Park laboratories. After cleaning the compressors, the engines' performance returned to original. In fact, there were documented cases of cleaned high-mileage turbines that had higher output after cleaning than they did when they were brand-new.

Another anomaly discovered in the program was the deterioration of the transmissions in the Ghia Turbine Cars. The transmission was simply a modified Torqueflite, one of the most reliable automatic transmissions ever built. Still, many of the cars were turned in needing transmission overhauls. The fourth-generation turbine only put out 130 horsepower, a fraction of the power put out by many of Chrysler's other vehicles that used this transmission without such problems.

At first the engineers thought the problem may have been caused by the band adjustments made when adapting this transmission to the turbine car. When they examined the long-term tests being performed by a professional test driver, the transmission did not suffer the same problem the user cars had experienced. The turbine team determined that the problem most likely did lie with the users. By trying to make the car drive a bit peppier, many drivers manually shifted the car from "Low" to "Drive," probably a little later than the transmission would have performed the shift.

Meanwhile, the scientists and engineers continued to refine their experiments and work out various technical problems. Dr. Amedee Roy, who had overseen the work making the turbine fans less expensive and more heat tolerant, presented a paper at the ninety-fourth annual meeting of the Metallurgical Society of the American Institute of Mining, Metallurgical, and Petroleum Engineers. On February 15, 1965, he explained "Development of New Iron-Base Superalloys for 1500 Degree Fahrenheit Applications" to the select few on the planet who could expect to understand the topic. As he pointed out in his paper, "gas turbine engines and new superalloys have made parallel progress. This is not surprising since each new development in either field is a stimulating challenge to the other." During his presentation, Roy walked his audience through the tests he had conducted at Chrysler and the amazing characteristics of the materials with which he had been working. Still, he gave nothing away. Dr. Roy simply referred to the alloys by their CRM numbers.

———

The last of the test drivers was an executive secretary from Chicago named Patricia Anderson. She parked her 1960 Corvair for three months and put 2,641 miles on the odometer of a Ghia Turbine Car. When she turned it back in to Chrysler on January 28, 1966, the Ghia Turbine loaner program officially ended.

Even though Chrysler did not say for a while what its consensus was, local newspapers deemed the experiment a success. Robert Irvin of the *Detroit News* wrote that the cars were "regarded a success in at least one area. The turbine program helped change the firm's image. It came at a time Chrysler was trying to make the public forget the management squabbles and dissention [sic] that marked its leadership in previous years."

Before the program ended, however, the Vlahas—the first users—wrote to Chrysler and asked if they could have the car again. They hoped that Chrysler might let them be the last users as well, for a sort of poetic finish to the program. Patricia Vlaha admitted to reporters that they just liked the car so much they'd try anything to get the car back. "We're keeping our fingers crossed. We'd love to drive it again."

The Vlahas got their wish in a roundabout way. After the user program ended, Richard Vlaha asked Chrysler if he might be able to borrow a car to use while he visited New York City for training with IBM. Chrysler obliged, and the Vlahas—Patricia came to New York for the trip—got to take one last spin in the car. They showed it off to everyone at work, and brought it to a local country club where IBM was holding a function.

Chrysler decided one last tour was in order for the Ghia Turbine Cars and the various displays it had made for them. The cars went on a tour of college campuses around the country. Engineering departments welcomed them like conquering heroes. Turbine engineers gave lectures and seminars on turbine power, and the cars drew crowds of college kids outside the school buildings. Jerry Gross was one of the engineers sent on the tour; he showed off the Ghia to schools in Boston and Rhode Island.

One VIP who got to drive the Ghia Turbine was Bill France. Big Bill, as he was known, the founder and benevolent dictator of NASCAR, opened up the Daytona motor speedway in 1964 to the turbine car. The track was the centerpiece of NASCAR's season, and this particular year saw a strong contingent from Chrysler, powered by the new Hemi engine, getting ready to square off against Ford. The huge track was two and a half miles around, with steep banked turns. Carry took the Ghia to Daytona for the week. Big Bill took a few laps behind the wheel on the Daytona oval and was impressed.

Tom Golec and a few others also took one of the Ghias to Denver to see how it would run in the thin mountain air. Unexpectedly, the starter began malfunctioning. On the Ghia cars, the starter doubled as a generator, so the unit got a lot more wear than a typical starter that a consumer might only use a few times a day. This unit was in use whenever the car was running. Golec crawled underneath the car himself to see what the problem was. He saw that the brushes were worn out, even though Ghias with much higher mileage back in Detroit had never encountered this problem. Golec and the others replaced the brushes and chalked it up to the thin air and its impact on the oxidation of the material. Later on, the cars were equipped with separate starters and generators to avoid this problem altogether.

———

Bill Carry oversaw the creation of a training manual for the Ghia Turbines, so that if Chrysler launched a turbine-powered product line, service manuals would be available to send to dealers for the technicians to consult. One thing he did for research: he spent a day at the Chelsea Proving Grounds, driving the Ghia in and around a road course and then for a lap or two on the huge oval, over and over again. He spent a whole day doing it, and when he was done he was glad that he didn't work at the proving grounds on a full-time basis. Carry still has the draft of the Ghia Turbine "training manual." His draft's cover does not bear any indication that it was for the turbines—the title page on the inside read, "Chrysler Gas Turbine Training Guide."

It is an interesting document. Service manuals exist for most production cars, and they follow a relatively common format. Because this was the manual for a car that had a never-before-publicly-used engine type, it contained quite a bit of basic information on turbine operation. The manual included diagrams of the various systems as well as step-by-step repair procedures. The troubleshooting portion looks familiar in layout to those found in most service manuals, but it is a little more interesting because of the turbine theme. Your turbine suffers from a relight "pop"? See Section VIII. You are advised to double-check the igniter, and if that doesn't solve the problem, try a better fuel, such as kerosene. If not, you may have a problem with the air nozzle or the air pump.

As the program progressed, Carry and the others examined the comments from the users to see how they rated their experiences with the car. Not all the feedback from consumers was useful, however. As one might imagine, a cross-section of the public could occasionally draw someone who didn't know what he was talking about. "One of the users was quoted as saying that there was a governor on the car that kept it from going more than seventy miles an hour. Now, where the hell the guy got that idea I haven't the slightest idea, but there certainly was nothing like that on the car," Carry said years later. The car not only didn't have a governor, but it could easily go over a hundred miles an hour.

Users also remarked on the turbine cars' poor fuel economy, though Chrysler noted that consumers tended to drive the Turbine Cars a bit less economically than they normally might. Neighbors wanted rides around the block, and most people took every opportunity to drive the car, no matter how short the trip might be. Carry once drove a Ghia Turbine through several states, accompanied by a full-size Chrysler car with a V-8. The two cars traveled the distance using the same amount of fuel.

Some of the facts and figures of the turbine engine were notable, especially to those who were familiar only with the characteristics of a piston-engine car. The Ghia's engine gulped huge volumes of air. Measured in pounds, it took in about 2.2 pounds of air per second, about four times what a piston engine car devoured. At 60 MPH the engine in the Ghia burned about half a pound of fuel per minute. The stream of hot air through the turbine reached speeds of 1,900 feet per second—just a tad below 1,300 miles per hour.

Many people questioned how it was possible for a device that spun at 44,000 RPM to be put to practical use. How was that astronomical speed utilized? It was done with gears. The output shaft of the power turbine spun at ridiculously high rates of speed as well, but it turned a small gear that was coupled to a large gear on the input shaft to the transmission. The reduction rate was a factor of ten to one, more in the range of usefulness.

———

Some people wondered what would happen if a Turbine Car were brought in for service to an old-fashioned mechanic unfamiliar with turbine engines and without access to the technical expertise of a Chrsyler-affiliated dealership. Sixty years of working on piston engines would presumably create a skill vacuum at these repair facilities, since almost none of the experience of working on piston engines would help a technician diagnose or repair a turbine engine.

Chrysler's Turbine Car program proved that this would not be a problem. For the fifty-car test fleet, Chrysler employed five field service technicians and two supervisors. These seven oversaw the repairs and maintenance of all fifty cars for two years to all four corners of the country. Even with the small crew, repairs on the Turbine Car fleet were swift and easy. Early in the program, the total downtime for the cars was 4 percent. By the end of the run, the technicians had reduced the downtime to 1 percent. Chrysler proudly pointed out that much of that downtime was taken up by the time it took to ship parts from Detroit to wherever the car sat. Presumably, if there were a dealer network with a supply of parts on hand, the downtime would have become a fraction of 1 percent.

Bill Carry headed the service program for the Ghia Turbine Car program throughout the nation. His conclusion at the end of the program was that turbine technology posed "no greater problem to the Automotive Service Industry than the introduction of the automatic transmission did some years ago."

9

Wrap-Up of the User Program

When the fifty Turbine Cars found their way back to Chrysler, the consumers' responses were largely enthusiastic. And it's not that the users didn't run the cars through the wringer. At least thirteen of the cars were returned with over ten thousand miles added to their odometers in the three months they'd been borrowed. The drivers also came from a huge cross-section of the driving public. They ranged in age from twenty-one to seventy and included ministers, a retired rear admiral, a surgeon, a bus driver, and virtually every other imaginable occupation. The totals were impressive: the 203 users in the program racked up over a million miles on the cars.

And for the sake of accuracy, it should be noted that of the fifty-five cars built by Ghia, only fifty cars were allotted to the user program, with the last five considered prototypes. Technically, only forty-six of the fifty user cars were lent out; the remaining four were used for promotional purposes—two at the World's Fair and two on a national dealership tour.

On April 12, 1966, Chrysler held a press conference to announce its findings with respect to the user program. The conference was held at the exclusive Boat Club on Belle Isle, a small island in the Detroit River, connected to Detroit by a bridge. David F. Miller, manager of marketing and consumer research at Chrysler, spoke to the press and handed out a six-page press release. With him stood George Huebner and a vice president named Harry E. Chesebrough. Miller's comments and the press release, incorporated into many newspaper stories, described the rationale behind the program and its unique features, how the users were debriefed afterward, and what the findings of the program were.

The most obvious finding was that three out of four users singled out the smooth operation of the turbine engine as the car's principal advantage over other cars they'd driven. "People talked about a gliding sensation, similar to that experienced in a jet airplane. It seemed to matter little whether the car was idling or cruising at turnpike speeds. The real advantage was felt, though, on long trips. Time after time people would tell of driving 400 or 500 miles in a day and still feeling fresh upon arriving at their destination."

The next thing users focused on was the vehicle's reduced maintenance requirements. Although the program lasted only three months for each user, and Chrysler handled all the maintenance, the users knew the vehicle needed no oil changes or tune-ups. The car was also noted for its starting ability. In a time when most cars had carburetors and needed a pump or two of the gas pedal to start—and maybe more on a cold morning—the turbine always started instantly, regardless of outside temperature. Others noted the car's instant heat as well, and the quietness of the turbine's sound over that of a piston engine.

Miller admitted some users found problems with the cars, but he pointed out that the consumer reaction had been overwhelmingly positive. Chrysler was aware of many of the issues, such as the turbine's poor fuel economy, before the program even began. One in three users complained about the "lag" the engine experienced from a dead stop. The turbine car accelerated much more slowly than a piston engine, but that was something Chrysler thought could be easily resolved.

The issue of the noise the engine made was most interesting. One in five complained about it, while three out of five liked it. Miller never said which group Chrysler would cater to in the future. Most users, however, agreed that, at highway speeds, the car ran much quieter than a comparable piston-engine car.

The *Detroit News* managed to get a story into print that afternoon: "Turbines Please Test Drivers." Calling the report by Miller "generally optimistic," the *News* noted that Chrysler did not answer the question of when—or if—Chrysler would ever sell turbine cars commercially. The article quoted a Chrysler executive who had spoken at Miller's presentation, stating that that decision would be made later in the summer. There was hope for turbine supporters: "From what he said, it appears Chrysler has no intention of dropping the program, and in fact, the next logical step could be the first limited production of a passenger car turbine in this country."

The following morning's *Detroit Free Press* recapped the press conference and accompanied their article with a photo of a local woman who'd participated in the program. The caption read, "Chrysler's gas turbine powered cars were a hit with users when they were introduced late in 1963. This model was photographed while being driven by Mrs. Jeannine Goebel, of Bloomfield Township. The place: Washington Blvd, in front of the Sheraton-Cadillac Hotel." The press conference was even reported in Toronto's *Globe and Mail*, even though the user program had not sent any cars to Canada—all 203 users were in the lower forty-eight states and restricted from leaving the country in the car by the user agreement they signed.

More astute observers of the press conference may have been puzzled by Huebner's low profile. Usually one to take center stage at such an event, he let the others do the bulk of the talking. It may be that he had reservations about the program's results, and was disappointed that he couldn't announce the imminent production of turbine cars. Yes, the users had been pleased to drive their hand-built Ghia Turbine Cars around America for free. That, however, was not the real target of the turbine program. He had hoped the user program would be the last step before moving to production of a turbine car for sale to the public.

However, Huebner knew that the fourth-generation turbine engine still had problems, issues that would be formidable and expensive to resolve. He wouldn't state it publicly yet, but he believed the Ghia Turbines were too loud, even when they were simply idling. The lag at acceleration was also a problem, and the lack of engine "braking" would need to be dealt with. The gas mileage was a problem, and the Ghia cars did not have air-conditioning. At the time, air-conditioning was becoming a quite popular option, but the addition of a compressor under the hood would have wasted even more horsepower that the little engine couldn't afford to spare. While the public relations people spun the program as a wild success, Huebner knew it would just send his engineers back to the lab.

It wasn't just the users who were impressed with the cars; the technicians who worked on them remember the cars fondly as well. Years later, Al Bradshaw summarized his impression of the car: "The cars ran very good. For what they were, and as unique as they were, they were remarkably dependable."

———

After the cars were returned, Chrysler let some of the engineers who'd designed the cars borrow them for a week or longer. Jerry Gross loved driving the Ghia around for the week he had it for personal use. It was the culmination of a dream he first had in college: a turbine-powered car. Dr. Amedee Roy brought one to his home in a suburb of Detroit where many other auto executives lived. An engineer from General Motors whom Roy knew from the neighborhood stopped by to admire the car and Dr. Roy tossed him the key. He was startled—a Chrysler engineer letting him drive the car unsupervised? Dr. Roy laughed about it later. By now there were no secrets with the program. If anything, Roy knew the car would impress the GM engineer more if he had it to himself.

After the success of the Ghia Turbine Car program, some people within Chrysler began pushing to launch a turbine-powered car into the product mix for 1966, but with the fifth-generation turbine. A new car was being planned for launch that year, the sleek Dodge Charger. Bill Brownlie, one of the Charger's designers, said, "Lynn Townsend called Elwood Engel, myself, and others into a meeting during the time of the fifty-car program and we discussed actually offering a new turbine car on a limited basis to what would have been virtually hand-picked customers as a test of public acceptance. In that meeting it was decided to build a limited number of special-bodied turbines—that body became the '66 Charger fastback." Although Chargers did go into production, none were ever built with turbine engines. Later there was some debate about how close this program came to fruition.

While the engines had become more efficient with each generation, and strides were being made in making them run cleaner, there was nothing the turbine team could do to make the parts of the turbine easier to manufacture. The sixth- and seventh-generation engines still required the investment casting process to create the turbine disks, the ignition nozzle, and the nozzle blades.

The higher-ups at Chrysler had to examine the issue: could they mass-produce the turbine engines if they decided to put a turbine car into full-scale production? While Chrysler routinely overhauled assembly lines and even entire plants to make room for new cars, manufacturing the turbine engine would not be so simple. Chrysler was not making any similar parts by investment casting in-house at the time. To tool up a plant to manufacture turbine engines, Chrysler would have to set up a plant to start mass-production of parts by investment casting. Further, no one in the industry had figured out a faster way to make parts with investment casting. Each part would still need to be preceded by a wax model, the slurry mold would have to be made, the wax would have to be melted off, the molten metal would have to be poured into the mold, and then, after the part had cooled, the mold would have to be broken off the casting. Four of the most critical parts of the turbine had to be made this way—there was no way around it. Chrysler could not expect a company like Howmet to manufacture enough of these parts for them on the scale necessary to launch a whole new car line. After all, Chrysler built and sold *a lot* of cars. In 1966, their Dodge division would have three models that sold more than a hundred thousand units each. One car, the Coronet, would sell more than a quarter of a million units. If Chrysler was going to build turbine cars inexpensively enough to be economically competitive, these issues would have to be resolved on a scale to compete with these numbers.

————

In 1967, Chrysler decided to get rid of most of the Ghia cars. Various reasons are given for what happened next. Regardless of where the truth lies, it's a sad story. The most common version told is that the government told Chrysler it had to pay exorbitant import taxes on the Ghia bodies. This story has been largely discredited, but it is still repeated.

Some within the program felt the reasoning behind the cars' destruction was a bit simpler. "The reality was the import duties at that point would have been peanuts. They didn't want the cars just hanging around, getting into people's hands and messing up the image of the program, people getting them and putting V-8s into them, that was the real reason," Bill Carry explained.

As early as 1963, Chrysler had stated it would not sell any of the Ghia Turbine Cars to the public. A Chrysler vice president told *Look* magazine, "Our main objective is research, and we did not want turbines turning up on used car lots." If the cars had been sold to the public, it may have turned out even worse for Chrysler from a public relations perspective. Without spare parts to keep the cars running, they would have soon been consigned to scrap yards anyway. Or worse, after the turbine engines failed, the owners would have to shoehorn something else under the hood to keep the car running. The final result might have seen "turbine" cars being driven around with piston engines under their hoods. Automotive manufacturers routinely consigned their prototype and test cars to the scrap heap, and the turbine cars were no different.

Many people renewed their offers to buy the car. Richard Vlaha called up his contact at Chrysler and asked if he could buy one of the cars. He wasn't sure if he could afford it but thought it was worth a shot. Chrysler told him that the cars weren't going to be sold to individuals.

A very short item—by the standard of publicity the turbine program had usually received—appeared in the *Detroit Free Press* on April 15, 1966. "Chrysler Corp. will chop up most of the 50 turbine cars with which it has conducted a controlled driving experiment in the last two years. The corporation emphasized, however, that destruction of the turbines will in no way affect Chrysler's decision to produce the cars or abandon the program."

Chrysler put the word out that it would consider donating the cars to museums that might be interested in acquiring the cars for display. Only six museums accepted the offer. Five museums were public and one was private. Chrysler decided to keep three of the cars. The three retained by Chrysler bore the vehicle identification numbers ending in 30, 37, and 42. For many years Chrysler kept one of the cars at the Chelsea Proving Grounds and the other two at its archives and museum.

Many people associated with the program realized what was about to be lost. Jerry Wenk, the test driver from Chelsea, brought the turbine car from the proving grounds home and let everyone know that it was now or never. He told them it was their "one shot in a lifetime" to ride in the jet car. He took his mother for a ride, as well as all the members of his family and many of his neighbors. He spent the better part of a day driving around Chelsea with the car loaded full of passengers. Everywhere they went, the car turned heads. People yelled out, asking him to rev the engine for them.

———

On a day when many grown men at Chrysler cried, the last forty-six Ghia Turbine Cars were destroyed. Forty-five were sent to a scrap yard south of Detroit, where they were crushed and incinerated, and one was destroyed at the Chelsea Proving Grounds. Nine were spared.

Carry went to the scrap yard the day the cars were destroyed. "Talk about a bad day." Employees from the scrap yard punched holes in the gas tanks, took the fuel out, poured it into the Italian-crafted interiors, and then burned the cars. The entire process was filmed, presumably to make sure no one snuck off with one of them.

One car was destroyed at the proving grounds by an employee. Wenk said later that one of the men who worked at the proving grounds walked up to the car, without telling anyone he had orders to destroy it, and acted like he was angry about something, cursing as he took a hammer to it, smashing out the windows. After attracting a bit of a crowd, he told the others that the order had come in to destroy the car. That car was later dismantled and destroyed at the proving grounds, though some later reports said that the car was crashed in a collision test. It was unclear why Chrysler would crash-test a car that wasn't going into production.

Wenk recalled that a story went around that two more of the Ghia cars were at the bottom of the ocean. A cargo ship supposedly coming over with two crated Ghia bodies sank somewhere off the East Coast. This story is most likely a variation on the sinking of the *Andrea Doria*.

The museums that asked for cars soon got the few that avoided the scrap yard. Cars went to the Petersen Automotive Museum in Los Angeles, Harrah's in Nevada, and the Henry Ford Museum in Dearborn, Michigan. Another went to the St. Louis Museum of Transportation. The Smithsonian Institution soon housed turbine car 45. One didn't have to travel far to its new home; the Ghia bearing vehicle identification number 991225—car 25—was donated to the Detroit Historical Museum in January 1967. It bears a number 18 on its body, on the ceiling, above the rearview mirror. The receipt for its acquisition by the DHM described the car in cold, almost medical, terminology:

1-Automobile: Chrysler Corporation Turbine Car, 1964; experimental; color is Turbine Tan with black grained vinyl hardtop; black leather bucket seats front and rear; large drive tunnel with top consoles both front and rear between seats; has Chrysler Corporation Turbine emblem on left front edge of hood and in rear center of trunk lid; word "Turbine" in chrome near rear end of rear fenders; tires are 7.50 x 14 Goodyear whitewalls; 46,115 miles on speedometer; vehicle weighs 3900 pounds; has aerial at rear quarter panel which is 19½" high; like new except for metal curled under below rear edge of trunk lid, almost unnoticeable; wheelbase =

110" x 59", overall length = 196", overall width at wheel wells = 74", overall
height = 56". Title in Acc. Corres.

A few of the details in the receipt are mistaken, however. The bucket
seats in this car were turbine bronze, just like all the others from the user
program. The other errors are minor, but one is striking. The receipt gives
a "Value," presumably what Chrysler suggested the car was worth at the
time: ten thousand dollars. The same receipt describes an engine that
accompanied the car—not the one under the hood—on a pallet made of
oak, valued at five thousand dollars. Neither of those prices, however, had
any connection to reality. The car could easily have been sold for over ten
thousand dollars at the time, and George Huebner had even said the cars
cost more than fifty thousand each to build. The DHM Ghia car also still
had its four original whitewall tires on it. Carry mentioned later how most
of the original whitewall tires had been replaced, so it was a bit unusual for
this car—at forty-five thousand miles—to still have its original tires.

The receipt for the car also showed that Chrysler donated a collection of
literature, including a service manual, to the museum. The DHM passed
these documents along to the Detroit Public Library's National Automotive History Collection. Also among those documents were the various
press releases from the venture and many newspaper articles that featured
the car. The cover letter accompanying the service manual was drafted by
Bill Carry, who explained the evolution of the document through the program's run. "The manual is no longer completely up to date. There were
a number of wiring and miscellaneous changes made to the Turbine cars
during the time they were on the road. These changes were issued in an
informal manner to our Service Representatives and so are not reflected in
the manual." No doubt, if the car had gone into production, Carry would
have seen to it that the revisions were made.

———

To offset the gloom of seeing most of the turbine cars destroyed, Chrysler
announced that the user program had succeeded in proving the viability

of the cars. Huebner told the press he was "gratified" by the results of the program. "Based on our inspections of high-mileage cars in the program, we believe most of the turbine engine parts will enjoy far more than 50,000 miles, and pass the 100,000 miles that are generally considered acceptable for passenger cars." Chrysler also pointed out how the consumers had almost universally praised the car's smooth ride, easy starting, and quick warmth, as well as the variety of fuels it could burn. He noted that the primary complaint, which was almost universal, was that the users wanted to keep the cars longer.

Chrysler had also pushed the limits of what it could get the little fourth-generation engine to do. To put the engine into a full-sized car, especially one with air-conditioning, would have required engineers to get more power from the turbine. They knew this would require higher internal temperatures and reconfiguring some of the elements of the engine. While Dr. Roy and the metallurgists had found ways to make the internal parts of the fourth-generation turbine from low-cost alloys, future engines would be more expensive. It would be back to the drawing board—or laboratory—for anyone who wanted to try to make the turbine run hotter with inexpensive parts.

———

In September 1966, Harry Chesebrough, the vice president who had spoken at the Detroit Boat Club, issued a statement of Chrysler's intentions. After recapping the "unprecedented" user program and the benefits Chrysler had gained from interviewing the users afterward, Chesebrough announced that Chrysler was going to launch the fifth-generation engine. He made no mention of a specific car it would power, or if this engine would be part of a bigger project. It looked as if Chrysler was not quite sure what it would do with the engine. Chesebrough did say this new engine would put out a little more horsepower and have faster throttle response than the one in the user program. The engine would have to be placed into a regular test car and run at the proving grounds rather than on a public stage like the Ghia car program.

———

For the most part, the turbine cars would never be publicly displayed again.

Some people wondered why Chrysler couldn't simply start building and selling turbine cars, and just work out the bugs of the program as they arose. There were several obvious reasons, although Chrysler did not widely admit these points yet.

Without resolving the issues that prevented it from mass-producing the investment cast parts, any turbine engines Chrysler built would have to be—in essence—built by hand, one at a time. If it just built fifty Ghias, and then five hundred Coronets or Chargers, and so on, Chrysler could probably make enough engines to put the cars on the road, but it would never be able to overcome the final mass-production hurdle. Furthermore, even a small number of turbines on the road would require a network of trained mechanics, a supply line of spare parts, and so on.

One of the people who would have been in that "supply line" was Bill Carry. Whenever he asked about the probability of the program moving from prototypes to production—that is, with cars being sold to consumers—he was told there were still large hurdles to be cleared. "Nobody was willing to say that they wanted to spend the money on major tooling; it would have been an enormous investment to tool up for wider production. That's what killed it." People within the program knew that they couldn't sell five hundred cars to the public without the needed support in place. Otherwise, they risked putting five hundred "orphans" out there, as Carry put it.

Chrysler's turbine engineers had been designing a fifth-generation turbine during the two years of the Ghia program. First, they simply updated the two most obvious aspects of it for performance: they made the regenerators larger to capture more of the exhaust heat, and they stepped up the temperature in the burner stage to make the engine run hotter. They had known for a long time that increases in the combustion temperature translated to higher power output for the turbine. Shortly after, they dropped the fifth and moved on to the sixth-generation engine.

It looks as if the turbine engineers rushed to get the fifth-generation finished so it would have been ready if Chrysler wanted to offer a turbine car for sale to the public at the end of the Ghia program. In a report written in 1979, Chrysler said the fifth-generation engine was abandoned for two reasons: "economic conditions prevailing at the time and because studies revealed that substantial burner development was still required before this engine could meet strict requirements limiting emissions of oxides of nitrogen." So, without the burning need to put an engine on the road right away, the engineers went back to the "skunk works" to revamp the entire engine, using things they'd learned from the program and some other ideas they had cooked up in the lab over the previous few years.

———

In 1967, Chrysler unveiled its next version of the turbine, the sixth generation. This one, it claimed, finally had the performance characteristics to match a contemporary V-8 piston engine. Not only was its performance on the mark, it had been strenuously bench-tested for durability. Huebner told the press the engine had run in a test cell for over 3,500 hours without problems. At the time, he considered one thousand hours of test cell time the equivalent of fifty thousand miles of consumer driving. The engine was bulletproof, according to the engineers who performed the endurance testing at the laboratory.

The engine had just one problem: its NOx output was too high. These oxides of nitrogen (NO and NO_2) were often abbreviated as NOx. They are a chemical by-product of combustion. One factor influencing the amount of NOx created is the length of the combustion event. In an automobile piston engine, often called a "four-stroke engine," the fuel only burns for a moment. The combustion, or "power," stroke is then followed by the exhaust, intake, and compression strokes. During the last three strokes, there is no combustion taking place in the cylinder. On the other hand, the turbine engine, once running, is constantly burning fuel. While the amount of fuel might increase or decrease, the combustion process is continuous. The engineers knew that increased NOx output was a by-product of a continuous burn.

The problem was that there was no easy fix. It was something Chrysler engineers would struggle with during the entire run of the program. Huebner didn't say what the NOx numbers were, but he hinted that Chrysler was making strides in this direction. He told the press that if Chrysler could simply solve this one last problem, the turbine cars would go into full production by "the late 1970s." Why so long? The NOx problem was nowhere near being solved, and mass-production of the cars would require constructing a plant from the ground up. Rather than make bold predictions of short deadlines, he pushed the date off into the distant, vague future.

Chrysler hinted it might build a test run of Dodge Coronets with turbine power, and built up a running model for demonstration with the sixth-generation engine under its hood. The Coronet was one of Chrysler's more popular models at the time, and Chrysler thought such a marriage might work. Like its predecessors, Chrysler lent the new turbine prototype to reporters and auto writers to generate press and publicity. Now, however, it seemed anticlimactic. After the user program had generated such immense publicity, how could a single car—one that looked "normal"—expect to get headlines?

Previously, automotive writers had not always been kind to the turbines, but a writer who drove the 1967 Turbine Coronet liked what he saw in the latest version. "On-the-road performance is comparable to that of a big V-8. Also unlike a piston engine, a gas turbine produces maximum torque at zero speed. So it provides excellent acceleration and flexibility at low speed and throughout the cruising range, adapting to changing conditions without special attention from the driver and with minimum transmission shifting." After talking about the performance aspects of the car, the writer felt the need to dispel a few myths about turbines. "The dire predictions that turbine noise would injure ear drums and set the neighborhood dogs to howling just isn't true either. In fact, during the 50-car turbine program conducted with the noisier 4th-generation engine a major complaint from the test 'owners' was lack of engine noise! Drivers, it was discovered, wanted more turbine sound to let them feel as if they were driving a jet plane, Huebner says."

The sixth-generation engine was a refinement of its predecessors. It was more efficient, gave quicker throttle response, and was even a bit quieter than its predecessors. One major advance in its design was the placement of the auxiliary drives. In the Ghia cars, the generator and fuel pump were driven off the front turbine—the compressor. This meant that these accessories were always being turned, and when the engine was accelerated, the accessories slowed down the gas generator as it spooled up to full speed. On the sixth-generation engine, the engineers moved the auxiliary drives to the power turbine—the back end of the engine. There, the drives would not hinder the gas generator upon acceleration—slow throttle response was also something that Ghia users had complained of—and much of the noise they made would not be as apparent.

When the drives were at the front of the engine, and always turning, the gear noise was more obvious. But when the devices were moved to the rear of the engine, they were not turning as much and they were buried deeper inside the car, making them harder to hear. The new placement of the auxiliary drives on the power turbine also added to the engine braking effect—again, something that made it "feel" more like a piston engine. And, by removing the auxiliary drives from the compressor, the engineers discovered they could get the engine to easily start with a twelve-volt starter. This allowed them to stop worrying about the intricacies of having the oddball twenty-four-volt starter in a car when most cars used twelve-volt electrical systems.

———

Dean Musgrave was a Stanford- and MIT-trained engineer who joined the turbine program in 1972, after the Ghias had already been destroyed. He came to Detroit looking for work on turbines and began working on the 1967 Coronet with the sixth-generation engine. Since this car was rarely—if ever—seen by the public, there was no need to put the engine into a "newer" car each year. As a result, the Coronet had been used for several years as a test car. It was still being used when Musgrave signed on with Chrysler.

The engine put out 150 horsepower, and those who drove it said it performed as well as any comparably equipped V-8 on the road at that time. Musgrave had several opportunities to drive the newer turbine cars in the post-Ghia period. The Coronet with the sixth-generation engine impressed him. "It felt like it was pretty close to being sellable, to tell the truth," he said.

Based on some of the things it learned from the Ghia user program, Chrysler also considered placing this engine into the largest and most expensive car in its lineup. Many of the users who liked the Ghia had expressed hesitation when asked if they would consider buying the car if it cost much more than a typical car of similar size with a piston engine. Chrysler decided it might be more palatable to the buying public if the engine were placed into a top-of-the-line luxury car. That way the price increase from the engine wouldn't stand out so much and the smoother engine operation could be used as a selling point.

The turbine engine was then installed into a Chrysler Imperial. Jerry Wenk got to test-drive the heavier car at the proving grounds, but he wasn't impressed by it. The car seemed terribly slow and sluggish. After driving the other turbine cars, something just didn't feel right about this combination. It appears the idea was scrapped shortly afterward. Would people with a lot of money to spend on a nice car want one that had a radical powerplant? Probably not.

Chrysler's continuing turbine experiments still made the news but were now pushed further back from the front pages. Many of the former users scoured the papers looking for information on the program, hoping that the cars would someday become available to buy. The Olsons—Alden and Mark—both hoped for the day they could purchase a turbine car, but as the years passed and interest in the program waned at Chrysler, it became obvious to them that the day would never come. Much of the goodwill Chrysler had gained from the grand experiment of lending the cars to the public evaporated.

George Huebner began working on turbines at Chrysler in 1945. Later, he became the company's director of engineering research. But he was always closely identified with the turbine car program. *Chrysler photo, courtesy of Mark Olson, www.turbinecar.com*

Werner von Braun (center) and Huebner (second from right) worked together on the Redstone rocket program as part of Chrysler's contract with the U.S. Army. *Huebner Papers, Chrysler Photos, courtesy of the Bentley Historical Library*

Sam Williams was the brilliant engineer who solved many of the earliest problems Chrysler encountered as it tried to scale down a turbine engine to fit into a car. Later, he would found Williams Research—eventually known as Williams International. *Courtesy of Williams International*

When a turbine powerplant was installed into an automobile for the first time, the men who worked on the turbine car program commemorated the occasion by posing for a group photo. Huebner is on the far right; Williams is standing immediately to the right of the car's engine compartment. *Chrysler photo, courtesy of Jerry Gross*

Members of the press applaud as Huebner takes the turbine car for its first public drive. Dr. Williams can be seen in the backseat. *Chrysler photo, courtesy of Jerry Gross*

The press still showed up at the official demonstration of the turbine car at the Chrysler proving grounds, even though the day was rainy and cold. *Chrysler photo, courtesy of Jerry Gross*

(above) A turbine engine was also installed into a 1955 Plymouth, which Chrysler engineers couldn't resist taking for a spin on Woodward Avenue. *Chrysler photo, courtesy of Jerry Gross*

(right) The turbine program saw the upgraded engines placed into newer-model cars as well. Here, the turbine powers a Plymouth Fury. *Chrysler photo, courtesy of Jerry Gross*

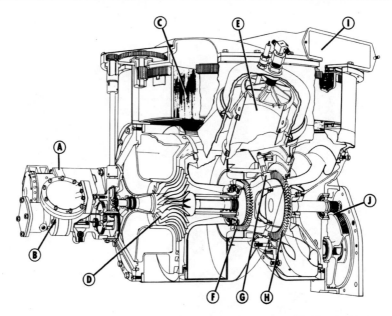

MAIN COMPONENTS OF THE CR2A gas turbine which powers the Dodge Turbo Dart are: (A) the starter-generator; (B) fuel pump; (C) regenerator; (D) compressor impeller; (E) combustion chamber; (F) first-stage turbine, which drives the compressor impeller and accessories; (G) variable second-stage nozzle; (H) second-stage turbine which supplies power to the driveshaft; (I) one of two exhaust outlets; (J) single stage helical reduction gear of 8.53-to-1 ratio which reduces power turbine rpm of 39,000 to 45,730, to a rated output speed of 4,570 to 5,360 rpm.

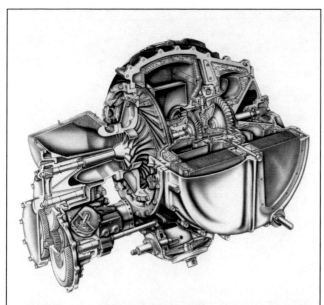

CHRYSLER CORPORATION TWIN-REGENERATOR
GAS TURBINE ENGINE

(above) While the automotive turbines developed by Chrysler looked nothing like their aerospace counterparts, they operated on similar principles. *Chrysler photo, courtesy of Jerry Gross*

(left) Chrysler touted the various innovations developed to make the turbines more efficient. To the right of this illustration, the heat regenerators can clearly be seen, on either side of the turbine's central shaft. The regenerator closer to the viewer is shown cut in half. *Chrysler photo, courtesy of Jerry Gross*

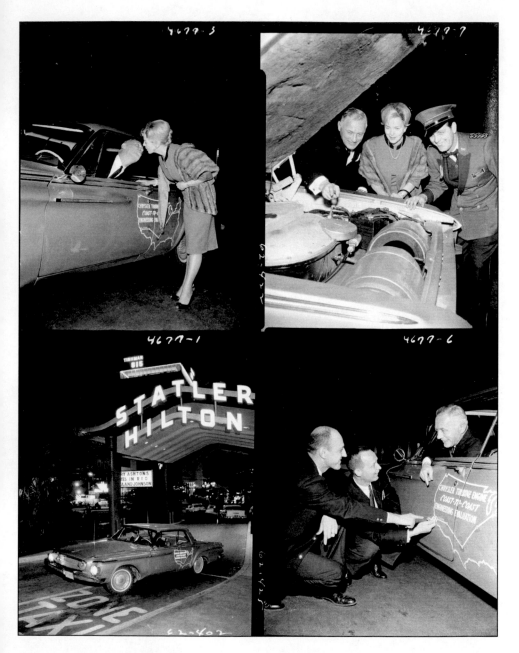

Huebner's cross-country trip in a turbine-powered Dodge Dart was a publicity bonanza. As such, it was well documented with public relations photos like these. *Huebner Papers, Chrysler Photos, courtesy of the Bentley Historical Library*

In case anyone wondered where the Dodge Turbo Dart was going—or where it had been—Chrysler put a convenient map on the door for reference. *Chrysler photo, courtesy of Jerry Gross*

The Ghia Turbine Car was styled by automotive designer Elwood Engel specifically to be a platform for the turbine engine. *Courtesy of the BruntBros*

The Ghia Turbine had space age touches throughout its design—including faux cooling fins everywhere, like these on the headlight bezel. *Courtesy of the BruntBros*

Inside the Ghia's engine compartment, Chrysler's fourth-generation turbine engine may not have looked cutting-edge to the unitiated. Even so, it represented the absolute state of the art. *Courtesy of the BruntBros*

In many respects, the styling of the Ghia Turbine allowed it to blend in with its contemporaries. It wasn't until people heard the whoosh of the engine that they realized the car was radically different from everything else on the road at the time. *Courtesy of the BruntBros*

The body lines of the Ghia were recognizably the work of Elwood Engel. Many people noticed the resemblance of the Ghia Turbine to another car he designed: the Ford Thunderbird. *Chrysler photo*

At first glance, the dash of the Ghia Turbine looked like those of its contemporaries. But the tachometer went to 60,000 RPM. *Courtesy of the BruntBros*

Slim and streamlined, the control column of the Ghia housed the gearshift and all of the switches and knobs for the vehicle's accessories. *Courtesy of the BruntBros*

Although "Typhoon" had been proposed as a name for the Ghia, the car was simply christened "Turbine." *Courtesy of the BruntBros*

The Ghia cars were shipped from Italy mostly complete; the engine and transmission were installed at the turbine car assembly facility in Detroit. *Chrysler photo, courtesy of Jerry Gross*

Technician Bill Carry delivered many of the Ghias to the participants in the user program. He made a point to demonstrate everything in the car, especially when the press was on hand to document the event. *Chrysler photo, courtesy of Bill Carry*

Vehicle deliveries often became media feeding frenzies, because Chrysler's public relations people notified everyone in the local press about the upcoming event. *Chrysler photo, courtesy of Bill Carry*

The Olson family of Duluth, Minnesota, was one of the lucky families given a turbine car to use for free. Alden Olson (second from left) was officially user number 160; he took delivery of the car on May 13, 1965. *Courtesy of Mark Olson, www.turbinecar.com*

One of the fifty-five Ghia Turbine Cars was painted white and was not loaned out for the user program. Here, it is on a hoist while technicians are taught the finer points of automotive turbine repair. *Chrysler photo, courtesy of Jerry Gross*

One Ghia Turbine Car spent several months traveling the globe, arriving in its own custom-outfitted airliner. *Courtesy of Mark Olson, www.turbinecar.com*

The sixth-generation turbine engine was placed into several different cars, including a 1967 Coronet that bore nothing on its exterior to suggest it was turbine-powered. *Chrysler photo, courtesy of Jerry Gross*

A Plymouth Satellite equipped with a sixth-generation turbine engine sits behind the specially built dispenser Chrysler often used to demonstrated the multifuel capabilities of its turbine cars. *Chrysler photo, courtesy of Jerry Gross*

The sixth-generation engine was used as the baseline in later programs underwritten by the federal government. The engine embodied many of the solutions to problems Chrysler had discovered during the Ghia program. *Chrysler photo, courtesy of Jerry Gross*

The last turbine engine—the seventh generation—was developed with input from the Department of Energy. *Chrysler photo, courtesy of Jerry Gross*

Ghia car number 42 is now owned by Jay Leno, who occasionally drives it around town in Southern California. To the left of Leno is the author. *Courtesy of the BruntBros*

10

The Beginning of
Chrysler's Financial Decline

While Chrysler had done quite well when Lynn Townsend first took over, hard times hit the company in the 1970s. Townsend, an accountant by training, was ill equipped to deal with the various obstacles the auto industry ran into. The energy crisis hit all the car companies hard; Chrysler had no small cars in its lineup and saw a decline in market share. When the company's revenues sagged, Townsend thought it wise to cut spending and delay launching new models.

The other car companies did exactly the opposite—they did not cut spending or delay launches. As a result, they picked up the market share that Chrysler surrendered. Townsend did not know what to make of the situation, so he hired and promoted more accountants to help him out. Fellow bean counters could be found chairing the board of directors and filling many of the highest positions within Chrysler. Later, when Lee Iacocca came along and tried to straighten out the mess, he pointed to the "square pegs in round holes," his description of accountants working as sales managers or division managers. "I have never seen anything like it," he said.

The accountants at Chrysler's helm seemingly couldn't run the ship straight. They tried to implement a computerized system for ordering cars, but something went haywire. Hundreds of cars were accidentally built with unusual option combinations. Chrysler New Yorkers showed up at dealerships without automatic transmissions or air-conditioning. The cost of correcting these problems, and others that had worked their way into the system because of cost cutting, inspired Townsend to dump the five-year or fifty-thousand-mile warranty that had been touted earlier as Chrysler's proof of offering better-built cars to the consumer. Those who were unhappy with their Chryslers and how they functioned were instead given a phone number they could call to complain. Presumably, hiring someone to answer the complaint line was cheaper than fixing the cars.

All the while, Chrysler refused to build small cars until it was too late. With hints of fuel issues on the horizon, Ford, American Motors, and General Motors all had small cars in the planning stages. Soon Pintos, Gremlins, and Vegas appeared on American highways. While these cars were being sold in 1970, Chrysler waited until 1978 before launching its answer to the fuel shortages. The models known as the Dodge Omni and the Plymouth Horizon would have helped Chrysler much more if they had been introduced eight years earlier.

It is interesting that one of the biggest problems facing Chrysler at this time—skyrocketing fuel prices—could have been answered by the turbine Chrysler already had in development. Many people in the turbine program, such as Jerry Gross, thought the turbine's ability to burn alternative fuels could have been its saving grace. While gasoline prices hovered at the low levels of the mid-1960s, it was hard to imagine that someday gasoline would break the two-dollar-a-gallon mark. A car that burned gasoline when it was affordable, or anything else when gas prices rose, certainly held promise. Some Midwestern states already encouraged alcohol production for use as auto fuel, so the infrastructure for alcohol production—primarily from agricultural products like corn—was already in place.

Bud Mann agreed that the alternative fuel capability of the turbine could have benefited Chrysler, and the rest of the auto industry, greatly. After all, the later versions of the turbine got better gas mileage with lower emissions, and were still capable of burning all of the strange fuels that the Ghia had made headlines burning. With gasoline prices threatening to explode, gasohol and diesel suddenly looked like viable alternatives.

But the turbine program at Chrysler was doomed at this point, regardless of the technological advancements made by the engineers in the years since the Ghia cars first hit the road. Among the obstacles they faced were the nation's recent concern about smog and legislators in Washington who would reconfigure the entire automotive market in America.

11

The Problem of Smog

A small town in Pennsylvania named Donora made headlines in 1948. In the fall of that year, a thick haze of fog and smoke from a nearby zinc smelter covered the valley along the Monongahela River with a choking haze. The Friday night football game between the local schools was obscured. People in the stands could hear the referee whistles but could not see the players. Heartier people coughed their way through it and did the best they could, but those with respiratory ailments and the elderly didn't fare as well. Traffic came to a halt, and local emergency services became overwhelmed. The community center was commandeered as a makeshift morgue. By Saturday night, eleven people had died. Nine more died in the next few days. Estimates of townspeople sickened by the smog were placed at seven thousand—half the town. People had complained about smog before, but this time people died. Congress began looking at the problem.

Just a few years later, right around the time George Huebner rolled out the first turbine car from the shop in Highland Park, a strange weather phenomenon occurred in London. In December 1952, a cold snap inspired many Londoners to vigorously fire up their coal-burning furnaces. For almost a week, a cloud of smoky fog choked the city. The smog—a word invented by a Londoner in 1905 to describe the city's ugly combination of smoke and fog—became so dense it rolled into homes and buildings. Theaters canceled performances because audiences couldn't see the stage through the haze. After the better part of a week smothering London, the smog finally blew away with the wind. Most Londoners went on about their business and chalked the smog attack up to a freak of nature.

Three weeks after daylight returned, public officials released some startling figures: four thousand more people had died during the five-day smog incident than normal. The news hit like a shock. Unlike an earthquake or fire, the smog had come and gone quietly. Yet it left in its wake four thousand dead. Another eight thousand died in the months that followed, deaths also attributed to the smog. British officials, now that they had seen its deadly effects, began dealing with smog and its origins. The British parliament passed a Clean Air Act in 1956, dictating what materials could be burned as fuel in homes and limiting their uses in certain areas, particularly near London. Soon the smog problem disappeared. Some people in the United States may have even noticed.

———

The London Smog caused shockwaves in Europe, and the memory of Donora was still fresh in the minds of Americans. In 1955, Congress passed the Air Pollution Control Act—a predecessor of the Federal Clean Air Act. Although the law was not aimed solely at the auto industry, it eventually caused major headaches for the Big Three.

The auto industry would also discover one more adversary: the state of California. Los Angeles began studying automobile exhaust because of the ever-present smog that hung over the city. Smog had become a common occurrence due to the city's geographic location and population density, and the city suffered its first smog event in 1943. Shortly thereafter, the city established air pollution control boards and districts, with the aim of reducing smog. In 1951, they outlawed the use of backyard incinerators, and the following year a professor at the California Institute of Technology announced that he had discovered the origins of smog—cars.

Most Angelinos considered the news akin to announcing the discovery of the source of rain. Everyone believed smog came from cars. In 1954, Los Angeles came under another smog attack—this one even worse than the one in 1943. Although it didn't directly kill residents the way the London or Donora smog events had, it forced the closing of Los Angeles International Airport, and even Los Angeles Harbor.

Believing it had a lot at stake in the arena of automotive emissions, California became a strong force behind the move to clean up auto exhaust. In 1959, California passed legislation establishing air quality standards throughout the state that required motor vehicles to limit their emissions. In fact, California beat the feds to the punch and passed laws restricting tailpipe emissions from automobiles. It empowered the Highway Patrol to pull over vehicles and test their exhaust for smog ingredients.

The first two chemicals on the watch list were hydrocarbons and carbon monoxide. Although piston engines and turbine engines alike manufactured these by-products, the turbine designers had been focusing on making the turbine engine peppier. To now attack the emissions problem meant the program had to shift gears and refocus. Even worse for Chrysler and the rest of the auto industry, the federal government was about to update the Air Pollution Control Act and replace it with the Clean Air Act. The Clean Air Act specifically attacked tailpipe emissions. If passed, all automobiles sold in America would have to limit their emissions to only a small fraction of what the cars emitted in the 1960s.

Storm clouds were on the horizon—or perhaps they were clouds of smog from the west. Popular media fueled the drive to do something—anything—about pollution and smog. Politicians also spoke out. John Gardner, the secretary of health, education, and welfare, stated publicly at the end of 1966, "The automobile internal-combustion engine and the interests of the American people are on a collision course" with respect to emissions. *Popular Science* ran an article with that statement as its title. It spent four pages describing the poisons put into the air by cars—at least, piston-driven cars. After discussing a variety of methods by which some of the problems might be resolved—different carburetors or smaller engines, for example—the article called for action:

> The time has come to redesign the internal-combustion engine, with control of air pollution a prime consideration, not an afterthought. The automobile industry has a responsibility to look at all potentially practical ways of designing and building a "cleaner" engine. Looking a decade or more ahead, it seems clear that we dare not rely solely on the possibility of achieving truly effective control of pollution from even the best of improved internal-combustion engines. The stakes are too high for that. We—both government and industry—must explore all other propulsion systems that may produce little or no pollution, such as gas turbines . . .

It is unclear why Gardner thought the turbine was the answer. He may have been right, but it was not something many people had focused on previously. In its previous applications, the Chrysler turbine engine had most often been run on diesel or white gasoline. This was during a time when most cars on the road burned leaded gasoline. Much of what the EPA wanted to crack down on arose from the burning of the lead in typical piston-engine cars. The capability of the turbine engine to burn multiple fuels would have allowed the turbine to run entirely on unleaded gasoline, or perhaps even cleaner fuels such as alcohol. It just had the pesky problem with the NOx, which the turbine engineers had not been able to resolve yet.

———

To many within Chrysler, it felt like they'd spent twenty years perfecting the turbine only to have the rules change once they solved the puzzle. No longer was a turbine with the power characteristics of a piston engine enough. Now it had to burn cleaner than the piston engines it had been designed to match in horsepower. Of course, one of the oddities was that the emissions were being measured with the engines running regular pump gas. The turbine could run other, clean fuels, but they were not widely enough available to consumers for Chrysler to test them for EPA standards.

The turbine engineers at Chrysler knew they would have to revamp the engines to get better emissions or the whole program would be lost. When *Road & Track* interviewed Huebner for his thoughts on the sixth-generation turbine, he explained that a majority of recent work on it had been in the area of emissions. Federal standards stipulated that the exhaust of an automobile engine could not contain too much carbon monoxide, hydrocarbons, or oxides of nitrogen. The last—NOx—was the only problem for the turbine, and even that had been controlled for the most part. Standards at the time called for no more than three grams per mile of the stuff, and the turbine's exhaust fell below that threshold. The problem lay in the future; the EPA called for a huge reduction by 1975 to less than half a gram per mile, and the turbine engineers were still crunching numbers and doing experiments to see how to make that figure work.

———

Many people wondered how the car companies would deal with the upcoming Clean Air Act's restrictions on tailpipe emissions. Some thought the answer lay in scrapping the traditional piston engine altogether. In January 1967, *Popular Science* published a roundup of engines that could potentially rival the conventional piston engine. The article described the Wankel, an engine that found limited use with Mazda. The Wankel engine had pistons that rotated around a center line rather than reciprocating up and down. Although it still used gasoline, it eliminated some inefficiencies of reciprocating parts. The article stated, "Inventing a rotary engine is the easy part. The difficulty lies in making it a good rotary engine." Most rotary engines wound up being too complicated and unruly to justify the massive expenditure necessary to switch over from piston engines.

California's stance on air pollution compounded the problem. The activist state had passed its own pollution control laws, which were invariably harsher than the limits imposed by the federal government. The 1966 regulations had gone after hydrocarbons and carbon monoxide. In 1969, updated laws also limited sulfur dioxide and nitrogen dioxide and even further reduced allowable carbon monoxide levels from the previous limits. It seemed that every time the auto manufacturers met a standard set by Sacramento, the standard moved higher, further, more distant. The problem was amplified for the turbine engineers. They had only twenty years of technology and study to work from when attacking the new air standards, while the mechanics working on piston engines had over sixty years at this point working on their powerplants.

The rest of the auto industry struggled to meet those air quality deadlines as well. With piston engines, emissions could be lowered quite simply. The problem was that to lower emissions they had to lower fuel economy as well. Some within the industry noted there would be a 15 to 20 percent "penalty" in fuel consumption to make up for the smog restrictions. With the government mandating the changes, the engineers shrugged their shoulders—the cars would cost a bit more from the engineering, and they'd burn a bit more gas along the way. At thirty cents a gallon, who cared about the extra gas?

———

Around 1970, the public's awareness and concern over pollution reached a crescendo. *National Geographic* published a themed issue in December 1970: "Our Ecological Crisis." Among the usual glossy photos one might expect of the magazine appears a familiar face. On page 762, George Huebner stands in front of the Coronet with the sixth-generation engine. He holds a turbine compressor in his hand, and the caption points out that the turbine engine Chrysler had developed now put out less carbon monoxide and hydrocarbons than a typical piston engine. Still, those pesky NOx emissions were no better than those of the piston engine.

In 1970, the Clean Air Act passed, mandating new "tailpipe" standards for all cars sold in the United States. It contained the radical restrictions the automakers feared. The most ominous portion of the Act was the requirement that the 1975 models from automakers emit no more than 10 percent of the tailpipe emissions of hydrocarbons and carbon monoxide when compared to the fleet average of 1970. This 90 percent reduction in emissions also applied to another exhaust component called "oxides of nitrogen." These had to be reduced 90 percent from the 1971 standards.

The auto companies complained in unison, and loudly. They claimed that the figures were drawn arbitrarily by legislators, and that the standards would be impossible for anyone to meet, regardless of which technology they used. Each of the Big Three automakers went to Washington and asked for time extensions to try and meet the new standards.

Huebner and others from Chrysler spoke to the Environmental Protection Agency panel on several different occasions. They pointed out the dilemma the new law created for Chrysler. Piston engines required new technology to meet the new standards—things like catalytic converters, which required rare and exotic metals to produce and promised to be quite expensive.

The turbine engine Chrysler had spent the last thirty years developing met two of the three requirements of the Clean Air Act; it just couldn't meet the oxides of nitrogen requirements yet. Huebner noted that Chrysler, the smallest of the "Big Three" automakers, had a limited research budget. Chrysler faced the choice: invest in solving the last problem with the turbine, or scrap the turbine program and invest the money in figuring out how to make the old piston engines run cleaner.

The EPA official was unmoved. Robert Sansom accused Chrysler of spending too little money on emission control devices. Many of the engineers from the turbine car program were pulled out of their departments and reassigned to work on reducing tailpipe emissions from piston-engine cars.

Huebner spent much of his time in Washington, trying to convince lawmakers that Chrysler was willing to cooperate, if only given the time necessary. He spoke to a group from the Department of Transportation and outlined the work Chrysler had done in the field of alternative powerplants. It had tried electric and steam as well as turbines in the search for a better engine. He explained that electric and steam cars had had their heyday already, but were replaced by piston technology. That displacement didn't take place overnight. Now the only engine that showed promise—to burn cleaner and use less fuel—was the turbine, but it would take time. Huebner boldly told them, "The prospect of a new powerplant does not frighten us, we thrive on novelty, that's how we grew up. Where power-plants, old or new, are concerned we know what has to be done and we think we know how to do it."

———

In April 1971, Huebner returned to the University of Michigan, his alma mater, and spoke to the graduate school of business administration about the problems facing the auto industry in trying to meet the federal pol-lution guidelines. He criticized the government's meddling, although he addressed the issues gingerly. He noted how the government often spoke of pollutants and how many tons of pollution were being dumped into the air by automobile tailpipes. In reality, he told his audience, the government was comparing apples to oranges. A ton of sulfur dioxide is two hundred times more harmful than a ton of carbon monoxide, and so on. He then noted something that perhaps only auto engineers would even know: a lot of the pollutants from cars came from the crankcase and from evaporation of fuel and oil, neither of which exited the car through the tailpipe. Chrys-ler had made huge strides in limiting these two other sources of emissions, but it would not get credit for them because they did not lessen what came out the tailpipes of their cars.

Chrysler had even gone so far as to create a "Cleaner Air Package" that could be retrofitted onto used cars—those already on the road—and would reduce the tailpipe emissions from cars that had hit the road with engines that were legal at the time but ran dirtier than the new models. Again, it gained Chrysler some goodwill, but it did nothing to ease the burdens of the EPA hurdles for new cars.

If anyone in the audience wondered about Chrysler's turbine program and what, if any, impact that would have on Chrysler's reaction to the EPA standards, Huebner addressed that, too. "As you know, Chrysler has had a major program on the gas turbine, for example, but we must face up to the practical fact that there is no possibility of any of these alternate systems becoming a major factor in the pollution equation by 1975 simply because even if we knew all of the answers and they were completely developed they could not be made in time. The improvements must be accomplished on the internal combustion engine and this is what we are working on."

A parade of auto industry representatives appeared before the EPA to discuss the tailpipe standards and what other engines might be able to do to meet them. Herbert Misch of Ford Motor Company believed the turbine engine had "greater potential" than any other, but the NOx problem appeared to be insurmountable, at least in the near future. A representative from Nissan had hopes for the turbine, but so far could not get its version to meet the standards. Shoji Hattori from Toyota said that his company had investigated many alternatives, but none of them, including the turbine, could meet the time limits. The president of General Motors said the company had tested a variety of engines and believed the turbine showed the most promise. But the NOx problem could not be solved in the short time frame mandated by the EPA. "At the present state-of-the-art, therefore, the most practical avenue for near-term progress in vehicle emissions control is to continue the clean-up of the gasoline internal combustion engine." Similar arguments were made by American Motors and the chief scientist of the U.S. Tank-Automotive Command.

Chrysler would do its best to cobble something together to clean up the piston engine technology it had been using all along. It was unclear if it would do this by using catalytic converters—something they had not had much success with—or by re-plumbing major systems under the hood so that vapors and gases would be routed around and re-burned as necessary. Again, it all looked expensive and complicated, but at least it was technology Chrysler knew it could work with. Huebner ended by pointing out something that only the government could have conceived: one of the EPA's proposed air standards called for tailpipe emissions to be cleaner than the ambient air in the area where a car might be driven. With his tongue planted firmly in his cheek, he noted, "This will be an elegant problem."

Interestingly, Sam Williams, the engineer who had gone solo in the 1950s and started his own company to exploit turbine technology, announced in 1971 that his company had created a turbine engine that met the EPA standards for 1975. He hoped to have one soon that would meet the 1976 standards, but this just illustrated the problems the EPA's rules caused engineers. With the standards changing often, sometimes every year, engineers were shooting at a moving target. Williams also believed his company could mass-produce the engines if need be, but he would have to find a buyer for them: Williams did not make cars, just engines.

Still, Dr. Williams believed it could be done if someone were willing to make the capital investment. He compared the tooling required to create an engine—piston versus turbine—and pointed out that, from scratch, the two technologies were even. While the tolerances within a turbine engine were much more critical, there were fewer of them than in a piston engine. "The number of wear surfaces alone on a piston engine that must be machined to close tolerance is overwhelming from a mass production point of view." Why hadn't anyone exploited this? Williams suggested the reason was money. He told an interviewer he believed the turbine programs had not been funded properly by those in a position to make the switch in technology: the government and the car makers.

———

Soon, however, the program encountered a new obstacle. Rising fuel prices not only threatened the pocketbooks of America, they inspired Washington to meddle further with the auto industry.

By 1973, OPEC had added more oil-producing countries to its roster of members. Qatar, Indonesia, Libya, the United Arab Emirates, Algeria, Nigeria, and Ecuador were previously countries few Americans thought of—or even knew existed—but that was all about to change. On Yom Kippur 1973, the holiest of days in Israel dawned as Egyptian and Syrian armies poured over the Israeli borders. Although intelligence had existed for months warning the Nixon administration that such a conflict loomed, the United States was caught almost entirely unprepared for what happened next. While the battle raged, OPEC leaders met in Vienna to discuss the price of oil in the world market. The members from Arab nations found themselves negotiating with executives from U.S. oil companies while the U.S. government was providing arms and supplies to the Israelis. It didn't matter to OPEC that the Soviets were supplying weapons to Egypt and Syria at the same time, and the U.S. rationale for involvement was typical Cold War "U.S. vs. U.S.S.R." Suddenly OPEC had a rallying point: its members should cut supplies and raise their prices to the Americans, who were apparently taking sides against the Arab nations in the Middle East. For the first time in its history, OPEC had what appeared to be full cooperation of the world's oil producers.

Before the war started, in October 1973, crude oil sold for $2.59 a barrel. What followed, the "energy shortage" or "gas shortage," is well remembered by those who drove cars or owned homes during that fall and winter. By March 18, 1974, the price for benchmark Saudi light crude oil had increased from $2.59 to $11.65 per barrel—a jump of more than 400 percent. The prices for all petroleum-based products shot up as well, including gasoline at the pump. Gas had cost around thirty cents a gallon at the beginning of the shortage, but it cost around $1.20 by the end. Suddenly drivers felt less concerned about pollution and horsepower. Now they wanted a vehicle that achieved good fuel economy.

Congress could not ignore the skyrocketing fuel prices, but there was little politicians could do to lower them. In an attempt to show that they were doing *something* constructive about the issue, Congress passed the Energy Policy and Conservation Act. This law would affect the auto industry in many of the same ways the Clean Air Act had, with policymakers in Washington dictating standards to the auto industry. This time the issue wasn't tailpipe emissions, it was mileage achieved by the cars. Once again, the automakers complained that the legislators were simply dictating arbitrary numbers for the companies to meet to sell cars. In 1973, a couple years before the law was passed, the Corporate Average Fuel Economy— later more commonly referred to as the "CAFE standard"—for American cars was thirteen miles per gallon. The new law required car companies to double their CAFE numbers within ten years.

To people within the industry, this meddling by politicians seemed malevolent. The CAFE standards would have to be met by cars that also met the EPA tailpipe standards! The requirements of the CAFE standards wound up costing the auto companies more than the tailpipe standards did.

———

Chrysler and the other automakers went to Washington and tried to cajole the EPA and Congress into giving short extensions of time to allow the carmakers to build the vehicles the legislators now required. If nothing else, could they have just one more year? Could the 1975 standards be pushed back and implemented in 1976? In an argument that probably cost the company much of its public relations clout, a vice president of Chrysler went to the EPA and tried arguing that auto pollution was not a threat to anyone's health, even in crowded cities. To some, the argument sounded silly and desperate. Even so, the EPA granted the automakers a reprieve: they would have two extra years to meet the new tailpipe standards.

George Huebner also spoke to an EPA panel in 1973. He told them that—as he had predicted—Chrysler had been forced to curtail its turbine program to focus its efforts on trying to meet the tailpipe emission standards. One of the EPA administrators asked Huebner and the others if they could come up with an alternative to the piston engine during the extension they had been given. The National Academy of Science had issued a report, which they had given to the EPA, and the EPA had confirmed the gist of the report with its own study performed by its own staff: given all the variables and options, the best answer to the emission needs of the country lay in alternative—that is, not traditional piston-driven—engines. One report liked a new engine from Honda. Another engine it liked was the Wankel.

Huebner and the other automakers were dumbfounded. He told the panel that the turbine cars could have already been in mass production at that time—1973—if the onerous tailpipe standards hadn't been forced on them. The only issue the turbines had—their one failure—was in NOx emissions. As he had stated repeatedly before, Chrysler could have solved that problem if it had been given a little more time when the Clean Air Act went into effect.

Huebner could have pointed out to the panel that experts from the auto industry had appeared before them a couple years earlier and had unanimously told them that more efficient engines—cleaner and with better gas mileage—could have been made if the government had only given the companies a little longer to meet the guidelines. In 1971, one of the eight witnesses who appeared before the EPA at a public hearing was Ralph T. Millet, president of the Automobile Importers of America. He had summarized the dilemma: "The effort devoted previously to alternate power sources has not been increased and very possibly and in all probability has been diminished because of the work that must be done to meet the immediate requirements of 1975–76."

Ironically, in the face of approaching smog restrictions from Washington and California, some thought the playing field was being leveled between the turbine and the piston engine. A writer for *Road & Track* wrote, "The government may not have to legislate internal combustion engines out of existence. If industry predictions are even half right, the 1976 piston-engine cars may be so bad that people may simply refuse to drive them." The assumption there, of course, was that the smog devices added to piston engines would severely hamper their performance. But this assumption was mistaken. The auto manufacturers had done enough research on the problem to be able to work around many of the restrictions and still be able to squeeze some horsepower out of the choked-down piston engines. It would just take more gasoline.

———

Someone within the Environmental Protection Agency apparently began to wonder if Chrysler might have been right all along. Could the company develop a clean-burning turbine engine if it didn't have to assign its engineers to the emissions problem? Chrysler claimed it needed more money to solve the problem, so the EPA asked the auto companies—including Chrysler—to bid on a project to develop a gas turbine for automotive use. The EPA would provide funding, thus removing the one obstacle Chrysler claimed to have encountered. The goal of this program was to see if one could be built that would be lower in emissions.

Chrysler gave Bud Mann the job of submitting the bid package. March 1972 was the most hectic month of his career as he tried to put all of Chrysler's turbine knowledge into a single document. After meeting with local

EPA officials and fine-tuning the bid package, Mann shipped a final draft off to Washington. Chrysler was clearly favored to get the project in light of the huge strides it had made previously with turbines. The EPA responded to Mann and his proposal with a question: "Did you really mean to label the cover of the proposal as 'The Environmental Pollution Agency'?"

On November 22, 1972, despite the huge typographical error—and the ensuing embarrassment and apologies—the EPA awarded Chrysler a contract that funded enough research for Chrysler to triple the size of its turbine department. The new project meant, however, that now Chrysler had to work within the framework of a government agency, with the accompanying paperwork and regulations. The goal of the project was to develop an automotive gas turbine engine capable of meeting 1978 federal emission standards for hydrocarbons, carbon monoxide, and oxides of nitrogen. Some people wondered if the EPA hadn't finally accepted that the engineers had been telling the truth: lowering emissions on automobiles wasn't simply a matter of picking numbers out of thin air. Chrysler was given $6.4 million to get the job done.

Probably one of the reasons Chrysler won the contract was because it had such a head start on the competition in this field. When they found out they had won the contract, Chrysler's turbine engineers simply pulled their sixth-generation engine off the shelf and began experimenting. They did not need to design a new engine to begin the race for a clean engine. They believed that if they had the money, they could reach the goals they had set for the engine when it was first unveiled in January 1965.

Chrysler used one of the engines as a baseline, and then dropped another engine into a modified 1976 Aspen four-door for real-world testing. This car was a far cry from the Ghia—it was too ugly and unremarkable to contain such an advanced powerplant. The engineers quickly threw all their know-how at the problem, implementing all of the ideas they had thought would work if they had been given the time and money before. They installed a transmission with a "lock-up" torque converter, which eliminated much of the power loss from the transmission at highway speeds. They put all the accessory drives—the pulleys and shafts that ran things such as the air-conditioner and the alternator—on the power turbine. In previous engines, they had been up front, on the gas generator. By moving them to the power turbine, this engine would respond much more quickly to the throttle.

But perhaps the place where the bulk of the money was spent was on the electronic engine controls Chrysler developed under the EPA program. Its engineers had known for years that much of the turbine's inefficiencies in completely burning fuel came from simple mechanical issues. For example, when the Ghia engine was shut off, a small amount of fuel sprayed into the combustor that did not burn. When the car was started while the engine was cold, the regenerator did not warm up for a few seconds. These little issues could all be dealt with by mechanical fixes, and the engineers set about to correct them. Much of what they did involved installing new-fangled electronic controls. These pre-computer devices used transistors, but they still took up a lot of space. The test cars had the electronic control devices placed in the trunk, and the turbines were now fitted with sensors that measured speed, position, temperature, flow, and pressure of the different activities inside the engine. Like the cars of today, the device read the various vital signs and then made immediate corrections to keep the engine's performance in line with what the engineers were looking for.

Reporters who drove the cars with the latest electronically controlled turbine engines loved them. A well-known travel writer from the *New York Times* named Paul J. C. Friedlander drove the sixth-generation turbine car in traffic. He described the car's moves as "fast and flashy." He claimed the turbine was as responsive as any of the "emission-controlled sluggish" cars being built that year. He asked Huebner how much this car had cost to build. The price tag was still outlandish; Huebner told him it had cost three hundred thousand dollars.

———

These measures may have been the last effort to keep the turbine car program alive. As *Popular Science* reported in late 1973, the EPA said about the ongoing experiments being run by Chrysler with the turbine engines: "If the results meet or better the goals, Chrysler can be expected to start tooling up for turbine cars; if not, you can forget about turbine cars."

Another obstacle keeping the turbine from going into full-scale development was Huebner's retirement from Chrysler—he retired in September 1975. Huebner had been at Chrysler over forty years and remained quite active in the engineering community. The Society of Automotive Engineers elected him their international president the same year. Apparently he still looked good. After he gave a talk at an SAE event in 1975, he received a handwritten note from syndicated advice columnist Ann Landers, who had been in the audience. "The most fun of all was you. You're a most attractive guy and just to look at you inspires confidence in anything you're connected with. Cheers!"

As news of Huebner's retirement spread through the automotive community, letters of congratulations poured in. Everyone knew who he was and what he had done, and he would be sorely missed. An assistant comptroller wrote, "I very much regret the fact that retirement may not permit you to prove me wrong for saying they would perfect an electric car with an atomic battery before you ever got the kinks out of your turbine. I really wanted you to win."

Lynn Townsend retired the same year as Huebner. His departure was probably not mourned the same way Huebner's was. While Townsend's earliest years at Chrysler had seen some successes, the accountant-turned-auto-executive did not have the expertise to guide the corporation through the late 1960s and into the '70s. Townsend expanded Chrysler's portfolio with investments in companies abroad and in real estate in America, neither of which helped the company's bottom line. Worse, the quality problems Chrysler had dealt with back in the late 1950s now returned. This time, American auto buyers had more options than before. Imported cars were being sold in America that got better gas mileage than their American counterparts, and many of them were built much better than the cars Chrysler was trying to sell. Townsend didn't seem to understand the problem. When someone asked him if perhaps Chrysler ought to build a small car, he answered: "The subcompacts are just too small. The American people won't climb into them. They have to give up too much in creature comfort. I think even a compact's a little small. I would think that probably the most popular car size you'll see 15 years from now will be like our intermediates today."

Townsend's mismanagement left the corporate ship in rough shape when his successor took the helm. The next few years saw Chrysler's brand decay even further. The new Aspen and Volaré—many of Chrysler's products were launched in pairs, one for Dodge and one for Plymouth—had been met with fanfare. Soon the vehicles were recalled for stalling, failed brakes, and hoods that popped open randomly. These recalls cost Chrysler hundreds of millions of dollars. To make matters worse, the cars suffered from premature rusting on the front fenders. After squabbling for a while with the Federal Trade Commission, Chrysler agreed to replace the fenders for consumers whose cars suffered from the problem. Customers who had done the fix themselves were reimbursed. Another forty-five million dollars was thrown out the window on that problem alone.

————

With Huebner gone, the turbine engineers continued to work with the electronics, trying to make the engines run cleaner. It was all terribly expensive, but for the most part it worked. In 1976, Chrysler engineers presented the results of their work to the SAE convention in Detroit, where Huebner had impressed Ann Landers the year before. They concluded, with graphs and charts to support their work, that the gas turbine engine was a viable alternative to the piston engine when it came to emissions. They had managed to reduce emissions across the board so that the engine would meet EPA standards. Now the obstacle was the cost of building the engines—a major component of which would be the parts requiring investment casting—with the added cost of the expensive electronic control units required to keep the engine behaving and getting the mileage of the vehicles to meet CAFE standards.

Huebner had hinted at this problem earlier, before he retired. In an interview with the *Automotive News* in 1973, he told a reporter:

> If gas turbines are to make a significant contribution to clean atmosphere, they must be used in large numbers, so most studies have been made for high volume production. Here is the heart of the problem. Gas turbine

engines have never been produced in automotive quantities by anyone. To do so will require replacement of current manufacturing techniques never previously used in large volume manufacturing. These techniques do exist and many of them are used for moderate volume production but the labor content is prohibitive. Processes like precision investment casting must be automated before they are practical for automotive purposes.

Again, they knew the problem: to make the turbine work within the current framework laid down by Washington would require substantial amounts of money. Chrysler did not have the kind of money necessary, even if it did have the technical expertise.

Meanwhile, some people wondered what effect the new tailpipe standards actually had on air pollution. Many people noticed that smog in some urban areas seemed just as bad as it had always been. In 1976, the EPA pondered declaring "Federal Smog Days"—telling government employees to stay home and not drive when the air pollution was particularly bad in Washington, D.C. Unsure of how to study the problem or what data to use, an EPA policy analyst polled his own workers, who had gotten the day off unexpectedly when the air-conditioning in their building failed. He distributed a written questionnaire to them, asking what they did on the unexpected day off, if they drove that day, and a few other questions. More than half of the EPA employees did not bother to return the questionnaire. From the 48 percent who responded, the analyst concluded that automobile usage by federal employees might be reduced by 18 to 42 percent on a declared "Smog Day." He was not sure what that would mean in the grand scheme of things; not everyone in D.C. worked for the federal government. He also thought the chances were good for workers to simply go shopping on a "smog day" as if it were just another day off.

———

Chrysler continued working on the turbines, and decided it was time to move to the next-generation turbine. This, the seventh, would be the last. One of the more radical updates appeared in the regenerator section—the metal developed by Dr. Roy was replaced by ceramic. One of the engines was placed into a 1978 Chrysler LeBaron and another was installed into a turbine "concept" car given to the Department of Energy.

In 1979, Chrysler wrote a report summarizing its turbine engine program. The company had met most of its goals. Chrysler had developed a turbine engine that met the 1975 exhaust emission standards; however, it had not gotten one to meet the new standards for 1979. It seemed that government regulators pushed the bar higher each time the engineers figured out how to meet the previous standard.

To get higher horsepower outputs with the lower emissions, the engineers knew what they needed, and it was expensive. They needed to make parts of the turbine sturdier in extremely hot environments. Dr. Roy and his engineers knew which metals could accomplish the task, but they were rare and costly. This was the driving force that led many in the industry to turn to ceramics.

———

In 1979, another group of federal officials began wondering about the viability of the turbine engine. Rather than aiming to meet the ever-changing federal guidelines, what would a state-of-the-art turbine car look like? This time it was NASA asking to see what the car companies could create. One group of companies, led by Chrysler and Williams Research, submitted a single bid on a contract to build an Advanced Gas Turbine car. This group said if they had the money, they could develop a viable turbine-powered car using everything they had learned so far. The new engine would make extensive use of ceramic parts, the car would have a continuously variable transmission, and the entire project—design, testing, and manufacturing— would take 1.3 million man-hours to complete. They were not the only bidders, however. General Motors and Ford each submitted bids as well.

Each of the Big Three approached the bidding process differently. Chrysler's bid suggested studying two different turbine designs. One was the two-spool setup, like the one in the Ghia car. One turbine, or spool, located in the front, generated the gas that was then blasted over the power turbine, the second spool. Chrysler hoped to use the federal money to compare that with the single-spool turbine, where the turbine's shaft is simply run into a transmission or a gearbox. While this second method lost less power, it caused headaches because of the difference in speed between the turbine and the gearbox. The turbine shaft might turn at 50,000 RPM. Running that speed into a gearbox would require a reduction by at least a factor of ten to make the output comparable to a typical automotive engine. Ford and GM each proposed their own methods. Ford suggested a single-spool; GM proposed a two-spool.

Surprisingly, Chrysler did not receive the contract. Later, engineers who worked at Chrysler at the time said that Chrysler probably lost the bid because its bid appeared to be redundant when compared to the other two. They believed that if they had simply picked the system they were most familiar with—the two-spool—and submitted that as their bid, they would have received the contract.

The loss of the contract was the final nail in the coffin for the turbine program at Chrysler. The company decided not to continue investing in the technology, and called the team together to deliver the news. Chrysler gave the engineers who had been working on turbines a week to find another job—within Chrysler or elsewhere.

———

The bidding process for the AGT program provides a detailed snapshot of the state of turbine technology toward the end of Chrysler's experiment with the technology. It also provides insight into the precise obstacles to Chrysler commercially producing the cars. The bid package asked for the specific criteria the bidder would use to make the decision to move forward with production. The Chrysler bid specified six concerns: fuel economy, emissions, reliability, manufacturability, cost, and drivability.

Chrysler was optimistic that these concerns—except for manufacturability and cost—could be addressed adequately. In the bid, engineers noted the "uncertainty with respect to practical means for machining, processing" and other aspects of mass-producing turbines on the scale necessary to market them competitively with traditional automobiles. Chrysler noted in its bid package that if the decision was made to go ahead with production—if all of the obstacles were overcome—they would need to produce around three hundred thousand units in a year. The program called for Chrysler and Williams to develop the engines and perform the testing over the next several years.

Around 1980, the Department of Energy published a summary of the development of the turbine, since the time the government had begun financing the work. The DOE was in charge of the program, after several government agencies had been consolidated. Now, it seemed, someone had finally figured out how useful the turbine could prove to be in a world with rising fuel prices. "At first the emphasis was on reducing air pollution caused by exhaust emissions, but with the uncertainty of gasoline supply and the certainty of ever-increasing petroleum prices, fuel economy became as important a consideration as cleaner air."

One of the charts in the DOE's summary showed the variety of fuel sources the turbines could use. Some came from petroleum, such as gasoline, kerosene, diesel, and heating oil. Synthetic fuels could be made from oil shale and coal, and alcohol could be derived from biomass. Now the government was giving development money to a variety of auto companies and their suppliers. Ford, General Motors, Detroit Diesel, and others were all working on engines or parts for the program.

The program promised to help industry study and develop turbine engines with an eye toward lower emissions and better fuel economy. The results of the project would be made available to auto companies "so that they can decide whether to put this engine into a production program." A chart below that conclusion suggested that turbine-powered cars could be in mass production by 1991.

———

As for the government program, interest in it fizzled during the Reagan administration. In 1981, the EPA funding for the turbine project ran out and Chrysler canceled all work on turbines. Gas prices appeared to have settled down to reasonable levels and the auto manufacturers had all managed to tweak their piston engines to meet the EPA and CAFE standards. The Department of Energy—which had funded the work—had been created by President Jimmy Carter. His successor—Ronald Reagan—was notorious for cutting federal programs. The government giving tax dollars to private companies to do research contradicted everything Reaganomics stood for.

Bud Mann was given the job of "redistributing" the thirty-three engineers who worked in the department with him. In many cases, that meant firing them. Mann later pointed out that although the program never produced a turbine car for the market, many of the lessons they learned applied to the department's successor: Advance Power Plant Engineering. Mann and his co-workers spent their time there improving fuel efficiency and emissions on the piston engine. After eight years spent on the program, the end result was not much more than a huge hangar at NASA filled with experimental turbines and equipment.

——————

Huebner later said that Chrysler had come close to manufacturing a turbine-powered car. How close it came was not revealed until many years after the program was killed. "We had the tooling," Huebner said. Chrysler "had bought the tools and laid out the production line for a much larger run of vehicles. Those would have appeared as 1966 models. So it became a very serious project. Very serious, and it remained serious through 1973 and '74. There were still plans to bring out a limited production run of vehicles. The NOx problem had been put to rest, and the production vehicles would have been successful. The problem was, though, that Chrysler Corp. went sort of broke at that point. The money ran out."

One issue Huebner did not publicly address was the sheer cost of building a plant specifically to manufacture and assemble automotive turbines. While Chrysler may have overcome many of the obstacles making the engine viable—more power, shorter lag on acceleration, better emissions, and so on—it still had not found a way to cheaply mass-produce the vital internal parts of the turbine.

Many of the people familiar with the program, people who worked at Chrysler at the time, said that one number was often pointed to as the amount Chrysler would have had to commit to the turbine car project if it had been brought to fruition: one billion dollars. In the years leading up to the demise of the turbine program, Chrysler's best year had seen a profit of a little over $422 million. The only time the numbers on Chrysler's balance sheet reached into the billions during that time was when the company *lost* a billion dollars, something they did in 1979 and again in 1980. The fact that "the money ran out" was not the problem. Chrysler had never had that kind of money to begin with.

12

Chrysler's Financial Troubles

In the 1970s, Chrysler had financial problems that previously were considered unimaginable by American business standards. In 1960, the company carried about $250 million in debt, but it still sold over a million cars that year. In 1970, its debt had more than tripled while the company only sold about 1.7 million cars. The debt figure flirted with one billion dollars by 1980. Everyone with a stake in Chrysler became nervous—it had become painfully clear that Chrysler could not survive on its own.

Lee Iacocca was brought in to lead the company in November 1978, when Townsend and his allies left. Iacocca surrounded himself with talented managers. He soon realized he needed money to keep the company afloat while he restructured. He went to Washington and sought financial help in the form of loans or loan guarantees. While many people found this an odd place to look for financial help, it was not without precedent. Large entities had received government help in the recent past, including Penn Central Railroad, Lockheed, and even the city of New York. For added emphasis, Iacocca suggested that many of Chrysler's problems resulted directly from the recent federal regulations on tailpipe emissions and CAFE standards.

While the argument seemed dangerous to make, it was not without support. The Department of Transportation investigated claims made by the automakers about the cost of compliance with the various new laws on emissions and mileage. Its report concluded that there was indeed a huge cost to the automakers in meeting the new standards. While GM and Ford could probably survive the experience, Chrysler was pushed to the edge of bankruptcy. A similar study by the National Highway Traffic Safety Administration concluded the same thing, warning that simple fluctuations in the economy might be enough to topple Chrysler, when coupled with other economic hardships brought on by the regulations. With these reports to back him, Iacocca's position looked better.

Others joined him. Douglas Fraser, the head of the United Automobile Workers union, publicly blamed the financial crisis at Chrysler on the federal government and suggested the government should invest one billion dollars in the company. Iacocca instructed Chrysler's advertising firm to take out ads in the *Wall Street Journal* to let the public know it was not seeking a handout, simply a loan.

Legislation was passed guaranteeing loans of $1.5 billion. The federal government would, in essence, cosign these loans, while Chrysler had to find another two billion in savings on its own, or secure loans from others. The bill was signed into law in January 1980.

Even with the federal money, Chrysler's future remained in doubt. The company struggled for a few years before returning to profitability. In 1982, Chrysler sold one of its last profitable divisions, its defense contractor, to General Dynamics in a move to raise cash. Without that $340 million sale, the company would have still shown a $69 million loss that year. It wasn't until 1983 that the company was profitable enough to pay back its loans.

Chrysler still had problems, even if its finances were starting to shape up. After its return to profitability, Chrysler vehicles continued to be plagued by quality problems. Perhaps it was endemic. When the 1979 model year New Yorkers—and its sister cars, the St. Regis and the Newport—were launched, Chrysler's quality control personnel expected there to be a few more than ten claimed defects per car on average. That is, some cars might have more than ten defects—they used the euphemism "conditions"—and others might have fewer than ten. The idea that an auto manufacturer was willing to sell cars with that many defects in the normal course of business shows how far off course Chrysler remained.

13

Other Manufacturers and the Turbine

Some manufacturers other than Chrysler had shown more than a passing interest in the turbine cars. Chrysler even let other auto manufacturers take a closer look at its turbines. Tom Golec took the Turbine Coronet to the General Motors proving grounds and gave the GM people a ride in the car. One of his passengers was John DeLorean, who peppered Golec with questions about stainless steel. How much stainless was used in the turbine's powerplant? Golec answered as best he could, but he didn't understand DeLorean's fascination with stainless steel until DeLorean quit GM a few years later and began building the ill-fated DeLorean sports car—with its stainless steel body.

A few other companies experimented with turbine technology for automobiles. Williams Research, the company founded by turbine pioneer Sam Williams, developed an engine for use in a small car in the early 1970s. The city of New York's Bureau of Motor Vehicle Pollution Control contracted with Williams to purchase a turbine-powered car. It wanted to study the car to see if it might solve the air quality problems New Yorkers were starting to notice in the city. Williams bought a couple AMC Hornets and replaced their stock engines with turbines. Although the cars ran well in theory, they were not nearly as refined as the turbine cars Chrysler had built. Bill Carry, now working for Williams, had the opportunity to drive one of the Hornets out at Michigan International Speedway, which Williams rented for a day of testing. He later said the cars needed much more work to make them suitable for city driving. The engines furnished by Williams were more than adequate; it was the rest of the car that probably needed to be overhauled to adapt to the turbine engine. The project fizzled out shortly after that. Williams continued to make turbines of all shapes and sizes—mainly for the aircraft industry, and even to propel cruise missiles. A few years later, Carry returned to Chrysler.

General Motors began developing turbine engines in earnest in the 1960s, with an emphasis on larger engines for trucks. The thinking behind the move was that long-haul trucks spent so much time on the highway they could take advantage of the turbine's efficiency while running at constant speeds. Also, the diesel engines most commonly used in those types of trucks were more expensive and complicated than the gasoline engines in passenger automobiles. GM, and some others in the industry, thought it might make more sense to use the expensive turbines as an alternative to the expensive diesels.

Ford, likewise, spent much time developing turbine engines for use in large trucks. In some respects, Ford made it a little further than Chrysler did with its turbine program. In August 1972, Ford sold a turbine engine to a customer. The next month, GM supplied turbine engines to Greyhound for use in buses. In December, a fire department in Ohio made the news by taking delivery of a turbine-powered Ford fire truck.

Even though the fanfare of the Ghia program was a fading memory in 1973, others still touted the turbine's promise with respect to cars. An article in the *Sunday Times* (London) entitled "The Battle to Power the Car of Tomorrow" suggested they were just around the corner. A writer traveled from England to Detroit to visit with George Huebner, now recognized as the patron saint of the turbine, and got a ride in a turbine car, which Huebner told the man was his daily driver. Somehow the writer also got the impression that "wives of top Chrysler executives use cars like it to do the shopping."

After touring Detroit in the turbine car, the writer returned to England and spoke with a man whose career path paralleled that of Sam Williams. Noel Penny had run British Leyland's turbine program before branching off and starting a turbine manufacturing firm of his own. "I think use of the motor car is growing so rapidly the problems it will create are almost incapable of being solved. But the gas turbine's multifuel capability is attractive. It will use any known form of hydrocarbon fuel. All you want is heat."

British Leyland worked on the turbine powerplant, mainly for its trucks. Previously, its biggest trucks were powered by diesel engines, which were loud and produced a lot of pollution. One of the directors of Leyland said the company had built a turbine that ran cleaner than a comparable diesel, and quieter—so much so that the turbine made less noise than the sound of the truck's tires on the pavement. He was quoted saying the turbine "is the big prize in the noise pollution race." He was less concerned about the NOx question; he considered smog an "American problem." His optimism appears to have gotten the better of him. Leyland built a few of the trucks—half a dozen or so—but did not take the project further. It may be that Leyland simply encountered the same problems Chrysler had. Whether built for trucks or cars, the turbine still ran with parts that were exorbitantly costly to manufacture.

Over in Italy, Giovanni Savonuzzi reappeared. He had left Chrysler a few years earlier; now he was in Italy, working for Fiat. What was he working on? A turbine-powered car.

———

For the most part, turbine engines never achieved any widespread usage in the auto industry. The engines proved too expensive to mass-produce, especially if they had to meet the mandates of tailpipe emissions and CAFE standards. Occasionally a company came along and created a show car or a prototype driven by a jet engine. And, once in a while, someone even sold some to the public. Others, such as Fiat, experimented with the idea but abandoned it when the biggest players in the industry decided to quit working on turbines.

A company called Marine Turbine Technology has built and sold motorcycles wrapped around a Rolls Royce–Allison engine. MTT advertises that it builds only five of the bikes per year, and their prices start at around $150,000. It may be that not that many people want to drive a motorcycle that does over 220 miles per hour, or it could be that there are only that many buyers per year for a bike that expensive. Among the people who had to have one—according to MTT's Web site—are a sheik from the United Arab Emirates, Jay Leno, and the Bellagio Casino and Resort in Las Vegas, which displayed one for "an air of automotive luxury."

The owner of MTT told Leno he is a little leery of selling the bikes to just anyone. Leno said, "He'll warranty his engines for life, but to do that, he looks for people he calls 'turbine-worthy people who appreciate that this is both a great piece of art as well as engineering.' And he has a sense of humor about it. 'You've got to respect the power,' he insists. 'Pick the wrong customer and you have a ticked-off widow—or a happy widow, depending on the circumstances.'"

14

The Death of the Turbine Program

In all, Chrysler built seventy-seven complete turbine automobiles during the push for the turbine car. It also built quite a few engines and other experimental devices as part of the project. Some placed Chrysler's outlay in the venture at $23.8 million at the time, a rather hefty investment for a car company teetering, at times, on the edge of insolvency. A small portion of the cost was later defrayed by government grants and contracts.

In 1976, George Huebner wrote a short article about the fate of the turbine car. He penned the article, he said, in response to a question he'd been asked by Patricia Vlaha, the wife of the first official user in the user program. "Vlaha's wife asked the big question: 'What's happened to the turbine?'" Huebner summarized the user program and explained how Chrysler was making progress with turbines, even if they hadn't been sold to consumers yet. The problem, as he explained it, was the ever-changing rules from Washington regarding emissions and fuel economy, and the hard economic times recently experienced by Chrysler. He summed up with, "So, Mrs. Vlaha, that's what happened to the turbine car," and finally, after a bit of speculation about the future, "Any further questions, Mrs. Vlaha?"

One problem with the article is that it was fictional, at least as far as any questions coming from Patricia Vlaha. Decades later, she laughed about Huebner's questions and answers, and noted that she had never spoken with him. Nor did she write to him or pose any questions to him about the turbine car. She pointed out that, in the article, Huebner mistakenly wrote that the Vlahas still lived in the same house they lived in when they got the turbine car. The Vlahas had actually moved out of state well before Huebner wrote his article. Looking back on it, it is quite clear that Huebner merely wrote from a promotional perspective. He just included a bit of literary license.

———

Replacing the piston engine has been a holy grail of sorts in the auto industry. While the bulk of the industry is invested in piston engine technology, the visionaries and the consumers who pay at the pump wonder what would happen if the U.S. auto industry weren't married to the petroleum-drinking piston engines. After all, the Turbine Car could burn a variety of fuels other than gasoline. And turbine power isn't the only solution. Throughout the last few decades, a number of other options have been explored as potential replacements for piston engines.

What other ideas were floated at the time? In September 1968, *Popular Science* asked, "Is There a Steam Car in Your Future?" Although some of the earliest automobiles had been powered by steam, they fell by the wayside when gasoline engines became cheaper and easier to use. The steam engine had been revived in Washington earlier that year when a Senate subcommittee on air pollution asked for solutions to the problem of auto exhaust. Its direction came partly from a Department of Commerce report that described the nation's air as a natural resource and the automobile as its enemy. No such focus was given to fuel as a natural resource, and the report went on to state that electric cars and turbine-powered cars were "unsuited" to automobiles. One wonders if the Department of Commerce had heard of Chrysler's fifty-car, one-million-mile, two-year test program proving just the opposite.

With the preconceived idea that turbines were not the answer, the Senate subcommittee began examining steam cars—a technology that had peaked perhaps with the Stanley Steamer, a steam-powered auto that had some success in the years before the Great Depression. The Stanley took twenty-five minutes from starting to build up enough steam to actually drive, making it horribly impractical by today's standards. Other steam cars were developed later that were much more efficient and reliable. But by then the buying public had moved on to the gasoline-powered piston-engine cars.

Could modern technology perhaps bring the steam engine into contention with the piston engine? The Senate subcommittee heard from a variety of inventors who claimed that steam engines had indeed been perfected over time. They now took less time to get up to steam and were more reliable than the powerplants at the turn of the century.

Even so, no one had figured out how to resolve a few lingering problems of the steam engine. Because they used water, they were prone to freezing in northern climes. They were still larger and heavier than their piston-powered, internal combustion counterparts. Their only advantage, it seemed, was their ability to burn a plethora of fuels. Like the turbine, a steam engine could run on any fuel that burned. Chrysler even built a steam car during the early 1970s, but it quickly came to the conclusion that the device was not the answer. As legislators heard testimony about the pros and cons of steam engines, Chrysler executives shook their heads. The Turbine Car had solved all these problems and had all these advantages—six years earlier.

People who worked on the turbine program were certain that major improvements were just around the corner that—if the program hadn't been killed—would have occurred in the natural course of development. For instance, one primary factor in power and efficiency was how much of the hot gases snuck by the turbine fans without hitting the blades. It was a matter of clearance between the parts inside the engine, mere fractions of an inch. As the manufacturing processes were inevitably refined, these clearances and tolerances would have been reduced and the subsequent improvements would have resulted in better fuel economy, more power, and faster throttle response.

Likewise, the materials that Chrysler had used in the turbines were primitive by today's standards. Al Bradshaw pointed out that something as simple as the fluid used in the transmission and lubrication system caused problems in the 1960s but would not have been such an issue in following years. Advances in lubrication science and synthetic materials now would eliminate the "soak back" problem that turbine engineers encountered in the Ghia cars.

———

While turbines made slight inroads with the car companies—more so at Chrysler—they drew more attention from race car builders. Certain races—particularly the longer ones where the cars tended to run at full throttle for most of the time—seemed ideal for turbine power.

One such race was the Indianapolis 500. The annual classic had no requirements that engines be "stock," as in NASCAR, and in the past had allowed for variation and experimentation in body styling and engine design. Andy Granatelli entered a turbine-powered racer, driven by Parnelli Jones, in the 1967 Indy, and Jones led the race with just two laps to go. The transmission behind his turbine engine failed at that point, and his otherwise stellar run became another minor footnote of the turbine story. The turbine car came in sixth place overall, in a race won by A. J. Foyt. Yet some wondered if turbines might have a future at Indy—Jones turned the fastest lap of the race with a circuit of almost 165 MPH, while the average speed of the winner was 151 MPH.

Indianapolis racing officials began wondering about the future of their race and decided to clamp down on nontraditional engines. The restrictions didn't discourage nine more racers from entering turbines in the 1968 Indy, but only three of them made the starting field and none made a dent in the race. The cars Granatelli and the others entered did not run any specially built engines like the ones Chrysler created for its turbine cars. All of the Indy competitors ran jet engines built by Pratt & Whitney—a supplier of engines to the aircraft industry. The engine was an ST6 that produced 950 horsepower.

Another turbine-powered car had made quite an impression at the twenty-four-hour Le Mans race in 1965. Driven by the veteran racer Graham Hill, the car came in tenth place. It beat all other British cars in the field, and it also used less fuel than any other car in the race.

———

The parallel histories of the turbine car and the price of gasoline in the United States are intertwined in such a way that one wonders about what might have been. What if the Yom Kippur War had taken place five years earlier, and automakers had been told to focus on fuel variety, efficiency, and economy rather than emissions in the late 1960s? Or what if the price increases in crude oil had been gradual rather than sharply spiking during the oil embargo? The same forces that made the advantages of the turbine car less relevant were similar to those affecting an aborted push for synthetic fuels in the mid-1960s. Daniel Yergin, whose book *The Prize* described the history of the petroleum industry, wrote, "In the end, it was the ever-growing availability of cheap foreign oil that made synthetic fuels irrelevant and uneconomical. Imported petroleum killed synthetic fuels."

Years later, people wondered about Chrysler's turbine experiment. For all the fuss it caused in the early 1960s, it seemed like ancient history by 1980. For example, a retrospective of the car appeared in *Car Exchange* in March 1980, in which writer John Gunnell had to explain what the Chrysler Ghia Turbine Car had been. Gunnell wrote, "The car of the future isn't coming any more. It's been here and gone. Some 17 years ago, 203 American families got a chance to test-drive the car of tomorrow. In fact, this car, the 1963 Chrysler Turbine, still stands as one of the most dramatic and innovative American automobiles ever built."

———

General Motors tried a program in the late 1990s with an electric car—the EV1—that had some similarities to the Ghia Turbine user program. GM built more than a thousand of the cars and leased them mostly to consumers in California. At the end of the leases, the cars were all returned to GM. The verdict on the electric car was probably a bit harsher than that of the turbine cars. A *Los Angeles Times* article marking the close of the program in 2003 cited a GM source stating the program was a "dismal and costly failure." The California Air Resources Board—a governmental agency pushing for alternative-fueled cars in that state—was likewise cited for the principle that the cars were a "commercial failure."

Perhaps the most striking similarity of the two programs is where the cars ended up: GM also chose to destroy most of its test fleet, setting aside just a few for museums. Photographs appeared on the Internet, said to have been taken in December 2003, showing stacks of crushed EV1s at GM's proving grounds near Mesa, Arizona.

15

The Survivors

Of the various Ghia Turbine Cars, nine still exist, and most can be seen by anyone who wants to make a pilgrimage. Chrysler still has two, five are in various museums around the nation, and two are privately owned. The survivors were all members of the fifty-car fleet, so none of the five prototypes survived. This means that all nine of the cars look identical. Even the ignition keys are cut identically. When Chrysler pulled cars aside to be sent to the museums, engineers removed the fan assemblies from the gas generators in the engines to make the cars nonfunctional. That way the cars appeared for all purposes to be complete, but they were incapable of running. The same parts were removed from the "display" engines that were donated to the museums along with the cars. The average person could not replace a fan assembly without Chrysler's help.

One Ghia Turbine Car is on display in the main entrance of the Walter P. Chrysler Museum in Auburn Hills, Michigan. It sits on a rotating pedestal a dozen or so feet off the ground, so you can actually see the underside as well as the top by looking at it from the various levels of the museum. However, its elevated location will keep you from seeing the car up close.

Chrysler had originally retained three cars, keeping two at the archives and one at its Chelsea Proving Grounds. In 2009, they sold one of their cars to television talk show host Jay Leno.

There are also Ghia Turbine Cars at the Henry Ford Museum in Dearborn, the Museum of Transportation in St. Louis, and the Petersen Automotive Museum in Los Angeles. The Smithsonian has one, as does the Detroit Historical Museum. Sometimes the museums trade exhibits with others that aren't blessed with their own Ghia Turbines, so there are never any guarantees that a Ghia Turbine will be on display at any of these places unless you check in advance.

Each museum that received a car was later given a spare engine in running condition. In the early twenty-first century, the Detroit Historical Museum received criticism for leaving the vast bulk of its automobile collection inside a decaying warehouse where no one could see it. Among the cars hidden away was a turbine car. In 2005, the museum lent its car to the Gilmore Museum, outside Kalamazoo.

The St. Louis car may have been surprised to find itself at the transportation museum there. The Museum of Transportation is primarily a railroad museum, and it had no facilities to properly store or show the car when it arrived. In fact, there were very few automobiles in the museum at the time. "They were long on equipment and short on facilities," Al Bradshaw recalled later. In the 1970s, Bradshaw visited the turbine car with some Chrysler executives and was dismayed to see its condition. Although it was roped off, it had a flat tire and looked like nothing had been done to it since it arrived at the museum. "It was not being taken care of very well."

Around 1980, Bradshaw heard that the museum planned to restore the car and make it run. Bradshaw was skeptical, knowing there was a shortage of parts for it. He gave the museum advice and access to his technical materials, and soon enough they had the car running. The museum's people even fabricated some of the engine parts it needed. Today the St. Louis car is one of the few that run, and the museum even takes the car out to occasional car shows to let people hear what the turbines sounded like.

———

One Ghia Turbine Car found itself in private hands after it was sold off by the Harrah's museum in Nevada. It first traveled back to Michigan, where it joined a car collection owned by Domino's Pizza magnate and car collector Tom Monaghan. A few years later, he sold it at the Hershey rare car sale to Frank Kleptz of Fort Wayne, Indiana. It has been reported that the car changed hands for one hundred thousand dollars. Kleptz displays the car on occasion and even managed to get it running, although he had some difficulty getting it in that condition. When Harrah's owned the car, it didn't have an operating engine. Later, when Harrah's was given a spare engine, the engine was sold separately to an individual and was no longer associated with the Harrah's Ghia.

NBC late-night host Jay Leno—an avid car collector and a friend of Kleptz's—spoke with Kleptz and asked him why the car didn't run. When he heard that all it needed was an engine, Leno called up his friend Bob Lutz—then a Chrysler executive—and asked how they might be able to secure an engine for the car. As a favor to Leno, Chrysler gave one of its spare engines to Kleptz—the supply of the fourth-generation engines was getting dangerously low—and soon the car was running again.

That is, until it suffered an engine failure. It is unclear what happened, although Bill Carry thinks he might have an idea. No one involved in putting the new engine into the "private" Ghia had any experience with the program. The engines were a bit trickier than a typical engine, and of course, they couldn't be idled for long periods of time—a problem for show cars.

Kleptz had the engine repaired and as of 2005 it was running again. It had about forty-five thousand miles on its odometer by that time, and was fully registered and licensed for road use. It is on display as part of the Kleptz Collection in Terre Haute. It has even been featured—running—in various car shows and in magazines. Kleptz said that he is often approached by former users from the user program, or people who rode in the cars during the program, who remember the car fondly.

Kleptz said that he likes the way the car runs so smoothly, but he's always a little worried when he fires it up. His past experience with the engine failure and the resulting difficulty in getting the car repaired make him leery. Otherwise he loves the car.

The turbine car, though it is one of only nine in existence, is not the rarest car in Kleptz's collection—not even close. Among the cars keeping the Ghia company are a 1940 plastic-bodied Pontiac that is the only one of its kind—one other was built, but it was destroyed long ago. Kleptz also has the 1933 Pierce-Arrow from the Chicago World's Fair—again, the only one in existence. His 1916 Scripps-Booth is more common, however. It's one of perhaps twenty survivors.

16

Going for a Drive in Jay Leno's Ghia

In 2009, I was surprised one morning to get a call from Jay Leno. I had spoken with him on the phone once before, so I knew it was him. A few years earlier, I had sent him something I wrote about the turbine car program.

This is one of those priceless stories that is too good to be made up. A bookstore in Michigan ran a newspaper ad for my previous book, *Death's Door*, that touted the book as a great holiday gift. Someone sent the ad to Jay Leno for his segment on funny ads from newspapers. After the bit ran, I got calls from friends all around the country, some of whom had caught my name in the fine print. I thought it was funny, so I gift-wrapped a copy of *Death's Door* and mailed it to Leno—after all, he had the ad but not the book. I had been researching the Chrysler Turbine Car program at this time, so I also sent a copy of what I had written on that along with a note saying that I thought the turbine car story was probably a little more up his alley than a book about the Italian Hall disaster. He called me to thank me and said he would hang onto my number.

When he called back in 2009, he had several questions about turbine cars. His questions were quite specific: Did I have a phone number for Bill

Carry? Did I still have a copy of the technical service manual? His questions sounded to me like more than simple curiosity. I asked him if he had bought one. He coyly sidestepped the question.

I started doing the math. "Well, there are only nine left in the world. I don't think Frank would sell his, so if I had to guess, you just got one of the cars out of the Chrysler Archives."

Leno admitted he had struck a deal to buy one of the three archive cars. He had been in town recently, performing stand-up for free at the Palace of Auburn Hills to benefit out-of-work Michiganians. The Palace is just minutes from Chrysler's World Headquarters. While he was in town, he swung by to talk cars. Of the three cars Chrysler kept, he had just purchased number 42—since all the surviving cars were identical, they are often referred to by the last two digits of the VIN. This car had been kept for a while out at the Chelsea Proving Grounds and was sometimes called the "proving grounds" turbine. Among the people familiar with the program, the proving grounds car was known to run a bit hotter than the others. Leno wanted to speak to Carry about maintenance on the car, and to find out if the hot-running engine was a problem that needed to be looked at. While the car was being transported from Auburn Hills to California, Leno arranged for Carry to come to California and give the car a once-over when it came off the car hauler.

Leno and Carry drove the car around for a while, and Carry told Leno that the temperature issue was nothing major. Something to keep an eye on, perhaps, but it was not worth tearing the engine down to trace. Carry had been working closely with the archives in keeping their cars running and was familiar with car 42 long before Leno bought it.

———

Leno's car resides in his collection, housed at his "Big Dog Garage" along with another hundred or so cars and almost as many motorcycles. Leno's collection is well known because of the fact that he keeps all of his cars in running condition; he actually drives them around southern California from time to time. With each additional car thrown into the rotation, Leno's options increase, so he might not drive his Chrysler Turbine Car on the streets very often. After all, he has a couple of Duesenbergs, a few steam cars, and even a turbine-powered motorcycle vying for his attention.

But he told me if I ever made it to California, he would let me drive the car.

We compared calendars and found a weekend we could both be in Los Angeles. I called my friends at *Mopar Action* magazine to see if they might be interested in a story about the turbine car Leno had just bought. ("Mopar" refers to all things Chrysler-related, so named afer the company's motor parts division.) They agreed to send Cliff Gromer, the editor of the magazine, out to take photographs and write an article about the rest of Leno's Mopars, while I would write an article about just the turbine car.

Gromer and I met in Los Angeles and drove over to Jay Leno's Big Dog Garage. Leno gave us a tour of the facility. It is really much more than a garage: it is actually several large buildings that contain his 105 cars, more than 80 motorcycles, and a complete facility for repairing, rebuilding, and maintaining the menagerie. After getting the quick tour, he fired up the turbine car and we all climbed in.

Soon we were tooling around Burbank and some of the roads into the nearby foothills. I had seen several of the cars before but had never ridden in one. On this warm Saturday in Burbank, traffic was light. The car ran quite smoothly. The turbine sounded like a jet taxiing along a runway; upon acceleration, the whooshing sound—there really is no other word for it—climbed in intensity. The engine's internal parts all spin rather than reciprocate, and the whooshing sound is very distinctive. It's nothing like the outboard motor rumble of a big block from the same era.

We pulled into a large parking lot so Gromer could take some pictures of the car. As we walked back to the car, I mentioned to Leno that he had promised to let me drive it. I wasn't sure if he would let me drive it in traffic, so maybe I could just drive it around this nice big parking lot for a couple laps? "Oh, no." He handed me the keys. "Drive us back to the shop."

I couldn't help but wonder: what if I wrecked his turbine car? I got behind the wheel and put the car in gear. I stepped on the gas and listened to the vacuum cleaner–like sound climb. The car inched forward. It was an amazing experience.

The transmission shifted as if nothing unusual was happening under the hood. We had the windows rolled down—the car does not have air-conditioning—and we talked about the car, and what might have been. As a car guy, Leno puts a lot of thought and study into all the cars he owns. "One of the problems with this car was probably that it seemed so much like any other car out there. People won't switch technologies unless there is a marked improvement going from the old to the new," he explained to us. And the way these cars were pitched to the public back then was that they were just like piston-engine cars. They were just cooler, used fewer parts, and would cost less to maintain. Buried deep within the literature something was mentioned about how they could run on multiple fuels, but no one seemed to notice that marketing angle much since other fuels held no advantage over gasoline, the cheapest fuel on the market back then.

I pulled the car into the driveway to the garage and shut it off. A few minutes later, Leno pulled the car back into the garage and parked it next to his EcoJet, not far from his turbine-powered motorcycle. A hundred feet or so away sat his 1970 Hemi Challenger and 1966 Hemi Coronet. The turbine car program may have died, but at least one of the survivors of the program has finally found a good home—a home where it will be treated like royalty, a home among friends. While we were talking, Leno told me he would be willing to write a foreword for my book, and to feel free to use that in my sales pitch while I searched for a publisher.

———

Mark Olson—whose family drove one of the turbine cars during the user program—runs a Web site devoted to these cars called www.turbinecar .com. I have corresponded with him for some time now, and he called me to let me know that Jay Leno had called him out of the blue one day. After I gave Bill Carry's number to Leno, Carry had told Leno about Olson and about how he had been trying to arrange a ride in one of the surviving turbine cars. Olson had a few near misses; one time he went to St. Louis, but the museum's car broke down before he arrived. On another occasion, he was promised a ride in one of Chrysler's archive cars, but the ride was canceled because of scheduling issues and the financial problems suffered by Chrysler in 2009. Leno had told Olson he would be happy to let him drive the car if he were ever in California.

The timing worked out so that I was in California visiting Leno before Olson. While making small talk that day, I mentioned to Leno about Olson's bad fortune in trying to get another ride in a turbine car. "If you wanted to have some fun, you could mess with him when he shows up," I said to Leno, who smiled.

A few weeks later, Olson called me to tell me about his trip to California. Leno had rolled out the red carpet for Olson and his wife and had even taken them out to dinner. When they got to the garage, though, Jay turned somber for a moment. "There is one problem though. There seems to be a problem with the turbine car." Leno is too nice a guy to take that joke any further, and he immediately told Olson I had put him up to it.

On the phone with me, Olson laughed. "You got me!" Olson did get to drive the car, over forty years after he drove the car his family had been lent by Chrysler.

———

A volunteer named Mike Eberhard watches over the car at the St. Louis Museum of Transportation. To make the car run, the museum had to take the nonoperational engine out and replace it with the crate motor Chrysler had sent them later. Eberhard has kept the car running for years, and he often takes the car out to shows. Leno has spoken with Eberhard to compare notes. After all, how many people in the world can have this conversation: "I was driving my turbine car the other day and I noticed that the temperature gauge read such-and-such. How does that compare with your turbine car?"

———

What about Chrysler's expensive foray into turbines? The company spent millions of dollars but didn't sell a single one to a consumer.

Was it worth it? Bud Mann reflected, "A lot of engineers learned a lot. Whether it was worth all the money and effort spent—only history can say."

Epilogue

George Huebner Jr. spent his entire career at Chrysler, championing the cause of turbine technology and working on other cutting-edge technologies. Among other accomplishments, he was heavily involved in the design and manufacture of the Redstone rocket program, which put America's first satellite into orbit. Even if he couldn't get the auto industry to follow his lead with turbines, he certainly earned its respect. He was active in the Society of Automotive Engineers, and the members elected him their international president in 1975, the same year he retired from Chrysler.

Among his many side projects, Huebner traveled to Sweden and spent eight years helping Volvo develop an automotive turbine. His resume wound up looking like that of an elder statesman, which is appropriate. President Richard M. Nixon appointed him to the Council on Environmental Quality, and he also served on a U.S. Army advisory panel. He spent much of his time devoted to his alma mater, the University of Michigan. He passed away in September 1996.

Sam Williams founded Williams Research after leaving Chrysler and began making turbine engines. Now based in Walled Lake, Michigan, and renamed Williams International, the company makes engines for cruise missiles and the aircraft industry, and dabbles in other turbine power applications. Williams never took the company public, so its finances are not as well known as those of Chrysler or Ford. Still, *Forbes* magazine guessed that Sam's company had annual sales in 1992 in the "$200 million dollar range." Much of that came from the sale of the wildly popular FJ-44 engine Williams developed; it was the least expensive jet engine ever certified by the FAA. In an interview in 2000, Williams said his vision of the future included the turbine engine displacing the piston engine. This time he wasn't thinking of cars; he was thinking of small planes.

Williams received many accolades during his career. He passed away in 2009 at the age of eighty-eight. In a later interview, he reflected on the advances in his industry:

> It's interesting to look back and see what the pioneers did and see how creative they were—and they didn't have the material that we do now. We must always be thinking of the next invention. You never reach a mature technology—it always improves and can be quite dramatic—there's no end to the future of improvement.

Many of the engineers from Chrysler's turbine program followed Sam over to Williams Research, including Dean Musgrave. One program Musgrave worked on while at Williams was a hybrid turbine-electric engine for GM. The GM EV1 electric car had been on the road for a while, with its primary complaint being short battery life. Williams made a small turbine that fit in the trunk of the car to help recharge the batteries from a small gas tank while the car was on the road. Although the program was successful—as far as the turbine from Williams—the EV1 program was eventually scrapped.

After his work on the turbines, Tom Golec worked on a variety of projects for Chrysler, including a three-cylinder engine and a straight-eight cylinder show car. After he left Chrysler, he helped with the durability testing for the engines in the Mini Cooper.

Bill Carry worked for Chrysler for a few more years after the Ghia Turbine project and then went to work at Williams Research. After a few years there, he returned to Chrysler, where he worked until he retired. He is still active in the turbine community, and he even helped the Chrysler Archives replace an engine in one of the three Ghias Chrysler kept for itself when it terminated the program. The engine he placed in the archive Ghia was the last spare engine Chrysler had. He carefully uncrated the unit, still delicately wrapped from when it was first built, and installed it in the Ghia. Thirty-seven years later, it fired right up.

In the late 1960s and early '70s, Carry and his wife were charter members of Michigan International Speedway, where they watched Chrysler cars driven by Bobby Isaac and Charlie Glotzbach do battle with the Fords in NASCAR. In 2009, Carry helped Jay Leno take delivery of a turbine car—much like he did so many times with the users during the Ghia program.

Jerry Gross retired from Chrysler in 2001, after working on the turbine program and then on regular "reciprocating" piston engine technology. Like many who worked on the turbine program, he lives in southeast Michigan and regularly corresponds with others who worked on the program.

Dr. Amedee Roy retired from Chrysler, hoping to spend more time working on his garden. Almost immediately, though, friends from Chrysler asked him to help them with a new project. Chrysler Defense—the Chrysler division sold to General Dynamics—was working on a new army tank design for the U.S. military. The state-of-the-art M1 tank would be powered by a monstrous 1,500-horsepower turbine engine. Roy helped General Dynamics solve some of its metallurgical problems, and the tank went into service. With some variations, the tank is still in service and has distinguished itself in several wars. The tank is particularly adaptive, capable of burning a variety of fuels including diesel, kerosene, gasoline, and jet fuel.

Roy then returned to gardening, not an uncommon pursuit for a retiree. Dr. Roy attacked the hobby much like he had the problems with the turbine engine. Neighbors are astounded by the array of flowers throughout the Roy yard, until they see what he's created behind his house. After years of applied science, Dr. Roy regularly grows tomato plants in his backyard that are over ten feet tall. The huge plants reach the power lines behind his yard, and the tomato yield is likewise amazing. From super alloys to super plants, Dr. Roy has quite a touch.

The Lively Set, the movie starring the Ghia Turbine Car, faded into obscurity, but not before it was nominated for an Academy Award. None of the actors were nominated, of course, but the film was nominated for Best Sound Effects. Perhaps the Academy liked the jet engine sounds while the Ghia raced on screen. It didn't win, however; it was beat out by *Goldfinger*. Other than turbine car fans, few appeared to like the film. One Internet critic called it a "dreadful piece of boring trash."

Jerry Wenk, who test-drove the car, spent his entire career at the proving grounds. He also test-drove the winged Charger Daytonas that would help Bobby Isaac win the 1970 National Championship, and probably drove every car Chrysler ever built or thought of building. As exciting as the job sounds to the car fanatic, many of Wenk's working hours were spent merely clocking miles onto cars to see what might wear out at fifty or a hundred thousand miles.

For an example of something that might liven up his workday, Wenk once had a twelve-point buck jump in front of a car he was driving on the track. The deer took off the roof of the car while Wenk covered his face and blacked out from the impact. When he came to, someone had pulled him from the car and asked him, "Are you alright?" "I don't know; I just got here!" he replied. Wenk made a full recovery but the deer wound up as food for a local prison. It was years before shards of glass stopped coming to the surface of his skin when he showered.

Al Bradshaw stayed with Chrysler until 1981. After the turbine car user program ended, he returned to training mechanics for Chrysler. His last position with Chrysler was in St. Louis, not far from the turbine car in the transportation museum. He remembers the experience as "a lot of fun."

Bill Hamer retired from Chrysler in 1989. He still fondly recalls his time with the turbine cars. Over forty years after the New York World's Fair, he still encounters people who tell him they recall riding in the car there.

When the Chrysler turbine program was officially shut down, Chrysler's regular engineering divisions swooped down on the rest of the turbine people and snatched up the highly skilled machinists, tool makers, metal-lurgists, and other specialists from Huebner's own little "skunk works."

———

From this point forward, Chrysler will have to either retrieve the engines it gave to the museums, scavenge parts from various nonfunctional engines left over, or maybe even consolidate parts from cars in its possession if it needs to keep its cars running. The population of cars and engines will continue to dwindle.

Chrysler abandoned and eventually demolished the six-story Highland Park building in which it developed its turbine technology. The Greenfield facility where the turbine cars were assembled now houses the Detroit Popcorn Company and an insurance agent's office.

Acknowledgments

The following people have all helped immensely with the creation of this book: Tom Golec, Bill Carry, Jerry Wenk, Dr. Amedee Roy, Bud Mann, Lee Pritchard, Virgil Exner Jr., Sara Young, Cynthia Young, Patience Nauta, Stuart Bicknell, Charlie Bicknell, Camilla Bicknell, Jerry Gross, Dean Musgrave, Frank Kleptz, Bruce Jolivette, Al Bradshaw, Bill Hamer, Tom and Mary Spademan, the Detroit Historical Museum, Neal Rubin, the *Detroit News*, Cliff Gromer, *Mopar Action* magazine, Curt Guyette, the *Detroit Metro Times*, Edwin Fox, Ray and Doris Fenstermacher, Mark Patrick, the Detroit Public Library (National Automotive History Collection), Brett Snyder, Heidi Lichtenstein, David Lucsko, Daryl and Simone McDaniel-Samano, Dave Reinard, Rich Bolzenius, Ed and Sue George, Mark Olson, Dick and Patricia Vlaha, Rick Vlaha (for purposes of the narrative, I refer to the father—Richard Vlaha—as Richard in the story. His friends call him Dick and the family refers to their son as Rick. All three helped me immensely with the story). Also, Bonnie Lippman and Shirley Herman, the users from Baltimore. And, of course, Steven Harris, my agent, and Yuval Taylor and Jerome Pohlen, my editors.

My brother Rick is an engineer at Williams International. He helped immensely in explaining concepts of the turbine to me in plain English and helping me understand the more technical aspects of this story so I could pass them along in an understandable and readable fashion. He also accompanied me to the Detroit Historical Museum to view their turbine car, and he pointed out many details of the car that I might have missed otherwise, especially during such a short visit. Still, any mistakes I make when describing turbine technology are entirely my fault.

My brother Ken is an automotive engineer who not only explained many of the automotive parts of the story to me but also managed to find me SAE papers on the turbine car project. Both Ken and Rick were invaluable in discussing the turbine car and helping me sound like I know what I'm talking about. In fact, a year or two before I decided to look into the Ghia car, Rick and Ken built a working turbine engine out of an automotive turbo charger. Repiping it and adding an igniter and fueling system, they had their "turbo charger" turbine spinning away in Rick's garage. At the time it seemed like a logical extension of their various garage projects; the previous year they'd built a working pulse-jet engine that they fired up at family gatherings. If you live near southeastern Michigan, you may have heard it run but not known what it was at the time.

William ("Bill") Carry was kind enough to both sit for an interview with me and lend me materials on the Ghia Turbine Car. Among his collection were two documents he created: one was the training manual for Chrysler turbine mechanics and the other was a report that summarized the turbine service program he oversaw. The latter document was unique, and he was generous enough to entrust it to me so that I could study it and make copies of it for later study. He also lent me many of the documents that were developed along the way—the Driver's Guide was one such example—and he also lent me photographs he had from the era—many that were one of a kind.

Tom Golec had a collection of documents and materials from the program that was invaluable. Amazingly, he had the wheels from the gas generator turbine of the five-thousand-hour test cell turbine. Forty years later, they looked virtually pristine.

Dr. Amedee Roy—the metallurgist—is a friend of my family's, it turns out. My brothers attended school with his children, and we always knew that "Mr. Roy" worked for Chrysler. It wasn't until many years later that I learned that *Dr.* Roy was one of the main protagonists of the Chrysler turbine story. When we spoke in 2005, he lent me a model he'd had made back in the 1960s of the fourth-generation turbine. The technicians in his lab had carefully cut one in half lengthwise and mounted the pieces on a plaque, creating a perfect scale, three-dimensional model of the major parts of the engine. Along with the exploded model, he lent me an example of the small Ghia car model that was given away as a promotion in the early 1960s. The one he lent me was still in the box, and I was probably the first to remove it when I photographed it in 2005.

I got to know Jerry Wenk, the test driver from Chelsea, while working on my previous book, on Bobby Isaac and the Charger Daytona. Wenk had test-driven that car and provided much valuable information about it. When I began looking into the turbine car program, someone mentioned to me that they had also been tested at Chelsea. A quick phone call confirmed that Wenk had indeed driven that car as well. He was kind enough to spend a few more hours with me, telling me stories from the proving grounds, and of the turbine car.

Bud Mann also spoke with me on several occasions, and even wrote a five-page summary of highlights of his time with the program. Mann's tenure with the turbine program—he was there for almost the entire program—allowed him to answer many of the questions I had regarding the precise timing of events.

Dick and Patricia Vlaha still enjoy their memories of the turbine car and their special role in the program as the first drivers. Thirty years later, when the History Channel ran a documentary on the turbine car, footage of the Vlahas driving the car appeared on national television. Richard laughed when he recounted how he got phone calls from people, telling him they saw him on television—again.

Bonnie Lippman—the daughter of the Hermans—married a man who'd attended elementary school with her years earlier. They didn't know each other then, but when they met later, he told her that he remembered her as the girl whose family had the turbine car. A few years after they were married, he told her he saw a turbine car at the car show in Hershey, Pennsylvania. No doubt he saw the car the weekend Monaghan sold it to Kleptz.

The Detroit Historical Museum has a Ghia Turbine Car as noted; the car is on display in Kalamazoo. The museum has little funding to show its extensive auto display. The Detroit Public Library has the National Automotive History Collection where some of the turbine car papers are kept, but the library isn't well funded either. People who don't live in Detroit must pay a ten-dollar fee to examine the collection, or buy a yearly pass for one hundred dollars. The people who staff these establishments are great to work with, helpful and cooperative. Unfortunately, their places of employment aren't appreciated by those with enough power to do anything about the problems they face. It is an interesting dilemma. As the auto industry goes, so goes Detroit. The city has suffered financially in the past few decades, as the Big Three struggle to stay competitive in a global economy. Perhaps everything would be different if the car companies had moved to turbines in the 1960s.

And of course, I have to thank Jay Leno—not only for contributing to this book but also for letting me drive his turbine car.

Notes

I. THE PROMISE OF THE JET AGE

the cartoon "stone age family" was the Flintstones . . . The Flintstones debuted in 1960, *The Jetsons* in 1962.

Kennedy delivered his "Moon" speech September 12, 1962, at Rice University.

Chrysler began researching turbines . . . This information is available from numerous sources. Some of the detailed information is from correspondence from Bud Mann in 2005.

a brilliant engineer named George Huebner Jr. . . . Huebner's biographical information is available in many places, including press releases issued by Chrysler and also from his personal files. Chrysler Corporation Press Information Service, "George J. Huebner, Jr. Executive Engineer—Research Engineering Division—Chrysler Corporation," press release, n.d.; "Candidate: George J. Huebner, Jr.," nomination form, National Academy of Engineering, n.d., ca. 1973, Huebner Papers, courtesy of the Bentley Historical Library, Ann Arbor, MI; Chrysler Corporation Press Information Service, "Biographical Data on George J. Huebner, Jr.," press release, n.d.; Earl F. Wegmann, "Chrysler's Diplomat in Coveralls," *Michigan Alumnus*, February 15, 1958.

Details about the A-86 aircraft turbine project come from Bud Mann.

The 1950 *Motor Trend* article: Griffith Borgeson, "Will Gas Turbines Propel the Car of Tomorrow?" *Motor Trend*, May 1950.

Biographical information on Williams comes from a variety of sources. "Freedom of the Skies," *Atlantic Monthly*, June 2001; Erick Schonfeld, "The Little (Jet) Engine That Could," *Fortune*, July 24, 2000; "United States: Inventor of the Small Gas Turbine Engine Passes Away," Al Bawaba (Middle East) Ltd., 2009.

By 1946, Williams was submitting patent applications . . . George J. Huebner Jr., Samuel B. Williams, and David Borden, "Arrangement of Component Elements of a Gas Turbine Powerplant" (U.S. Patent 2,795,928, filed October 29, 1953, and issued June 18, 1957).

The *Motor Trend* article referenced is Griffith Borgeson, "Will Gas Turbines Propel the Car of Tomorrow?" *Motor Trend*, May 1950.

Bud Mann's information was supplied to the author by Mann.

Before 1950, the United States was self-sufficient . . . One of the best narratives of the oil crisis is Daniel Yergin, *The Prize: The Epic Quest for Oil, Money, and Power* (New York: Simon & Schuster, 1992). See also Energy Information Administration, *Annual Energy Review 2003* (Washington, DC: U.S. Department of Energy, 2004), xix.

Meanwhile, the turbine team at Chrysler forged ahead . . . Again, this information comes from Mann.

Descriptions of Huebner's time with the Redstone program can be found in several places. Chrysler Corporation Press Information Service, "Biographical Data on George J. Huebner, Jr.," press release, n.d.; George J. Huebner Jr., "Rehearsal for Space," *Boys' Life*, September 1959.

Meanwhile, the turbine team finally developed an engine . . . Chrysler Corporation Press Information Service, "Compact Chrysler Gas Turbine in Plymouth Car," press release, March 25, 1954.

2. CHRYSLER'S FIRST "JET" CAR

decided it was time to unveil its first . . . Chrysler Corporation Press Information Service, "Compact Chrysler Gas Turbine in Plymouth Car," press release, March 25, 1954.

"Progress in Science." The text was used almost verbatim from the press release, punctuated by a few photos of the turbine car and its engine.

Sam Williams left Chrysler . . . and information about Williams Research and Williams International comes from Allan S. Brown, "Very Light and Fast," *Mechanical Engineering–CIME*, January 2007; "Fewest Parts = Lightest Turbofan," *Design*

News, September 4, 2000; Jerry Flint, "Corporate Jets for the Masses," *Forbes,* July 6, 1992; "Freedom of the Skies," *Atlantic Monthly,* June 2001; Mark Allen Gottschalk and Ann Allen Gottschalk, "Engineers Drive a Light Aircraft Revival," *Design News,* September 7, 1998; "Jet Engine Pioneer Inducted to Akron, Ohio, Inventor's Hall of Fame," *Akron Beacon Journal,* May 7, 2003; Dan Mayfield, "From Cruise Missiles to Commuter Jet, Eclipse Partner Enjoys the Challenges," *Albuquerque Tribune,* July 10, 2000; Dan Mayfield, "Getting Off the Ground," *Albuquerque Tribune,* July 10, 2000; "Sam Williams," *Automotive News,* July 6, 2009; Erick Schonfeld, "The Little (Jet) Engine That Could," *Fortune,* July 24, 2000; Brad Stone, "A Taxicab at 30,000 Feet: Aviation Mavericks Are Trying to Mint a New Class of Airplane—and Air Travel," *Newsweek,* October 6, 2003; Clint Swett, "If Idea Flies, Jet Travel Could Enter New Era," *Sacramento Bee,* July 14, 2002; "United States: Inventor of the Small Gas Turbine Engine Passes Away," Al Bawaba (Middle East) Ltd., 2009.

The proving grounds were huge . . . comes from Chrysler Corporation Press Information Service, "Chrysler Gas Turbine Combines Economy and Performance," press release, March 25, 1954, courtesy of Tom Golec.

"We kept it running . . ." is a quote of George Stecher's in *Automobiles: The Chrysler Turbine,* A&E Television Networks (1996).

The *Detroit News* article referenced is "New Engines in Action," *Detroit News,* March 26, 1954.

The starting difficulty . . . comes from *Automobiles: The Chrysler Turbine,* A&E Television Networks (1996), as does the *sense of urgency* and the details of the GM and Ford programs at the time.

All of the information about Bud Mann comes from Mann's correspondence with the author.

The story of Ford putting a jet engine into a Thunderbird comes from Michael Lamm, "Driving Chrysler's Bronze Blowtorch!" *Special Interest Autos,* January/February 1992.

On Friday, March 23, 1956 . . . newspaper coverage was extensive. One example is Leo Donovan, "Turbine Car Heads West," *Detroit Free Press,* March 27, 1956.

The *"final handshake"* comes from Earl F. Wegmann, "Chrysler's Diplomat in Coveralls," *Michigan Alumnus,* February 15, 1958.

Details of the trip come from Tom Golec—he was a member of the team driving the turbine car—and his logbook: Chrysler Corporation, "Chrysler Research Turbine Cross Country Log," plastic comb-bound, pocket-sized booklet, March 26, 1956, courtesy of Tom Golec.

Additional information about the cross-country drive comes from Huebner's own article: George J. Huebner, "A First in Automotive History: We Drove a Turbine Car Coast-to-Coast," *Popular Mechanics*, June 1956.

In fact, the driving crews even reported to the media . . . Leo Donovan, "Turbine Car Heads West," *Detroit Free Press*, March 27, 1956.

Stecher's comments come from *Automobiles: The Chrysler Turbine*, A&E Television Networks (1996).

turbine laboratory details, and comments about GM and Ford, are from Ralph R. Watts, "Chrysler Stresses Turbine Research," *Detroit News*, February 13, 1957.

Huebner told the press . . . in Leo Donovan, "Turbine Test Stepped Up," *Detroit Free Press*, February 13, 1957.

The Greenfield facility would house the assembly area . . . Details are from a variety of interviews by the author, including one with Bud Mann.

People at the U.S. Patent Office . . . Details come from the patents themselves: George J. Huebner Jr., Samuel B. Williams, and David Borden, "Arrangement of Component Elements of a Gas Turbine Powerplant" (U.S. Patent 2,795,928, filed October 29, 1953, and issued June 18, 1957); and Giovanni F. Savonuzzi, "Gas Turbine Engine Housing" (U.S. Patent 3,167,914, filed July 3, 1961, and issued February 2, 1965).

Savonuzzi's driving style was described in an interview with Bud Mann by the author.

Dr. Amedee Roy's personality was described by many members of the turbine team, interviewed by the author.

The next updated turbine engine went into a 1959 Plymouth. . . . Information is from *Chrysler Corporation Turbine Car*, film by Chrysler Corporation Audio-Visual Services (n.d.), courtesy of Bill Carry.

The *Detroit News* article: Ralph R. Watts, "19 Miles a Gallon Reported by Chrysler in Gas Turbine," *Detroit News*, January 11, 1959.

After this successful run . . . Ralph R. Watts, "19 Miles a Gallon Reported by Chrysler in Gas Turbine," *Detroit News*, January 11, 1959.

In May 1960, Huebner spoke . . . Details come from Fred Olmstead, "Third Chrysler Turbine Due for Auto Test Soon," *Detroit Free Press*, May 11, 1960.

In September 1960, on the other side of the world . . . "About Us," Organization of the Petroleum Exporting Countries, www.opec.org/opec_web/en/17.htm; and Daniel Yergin, *The Prize: The Epic Quest for Oil, Money, and Power* (New York: Simon & Schuster, 1992).

The story of Chrysler's struggles from the 1950s through the 1970s is told very well in Charles K. Hyde, *Riding the Roller Coaster: A History of the Chrysler Corporation* (Detroit: Wayne State University Press, 2003).

Lynn Townsend's biographical information comes from "Lynn Townsend & Chrysler's Comeback," *Time*, December 28, 1962.

On February 28, 1961, Chrysler unveiled its next . . . and information about the placement of the engine in the other vehicles comes from Chrysler Corporation, "History of Chrysler Corporation Gas Turbine Vehicles," report by Technical Information Engineering Office, January 1979. Information about the Studebaker and show cars is from *Automobiles: The Chrysler Turbine*, A&E Television Networks (1996).

After a few refinements . . . is from *Automobiles: The Chrysler Turbine*, A&E Television Networks (1996); and *Taming the Tornado*, film by Chrysler Corporation Audio-Visual Services (n.d.), courtesy of Bill Carry.

The press also widely reported . . . "Jet Auto Age Fired by Engine," *Pontiac Press*, December 27, 1961, courtesy of the Detroit Public Library, Automotive History Collection; Ralph R. Watts, "Turbine Test Ends Rumors," *Detroit News*, December 27, 1961.

"Huebner left little doubt . . ." and *"Our announcement will be greeted . . ."* "Turbine Cars Due in 1963," *Detroit Free Press*, December 28, 1961.

Chrysler's brochure: Chrysler Corporation, "America's First Gas Turbine Cars," four-page pamphlet showing images and details of the Turbo Dart and Turbo Fury, n.d., courtesy of the Detroit Public Library, Automotive History Collection.

Huebner's *3,100-mile, four-day trip* is described in *Automobiles: The Chrysler Turbine*, A&E Television Networks (1996); George J. Huebner Jr., "The Chrysler Regenerative Turbine-Powered Passenger Car," paper presented at the Society of Automotive Engineers, Automotive Engineering Congress and Exposition, Detroit, MI, January 13–17, 1964, document 777A; and in many Chrysler documents, including Chrysler Corporation, "Gas Turbine Vehicles," report by Engineering Division Technical Information Services, July 16, 1962.

Taming the Tornado, film by Chrysler Corporation Audio-Visual Services (n.d.), courtesy of Bill Carry.

Chrysler's public relations representative counted . . . George J. Huebner Jr., "Speech Given by G. J. Huebner, Jr., Dealer Enterprise," speech to unknown audience, Sheraton-Cadillac Hotel, Detroit, MI, December 9, 1963, Huebner Papers, courtesy of the Bentley Historical Library, Ann Arbor, MI.

Riding the Whirlwind, film by Chrysler Corporation Audio-Visual Services (n.d.), courtesy of Bill Carry.

That turbine engines sounded different . . . George J. Huebner Jr., "50-Car Turbine Program—Technical Results," remarks to the press, Detroit, April 12, 1966.

Information about the air cleaner assembly placement is from Chrysler Corporation Press Information Service, "NEWEST MODEL of Chrysler Corporation's gas turbine engine . . . ," press release accompanying press photo of the 1962 Plymouth Turbo Fury, n.d., courtesy of Tom Golec.

Information about the "silencer assembly" is from William J. Carry, "The Chrysler Corporation 50 Car Turbine Program: A Summary of the Service Program 1963–1966," unpublished personal summary, 1966, courtesy of Bill Carry.

In February 1962 the current lineup . . . Reported in Fred Olmstead, "Public Sees Turbine Cars," *Detroit Free Press*, February 2, 1962; and Ralph R. Watts, "Turbine Car Stirs Public," *Detroit News*, February 2, 1962.

Information about Jerry Gross, and his quotations, are from his interviews and correspondence with the author.

People in the automotive industry . . . is from "Candidate: George J. Huebner, Jr.," nomination form, National Academy of Engineering, n.d., ca. 1973, Huebner Papers, courtesy of the Bentley Historical Library, Ann Arbor, MI.

Chrysler sent both the Turbo Dart . . . Information comes from George J. Huebner Jr., "The Chrysler Regenerative Turbine-Powered Passenger Car," paper presented at the Society of Automotive Engineers, Automotive Engineering Congress and Exposition, Detroit, MI, January 13–17, 1964, document 777A.

Alden L. Olson and Mark E. Olson's experiences are described in their interviews and correspondence with the author.

"elicit and examine consumer reactions . . ." George J. Huebner Jr., "The Chrysler Regenerative Turbine-Powered Passenger Car," paper presented at the Society of Automotive Engineers, Automotive Engineering Congress and Exposition, Detroit, MI, January 13–17, 1964, document 777A.

Details of Chrysler at the Chicago Auto Show are from Chrysler Corporation, "History of Chrysler Corporation Gas Turbine Vehicles," report by Technical Information Engineering Office, January 1979.

3. THE FOURTH-GENERATION ENGINE:
CHRYSLER'S VIABLE AUTOMOTIVE POWERPLANT

The fourth-generation turbine was first placed . . . is from *Automobiles: The Chrysler Turbine*, A&E Television Networks (1996).

Chrysler issued a press release . . . Chrysler Corporation Press Information Service, "NEWEST MODEL of Chrysler Corporation's gas turbine engine . . . ," press release accompanying press photo of the 1962 Plymouth Turbo Fury, n.d., courtesy of Tom Golec.

Details of the engine's performance come from Chrysler Corporation, "Training (Chrysler Gas Turbine Training Guide)," unpublished training document for technicians who would work on cars in the Ghia program, n.d., courtesy of Bill Carry.

Stecher's comments come from *Automobiles: The Chrysler Turbine*, A&E Television Networks (1996).

Testing and endurance figures are from Gross's and Golec's interviews and correspondence with the author.

Information regarding investment casting comes from Mark McNeely, "Cast Components Increasing in Industrial Gas Turbines," *Diesel & Gas Turbine Worldwide*, June 2004. That parts of the engine required investment casting comes from Bill Carry's and Lee Pritchard's interviews and correspondence with the author.

Tales of endurance testing are from Gross's and Golec's interviews and correspondence with the author.

The story of Gross and Roy and the flaking material and its aftermath comes from both Gross and Roy, interviews and correspondence with the author.

The press release that mentioned fuels is Chrysler Corporation Press Information Service, "NEWEST MODEL of Chrysler Corporation's gas turbine engine . . . ," press release accompanying press photo of the 1962 Plymouth Turbo Fury, n.d., courtesy of Tom Golec.

The blade assembly can be seen in many places, including Chrysler Corporation, "Training (Chrysler Gas Turbine Training Guide)," unpublished training document for technicians who would work on cars in the Ghia program, n.d., courtesy of Bill Carry.

Descriptions of the fourth-generation turbine can be found in Chrysler Corporation, "History of Chrysler Corporation Gas Turbine Vehicles," report by Technical Information Engineering Office, January 1979; Chrysler Corporation, "Progress in Science," trifold document describing the early history of the turbine program, n.d.; Chrysler Corporation Press Information Service, "Strive to Perfect Turbine Engine," press release, n.d., courtesy of the Detroit Public Library, Automotive History Collection.

The burner "relight" problem was described in William J. Carry, "The Chrysler Corporation 50 Car Turbine Program: A Summary of the Service Program 1963–1966," unpublished personal summary, 1966, courtesy of Bill Carry.

4. THE GHIA TURBINE CAR

Bud Mann's quote comes from his interview with the author.

Chrysler decided to launch a major program . . . This information comes from many places, including *Automobiles: The Chrysler Turbine*, A&E Television Networks (1996).

Chrysler wanted a car whose appearance . . . William J. Carry, "The Chrysler Corporation 50 Car Turbine Program: A Summary of the Service Program 1963–1966," unpublished personal summary, 1966, courtesy of Bill Carry.

The methods of manufacture at Ghia are described in an interview with Virgil Exner Jr. by the author.

Details of the sinking of the *Andrea Doria* can be found many places, most easily at a Web site devoted to the event: www.andreadoria.org.

"You couldn't take the door off one . . .*"* Quotation is from *Automobiles: The Chrysler Turbine*, A&E Television Networks (1996).

The completed bodies were shipped . . . Michael Lamm, "Driving Chrysler's Bronze Blowtorch!" *Special Interest Autos*, January/February 1992.

The remainder of the information on the manufacture of the cars in the United States comes from William J. Carry, "The Chrysler Corporation 50 Car Turbine Program: A Summary of the Service Program 1963–1966," unpublished personal summary, 1966, courtesy of Bill Carry; and from interviews with Carry by the author.

Information about the prior use of the Greenfield building to make DeSoto taxis is from Leo Donovan, "Turbine Test Stepped Up," *Detroit Free Press*, February 13, 1957; and from an interview with Tom Golec by the author. The method of assembly at the plant is described in Michael Lamm, "Driving Chrysler's Bronze Blowtorch!" *Special Interest Autos*, January/February 1992, as is the date of the first car being completed in 1962.

For aficionados who want to distinguish . . . is from an interview with Bill Carry by the author.

Bud Mann's quotes and information are from interviews and correspondence with the author.

The fifty cars assembled at the Greenfield . . . Information about the cars comes largely from Chrysler Corporation, "The Chrysler Corporation Turbine Car," report by Engineering Staff—Technical Information Services, April 5, 1963.

At first the cars didn't perform . . . and *Chalking up slow throttle response* . . . come from Tom Golec in an interview with the author.

Jerry Wenk's experiences were related in an interview with the author.

Huebner's estimate of the price per car is found in Michael Lamm, "Driving Chrysler's Bronze Blowtorch!" *Special Interest Autos*, January/February 1992.

"Those 55 coupes were . . ." Michael Lamm, "Driving Chrysler's Bronze Blowtorch!" *Special Interest Autos*, January/February 1992. Virgil Exner Jr.'s statements are from his interview with the author.

Strangely, Chrysler never officially gave . . . Huebner repeatedly refers to the car as simply the "Chrysler Corporation Turbine Car" and never calls it a Ghia. See George J. Huebner Jr., "The Chrysler Regenerative Turbine-Powered Passenger Car," paper presented at the Society of Automotive Engineers, Automotive Engineering Congress and Exposition, Detroit, MI, January 13–17, 1964, document 777A.

others called it the Ghia or Ghia Turbine . . . is from numerous interviews with participants in the program at Chrysler.

The uncrating can be seen in *Automobiles: The Chrysler Turbine*, A&E Television Networks (1996).

All of the Ghias except one . . . comes from numerous sources, including interviews with Bill Carry by the author.

The cars came equipped with all the basic comforts . . . is information from the author's observations and is readily available in countless places. Descriptions of the interior of the car come from the author's own observations, having looked at, sat in, or driven three of the surviving cars. Many of these aspects can be seen in photographs of the cars as well.

Details of the Detroit Historical Museum car are from the author's own observations.

The key was described by Bill Carry in an interview with the author.

The power brakes on the Ghia . . . George J. Huebner Jr., "The Chrysler Regenerative Turbine-Powered Passenger Car," paper presented at the Society of Automotive Engineers, Automotive Engineering Congress and Exposition, Detroit, MI, January 13–17, 1964, document 777A.

Descriptions of the setup of the car and its transmission and drive train can be found in many places. The author also used interviews with Carry, and others.

The new film was *New Power for Progress*, film by Chrysler Corporation Audio-Visual Services (n.d.), courtesy of Bill Carry.

5. THE USER PROGRAM: THE ULTIMATE
PUBLIC RELATIONS EVENT

Many of the details and the rationale behind the user program were described in David F. Miller, "Remarks by Dr. David F. Miller, Manager of Marketing and Consumer Research," press release, April 12, 1966, courtesy of the Detroit Historical Museum.

When the cars were ready . . . Chrysler Corporation, "History of Chrysler Corporation Gas Turbine Vehicles," report by Technical Information Engineering Office, January 1979.

The second day of the event . . . Jack Crellin, "Chrysler Turbine Car Stalls, Causes Manhattan Traffic Jam," *Detroit News*, May 15, 1963.

"Auto engineers who dream . . ." "The Big Test," *Time*, May 10, 1963.

The immediate response from the public . . .Michael Lamm, "Driving Chrysler's Bronze Blowtorch!" *Special Interest Autos*, January/February 1992. The details of who responded are from Chrysler Corporation, "History of Chrysler Corporation Gas Turbine Vehicles," report by Engineering Office Technical Information, January 1964, revised August 1966.

Look magazine's feature: Al Rothenberg, "America's First Turbine Car," *Look*, June 4, 1963.

The brochures: Chrysler Corporation, "Turbine Car Information," four-page pamphlet showing images and details of the Ghia Turbine car, n.d., courtesy of the Detroit Public Library, Automotive History Collection.

The *Mechanix Illustrated* article: Tom McCahill, "Chrysler's Gas Turbine Car," *Mechanix Illustrated*, September 1963.

The information about Bill Carry comes from interviews with Carry by the author.

Al Bradshaw's information comes from his interview with the author.

Everyone who wrote to Chrysler . . . The letter each person received can be seen as John F. Bunnell, "A Letter from Chrysler Corporation," October 1963, reprinted at www.vlaha.com/turbine/.

Vlaha's story is from Chrysler Corporation, "History of Chrysler Corporation Gas Turbine Vehicles," report by Engineering Office Technical Information, January 1964, revised August 1966. Townsend's quotes and the rest of the paragraph are from *New Power for Progress*, film by Chrysler Corporation Audio-Visual Services (n.d.), courtesy of Bill Carry.

Detroit News article: Ralph R. Watts, "Public Test of Turbine Car Starts," *Detroit News*, October 29, 1963.

What the press did not know . . . is from an interview with Al Bradshaw by the author, as is *The press treatment the Vlahas received* and Jolivette's story.

Details of the delivery come from Carry, as did a copy of the checklist he used to make sure the users were acquainted with the cars. That checklist can be found in Chrysler Corporation, "Training (Chrysler Gas Turbine Training Guide)," unpublished training document for technicians who would work on cars in the Ghia program, n.d., courtesy of Bill Carry; and Chrysler Corporation, "Driver's Guide," glove box document included with Ghia car to instruct users on the vehicle's operations and controls, n.d. There are many places where the latter can be viewed, including Mark Olson's wonderful Web site, www.turbinecar.com.

The story of the Vlahas comes from Richard Vlaha's interviews with the author; information about the body shop is from Carry's interview with the author.

Al Bradshaw recalled seeing quite a few . . . comes from Bradshaw's interview with the author.

The Vlahas were impressed . . . is from the Vlahas' interview with the author.

The Ghia Turbines went like that . . . Chrysler Corporation, "History of Chrysler Corporation Gas Turbine Vehicles," report by Engineering Office Technical Information, January 1964, revised August 1966.

Chrysler Corporation, "User/Chrysler Corporation Turbine Car Agreement," contract users had to sign to participate in the Ghia program, n.d., courtesy of Mark Olson.

Details about consumer reactions and Chrysler's observations are from several sources, including Bill Carry.

Initially, Chrysler hoped to run. . . and *Carry also trained others* . . . are from interviews with Bill Carry by the author.

Bradshaw thought it was possible . . . is from an interview with the author, as is *Another time, Bradshaw and a few others* . . .

At the end of 1963 . . . George J. Huebner Jr., "Speech Given by G. J. Huebner, Jr., Dealer Enterprise," speech to unknown audience, Sheraton-Cadillac Hotel, Detroit, MI, December 9, 1963, Huebner Papers, courtesy of the Bentley Historical Library, Ann Arbor, MI.

The SAE papers: George J. Huebner Jr., "The Chrysler Regenerative Turbine-Powered Passenger Car," document 777A; W. I. Chapman, "Chrysler's Gas Turbine Car—Powerplant Design Characteristics," document 777B, courtesy of Tom Golec; and Amedee Roy, Frederick A. Hagen, and Claude Belleau, "Chrysler's Gas Turbine Car: Materials Requirements," document 777C. Papers presented at the

Society of Automotive Engineers, Automotive Engineering Congress and Exposition, Detroit, MI, January 13–17, 1964.

The draft of Huebner's paper with handwritten notes is in the Huebner Papers, courtesy of the Bentley Historical Library, Ann Arbor, MI.

The Jolivette stories all come from Bruce Jolivette, interview and correspondence with the author.

Bud Mann took a Ghia car home . . . Bud Mann, interview and correspondence with the author.

Every Ghia Turbine Car came with a Driver's Guide . . . Chrysler Corporation, "Driver's Guide," glove box document included with Ghia car to instruct users on the vehicle's operations and controls, n.d. There are many places where this can be viewed, including Mark Olson's wonderful Web site, www.turbinecar.com.

The third Ghia car to roll off the Greenfield . . . Details are from Jack Crellin, "Royal Oak Banker Tests Chrysler's Turbine Car," *Detroit News*, December 4, 1963. The follow-up story is found in Burt Stoddard, "How to Win Friends—Test Drive a Turbine," *Detroit News*, December 11, 1963.

Some consumers took advantage . . . is based upon data found in Chrysler Corporation, "History of Chrysler Corporation Gas Turbine Vehicles," report by Engineering Office Technical Information, January 1964, revised August 1966.

Chrysler shot another film . . . refers to *New Power for Progress*, film by Chrysler Corporation Audio-Visual Services (n.d.), courtesy of Bill Carry.

The shopping center campaign was described in Chrysler Corporation Press Information Service, "Chrysler Corporation Turbine Car Exhibition Round-Up Story," press release, n.d.

Mark Olson's family story is detailed in correspondence and interviews with the author.

In May 1964, Chrysler delivered a car to the Emmett family . . . George J. Huebner Jr., remarks to the press on delivery of a turbine car to a Cleveland-area motorist, May 28, 1964, Huebner Papers, courtesy of the Bentley Historical Library, Ann Arbor, MI.

Meanwhile, back in Detroit . . . Chrysler Corporation, "History of Chrysler Corporation Gas Turbine Vehicles," report by Engineering Office Technical Information, January 1964, revised August 1966.

The Chelsea Proving Grounds stories are from Jerry Wenk, interviewed by the author.

The story of Bill Carry's engine failure and the subsequent fix are detailed by Carry in interviews and correspondence with the author.

Dr. Roy's work diagnosing failures is described in interviews with Roy by the author.

Bill Hamer's story is from his interview with the author.

Automakers have always struggled . . . and the details of the engine installations and repairs in the field are from interviews with Bill Carry and Al Bradshaw by the author. Dave Jolivette's stories are from an interview with his son, Bruce Jolivette, by the author.

The history of car 28 is from William J. Carry, "The Chrysler Corporation 50 Car Turbine Program: A Summary of the Service Program 1963–1966," unpublished personal summary, 1966, courtesy of Bill Carry.

Mark Olson's story is related in Olson's interviews with the author.

Arthur Forrester of Oklahoma City had an adventure . . . is from Al Bradshaw, interviewed by the author, as is *Bradshaw found himself arranging* . . .

6. THE GLOBE-TROTTING GHIA

The bulk of the information regarding the Ghia's trip around the globe comes from *Passport to Five Continents*, film by Chrysler Corporation Audio-Visual Services (n.d.), courtesy of Bill Carry.

The president of Mexico, Adolfo Mateos . . . is told in Michael Lamm, "Driving Chrysler's Bronze Blowtorch!" *Special Interest Autos*, January/February 1992, as is the rumor about Chanel No. 5.

7. OTHER GHIAS IN AMERICA

Information about the World's Fair is from Bill Hamer, interviewed by the author.

The story of Huebner's drag race is in Michael Lamm, "Driving Chrysler's Bronze Blowtorch!" *Special Interest Autos*, January/February 1992.

Details about the scale plastic models are from an example owned by the author.

Information regarding the various fuels is found in many places; that it was a problem for the turbine users was discussed in an interview with Al Bradshaw by the author.

Meanwhile, the turbine's fuel economy . . . is from an interview with Bill Carry by the author.

Tom Golec recalled that part . . . is from an interview with the author.

Another Ghia spent its entire life . . . is from an interview with Jerry Wenk by the author.

The turbine's involvement in *The Lively Set* is described in Leon Dixon, "Yesterday's Cars of the Future," *Special Interest Autos*, June 1980. Details about the car on the set are from Al Bradshaw in an interview with the author.

Details about *The Lively Set* are from the movie itself.

8. THE USER EXPERIMENT

The story of the Bicknells comes from an interview with the Bicknells by the author.

The story of the Fenstermachers comes from an interview with the Fenstermachers by the author.

The story of Edwin Fox comes from an interview with Fox by the author.

The story of the Hermans comes from an interview with Shirley Herman by the author.

The routine maintenance details come from an interview with Bill Carry by the author, as does *Several months into the program* . . .

Bill Carry and Al Bradshaw told their respective repair stories to the author in interviews.

During the user program . . . is from Carry, in an interview with the author.

The "magic powder" is described in William J. Carry, "The Chrysler Corporation 50 Car Turbine Program: A Summary of the Service Program 1963–1966," unpublished personal summary, 1966, courtesy of Bill Carry.

Al Bradshaw's "magic powder" story is from an interview with the author.

a small port could be placed . . . William J. Carry, "The Chrysler Corporation 50 Car Turbine Program: A Summary of the Service Program 1963–1966," unpublished personal summary, 1966, courtesy of Bill Carry. Information about the lack of wear comes from several sources, including an interview with Tom Golec by the author.

Information about the deterioration of the transmissions comes from interviews with several people, including Bill Carry.

Roy's presentation is documented in Amedee Roy, Frederick A. Hagen, and Claude Belleau, "Chrysler's Gas Turbine Car: Materials Requirements," paper presented at the Society of Automotive Engineers, Automotive Engineering Congress and Exposition, Detroit, MI, January 13–17, 1964, document 777C.

The last of the test drivers . . . Chrysler Corporation, "History of Chrysler Corporation Gas Turbine Vehicles," report by Engineering Office Technical Information, January 1964, revised August 1966.

"regarded a success in at least . . ." Robert W. Irvin, "Chrysler Turbine's Happy Drivers Near Test's End," *Detroit News*, October 10, 1965.

The last story of the Vlahas comes from an interview with the Vlahas by the author.

Chrysler decided one last tour . . . From an interview with Jerry Gross by the author.

One VIP who got to drive . . . From an interview with Bill Carry by the author.

Tom Golec and a few others . . . From an interview with Tom Golec by the author.

Not all the feedback . . . came from Carry, as did *Users also remarked on . . .*

The Ghia's engine gulped huge volumes . . . Details and figures are from many sources, including George J. Huebner Jr., "The Chrysler Regenerative Turbine-Powered Passenger Car," paper presented at the Society of Automotive Engineers, Automotive Engineering Congress and Exposition, Detroit, MI, January 13–17, 1964, document 777A.

Some people wondered what would happen . . . is from Carry, in an interview with the author.

9. WRAP-UP OF THE USER PROGRAM

Details of the program can be found in many places, including George Huebner, "An Article Written by George Huebner in 1976 to the Wife of the First Turbine Car User," courtesy of www.turbinecar.com and Mark Olson.

And for the sake of accuracy . . . is from Carry and others, in interviews with the author.

On April 12, 1966 . . . Details come from David F. Miller, "Remarks by Dr. David F. Miller, Manager of Marketing and Consumer Research," press release, April 12, 1966, courtesy of the Detroit Historical Museum.

The Detroit News *managed to get a story . . .* Robert W. Irvin, "Turbines Please Test Drivers," *Detroit News*, April 12, 1966.

The following morning's Detroit Free Press . . . Roger A. Simpson, "Gas Turbine Car Is Great, But . . ." *Detroit Free Press*, April 13, 1966. *The press conference was even reported . . .* "Still Undecided on Turbine Car, Chrysler Plans Further Tests," *Globe and Mail* (Toronto), April 13, 1966.

Al Bradshaw summarized his impressions in an interview with the author.

The stories about Chrysler employees taking the cars home are from interviews with those cited, by the author.

The story of Bill Brownlie and the turbine Chargers comes from Leon Dixon, "Yesterday's Cars of the Future," *Special Interest Autos*, June 1980.

Details about the necessity of investment casting come from several sources, including Bill Carry and Lee Pritchard.

The story about the cars being destroyed was reported in "Chrysler Corp. Will Chop," *Detroit Free Press*, April 15, 1966; the reason for the destruction was explained by various sources, including Bill Carry's interview with the author.

As early as 1963, Chrysler had stated . . . is a reference to Al Rothenberg, "America's First Turbine Car," *Look*, June 4, 1963.

Richard Vlaha called up his contact . . . From an interview with the author.

Chrysler put the word out . . . is from several sources, including interviews with Bill Carry and Mark Olson.

The description of Jerry Wenk's last drive comes from his interview with the author.

Press coverage of the vehicles being destroyed can be found at "Chrysler Corp. Will Chop," *Detroit Free Press*, April 15, 1966. Bill Carry and Jerry Gross also addressed this issue in interviews with the author.

Wenk told the story of the car destroyed at the proving grounds in an interview with the author, as he did the tale about the turbines at the bottom of the ocean.

Details of the DHM car are from Detroit Historical Museum, accession document no. 67.142, January 1967.

The receipt for the car also showed . . . refers to a document from the Detroit Historical Museum.

To offset the gloom of seeing . . . is from Al Wrigley, "Gas Turbine Findings Lift Hopes," *Metalworking News*, April 18, 1966, courtesy of the Detroit Public Library, National Automotive History Collection.

Chrysler had also pushed the limits . . . Harry E. Chesebrough, "Statement of Policy—Chrysler Corporation Turbine Car Program," September 1966, courtesy of the Detroit Public Library, Automotive History Collection.

Some people wondered why Chrysler . . . is largely derived from interviews with Bill Carry and others; the fifth-generation information comes from Bill Carry and Lee Pritchard.

In a report written in 1979 . . . Chrysler Corporation, "History of Chrysler Corporation Gas Turbine Vehicles," report by Technical Information Engineering Office, January 1979. The report also details the sixth-generation engine.

Huebner didn't say what the NOx numbers were . . . refers to an event reported in Roger A. Simpson, "Gas Turbine Car Is Great, But . . ." *Detroit Free Press*, April 13, 1966; Al Wrigley, "Gas Turbine Findings Lift Hopes," *Metalworking News*, April 18, 1966, courtesy of the Detroit Public Library, National Automotive History Collection; and "Still Undecided on Turbine Car, Chrysler Plans Further Tests," *Globe and Mail* (Toronto), April 13, 1966.

The story of the turbine-powered Coronet was told to the author by several people, including Lee Pritchard.

Previously, automotive writers had not . . . is from Paul J. C. Friedlander, "Gas Turbines: Present and Future," *New York Times*, April 1973, Huebner Papers, courtesy of the Bentley Historical Library, Ann Arbor, MI.

Dean Musgrave's biographical information comes from his interview with the author.

The story of Chrysler's Imperial comes from an interview with Jerry Wenk by the author.

The Olsons' story comes from their interview with the author.

10. THE BEGINNING OF CHRYSLER'S FINANCIAL DECLINE

Chrysler's financial troubles and its response to them are told very well in Charles K. Hyde, *Riding the Roller Coaster: A History of the Chrysler Corporation* (Detroit: Wayne State University Press, 2003).

11. THE PROBLEM OF SMOG

The story of Donora, Pennsylvania, is from Jeff Gammage, "20 Died. The Government Took Heed: In 1948, a Killer Fog Spurred Air Cleanup," *Philadelphia Enquirer*, October 28, 1998.

Details of the London Smog events can be found in David Urbinato, "London's Historic 'Pea-Soupers,'" *EPA Journal*, Summer 1994. California's smog issues are from Gary Thornton, ed., "Headline History: Los Angeles County 1946 to 1962," *Los Angeles Almanac*, www.laalmanac.com/history/hi01h.htm.

John Gardner's quote headlines the article by John T. Middleton, "The Automobile Internal-Combustion Engine and the Interests of the American People Are on a Collision Course," *Popular Science*, May 1967.

Huebner's thoughts on the sixth-generation turbine are found in John Dinkel, "Turbine Drive," *Road & Track*, December 1972.

"Inventing a rotary engine is the easy part . . ." John T. Middleton, "The Automobile Internal-Combustion Engine and the Interests of the American People Are on a Collision Course," *Popular Science*, May 1967.

Around 1970, the public's awareness . . . Gordon Young and James P. Blair, "Pollution: Threat to Man's Only Home," *National Geographic*, December 1970.

The Clean Air Act is described extensively in Charles K. Hyde, *Riding the Roller Coaster: A History of the Chrysler Corporation* (Detroit: Wayne State University Press, 2003).

Huebner and others from Chrysler spoke . . . George J. Huebner Jr., "Alternative Powerplants," presentation to U.S. Department of Transportation Secretary Volpe and group, February 12, 1970, Huebner Papers, courtesy of the Bentley Historical Library, Ann Arbor, MI; and Richard A. Ryan, "Chrysler Blames U.S. for Gas Turbine Delay," *Detroit News*, March 14, 1973.

"The prospect of a new powerplant . . ." George J. Huebner Jr., statement before the Senate Committee on the Judiciary, Subcommittee on Antitrust and Monopoly, 90th Cong., 1st sess., September 26, 1967, Huebner Papers, courtesy of the Bentley Historical Library, Ann Arbor, MI.

In April 1971, Huebner returned . . . George J. Huebner Jr., "The Automobile—Pollution or Propaganda?" speech to the University of Michigan Graduate School of Business Administration, April 5, 1971, Huebner Papers, courtesy of the Bentley Historical Library, Ann Arbor, MI.

A parade of auto industry representatives . . . Richard A. Ryan, "Chrysler Blames U.S. for Gas Turbine Delay," *Detroit News*, March 14, 1973.

Chrysler would do its best . . . George J. Huebner Jr., "The Automobile—Pollution or Propaganda?" speech to the University of Michigan Graduate School of Business Administration, April 5, 1971, Huebner Papers, courtesy of the Bentley Historical Library, Ann Arbor, MI.

Interestingly, Sam Williams . . . Jan P. Norbye and Jim Dunn, "For the Gas Turbine Car, It's Now or Never," *Popular Science*, September 1973.

The story of OPEC and the rising cost of oil and gasoline is told quite well in Daniel Yergin, *The Prize: The Epic Quest for Oil, Money, and Power* (New York: Simon & Schuster, 1992).

CAFE standards are explained in Charles K. Hyde, *Riding the Roller Coaster: A History of the Chrysler Corporation* (Detroit: Wayne State University Press, 2003).

To people within the industry . . . refers to Richard A. Ryan, "Chrysler Blames U.S. for Gas Turbine Delay," *Detroit News*, March 14, 1973.

Chrysler and the other automakers . . . Richard A. Ryan, "Chrysler Blames U.S. for Gas Turbine Delay," *Detroit News*, March 14, 1973.

George Huebner also spoke to an EPA panel . . . Richard A. Ryan, "Chrysler Blames U.S. for Gas Turbine Delay," *Detroit News*, March 14, 1973.

A writer for Road & Track . . . John Dinkel, "Turbine Drive," *Road & Track*, December 1972.

the EPA asked the auto companies . . . and the following details of the contract work are from interviews with Bud Mann and Lee Pritchard by the author.

Reporters who drove the cars . . . refers to Paul J. C. Friedlander, "Gas Turbines: Present and Future," *New York Times*, April 1973, Huebner Papers, courtesy of the Bentley Historical Library, Ann Arbor, MI.

These measures may have been . . . Jan P. Norbye and Jim Dunn, "For the Gas Turbine Car, It's Now or Never," *Popular Science*, September 1973.

Huebner's retirement is well documented; correspondence referred to is all from the Huebner Papers at the Bentley Historical Library, Ann Arbor.

Lynn Townsend's retirement and accomplishments are detailed in Charles K. Hyde, *Riding the Roller Coaster: A History of the Chrysler Corporation* (Detroit: Wayne State University Press, 2003).

In 1976, Chrysler engineers presented the results . . . Peter R. Angell and Thomas Golec, "Upgrading Automotive Gas Turbine Technology: An Experimental Evaluation of Improvement Concepts," paper presented at the Society of Automotive Engineers Automotive Engineering Congress and Exposition, Detroit, MI, February 23–27, 1976, document 760280, Courtesy of Tom Golec.

Huebner had hinted at this problem . . . Bob Fendell, "Why Chrysler Nixed Turbine Car in '67," *Automotive News*, November 19, 1973.

In 1976, the EPA pondered declaring . . . Joel Horowitz, *Would Declaring Federal Smog Days Reduce Automobile Travel in the Washington, D.C. Area?* (Washington, DC: Environmental Protection Agency, 1976).

Chrysler continued working on the turbines . . . Chrysler Corporation, "History of Chrysler Corporation Gas Turbine Vehicles," report by Technical Information Engineering Office, January 1979.

Information regarding the opinions of Dr. Roy comes from his interviews with the author.

This time it was NASA . . . is from interviews with Bud Mann and Lee Pritchard.

Each of the Big Three approached . . . and details of Chrysler's proposal are from the bid package itself.

The Department of Energy summary and charts: U.S. Department of Energy, "The Gas Turbine: A Future Automotive Engine," trifold booklet, n.d., contains detached sheets describing "Ceramic Applications in Turbine Engines (CATE) Project," "Advanced Gas Turbine (AGT) Powertrain System Development Project," and "AGT 101: Advanced Gas Turbine Powertrain System Development Project," courtesy of Tom Golec.

Bud Mann was given the job of "redistributing" . . . From an interview with Mann by the author.

"We had the tooling" . . . can be found in Michael Lamm, "Driving Chrysler's Bronze Blowtorch!" *Special Interest Autos*, January/February 1992.

Information concerning the cost of building a plant specifically for turbine production comes from interviews with Bill Carry and Lee Pritchard by the author.

Chrysler's best year . . . Financial figures are in Charles K. Hyde, *Riding the Roller Coaster: A History of the Chrysler Corporation* (Detroit: Wayne State University Press, 2003).

12. CHRYSLER'S FINANCIAL TROUBLES

Chrysler's financial troubles and the arrival of Lee Iacocca are documented in Charles K. Hyde, *Riding the Roller Coaster: A History of the Chrysler Corporation* (Detroit: Wayne State University Press, 2003).

13. OTHER MANUFACTURERS AND THE TURBINE

Golec's story about John DeLorean is from an interview with Tom Golec by the author.

The story of Williams placing turbines in AMC Hornets was reported in Jan P. Norbye, "Tiny 80-HP Gas Turbine to Power Compact Car," *Popular Science*, March 1971.

General Motors began . . . "Those Tantalizing Turbines," *Ward's Automotive World*, November 1973.

Ford, likewise, spent much time . . . and the information on GM's turbines is from "Those Tantalizing Turbines," *Ward's Automotive World*, November 1973.

"The Battle to Power the Car of Tomorrow," *Sunday Times* (London), May 27, 1973, provided the information about the visit with Huebner, Leyland's turbine research, and Savonuzzi.

Information about Marine Turbine Technology comes from their Web site, www .marineturbine.com; information about Jay Leno's motorcycle is from www .jaylenosgarage.com.

14. THE DEATH OF THE TURBINE PROGRAM

In all, Chrysler built seventy-seven . . . Michael Lamm, "Driving Chrysler's Bronze Blowtorch!" *Special Interest Autos,* January/February 1992.

In 1976, George Huebner wrote . . . "George Huebner, An Article Written by George Huebner in 1976 to the Wife of the First Turbine Car User," courtesy of www .turbinecar.com and Mark Olson.

That *it was fictional* is from an interview with the Vlahas.

In September 1968, Popular Science . . . Devon Francis, "Is There a Steam Car in Your Future?" *Popular Science,* September 1968.

Al Bradshaw pointed out that something . . . is from an interview with Al Bradshaw by the author.

The story of the turbines at the Indianapolis 500 is mentioned in Michael Lamm, "Driving Chrysler's Bronze Blowtorch!" *Special Interest Autos,* January/February 1992.

Another turbine-powered car . . . "The Battle to Power the Car of Tomorrow," *Sunday Times* (London), May 27, 1973.

Discussion concerning the price of gasoline comes from Daniel Yergin, *The Prize: The Epic Quest for Oil, Money, and Power* (New York: Simon & Schuster, 1992).

"The car of the future" . . . John Gunnell, "Carrozzeria Ghia/Chrysler Turbine," *Car Exchange,* March 1980.

a "dismal and costly failure" . . . Bob Pool, "Drivers Find Outlet for Grief Over EV1s," *Los Angeles Times,* July 25, 2003.

15. THE SURVIVORS

Many of the observations about the surviving cars are simply those of the author. Bill Carry provided much of the information in interviews with the author; details of the Kleptz car are from interviews with Frank Kleptz and Jay Leno.

Around 1980, Bradshaw heard that the museum . . . is from an interview with Al Bradshaw by the author.

16: GOING FOR A DRIVE IN JAY LENO'S GHIA

The story of Jay Leno's turbine car is from personal experiences and interviews by the author. The story is partially told in Neal Rubin, "Jay Leno Gets Rare Chrysler, Author Gets Plug for Book," *Detroit News*, August 3, 2009, www.detnews.com/article/20090803/OPINION03/908030315/Jay-Leno-gets-rare-Chrysler--author-gets-plug-for-book.

"A lot of engineers learned a lot" . . . is from an interview with Bud Mann by the author.

Bibliography

A&E Television Networks. *Automobiles: The Chrysler Turbine.* 1996.

Akron Beacon Journal. "Jet Engine Pioneer Inducted to Akron, Ohio, Inventor's Hall of Fame." May 7, 2003.

Al Bawaba (Middle East) Ltd. "United States: Inventor of the Small Gas Turbine Engine Passes Away." 2009.

Albuquerque Tribune. "Almanac." October 29, 2001.

Allen Gottschalk, Mark, and Ann Allen Gottschalk. "Engineers Drive a Light Aircraft Revival." *Design News,* September 7, 1998.

Angell, Peter R., and Thomas Golec. "Upgrading Automotive Gas Turbine Technology: An Experimental Evaluation of Improvement Concepts." Paper presented at the Society of Automotive Engineers Automotive Engineering Congress and Exposition, Detroit, MI, February 23–27, 1976. Document 760280. Courtesy of Tom Golec.

Atlantic Monthly. "Freedom of the Skies." June 2001.

Automotive News. "Sam Williams." July 6, 2009.

Autoproducts. "Turbines: The Beat Goes On." May 1974.

Borgeson, Griffith. "Will Gas Turbines Propel the Car of Tomorrow?" *Motor Trend,* May 1950.

Brown, Allan S. "Very Light and Fast." *Mechanical Engineering–CIME,* January 2007.

Bunnell, John F. "A Letter from Chrysler Corporation." October 1963. Reprinted at www.vlaha.com/turbine/.

Carry, William J. "The Chrysler Corporation 50 Car Turbine Program: A Summary of the Service Program 1963–1966." Unpublished personal summary, 1966. Courtesy of Bill Carry.

Cars & Parts. "Domino's Pizza Cars." May 1988.

Chapman, W. I. "Chrysler's Gas Turbine Car—Powerplant Design Characteristics." Paper presented at the Society of Automotive Engineers Automotive Engineering Congress and Exposition, Detroit, MI, January 13–17, 1964. Document 777B. Courtesy of Tom Golec.

Chesebrough, Harry E. "Statement of Policy—Chrysler Corporation Turbine Car Program." September 1966. Courtesy of the Detroit Public Library, Automotive History Collection.

Chrysler Corporation. "America's First Gas Turbine Cars." Four-page pamphlet showing images and details of the Turbo Dart and Turbo Fury, n.d. Courtesy of the Detroit Public Library, Automotive History Collection.

———. "Chrysler Research Turbine Cross Country Log." Plastic comb-bound, pocket-sized booklet, March 26, 1956. Courtesy of Tom Golec.

———. "The Chrysler Corporation Turbine Car." Report by Engineering Staff—Technical Information Services, April 5, 1963.

———. "Driver's Guide." Glove box document included with Ghia car to instruct users on the vehicle's operations and controls, n.d. There are many places where this can be viewed, including Mark Olson's wonderful Web site, www.turbinecar.com.

———. "Gas Turbine Vehicles." Report by Engineering Division Technical Information Services, July 16, 1962.

———. "History of Chrysler Corporation Gas Turbine Vehicles." Report by Engineering Office Technical Information, January 1964, revised August 1966.

———. "History of Chrysler Corporation Gas Turbine Vehicles." Report by Technical Information Engineering Office, January 1979.

———. "Progress in Science." Trifold document describing the early history of the turbine program, n.d.

———. "Training (Chrysler Gas Turbine Training Guide)." Unpublished training document for technicians who would work on cars in the Ghia program, n.d. Courtesy of Bill Carry.

———. "Turbine Car Information." Four-page pamphlet showing images and details of the Ghia Turbine car, n.d. Courtesy of the Detroit Public Library, Automotive History Collection.

———. "User/Chrysler Corporation Turbine Car Agreement." Contract users had to sign to participate in the Ghia program, n.d. Courtesy of Mark Olson.

Chrysler Corporation Audio-Visual Services. *Chrysler Corporation Turbine Car.*

Film, n.d. Courtesy of Bill Carry.

———. *New Power for Progress*. Film, n.d. Courtesy of Bill Carry.

———. *Passport to Five Continents*. Film, n.d. Courtesy of Bill Carry.

———. *Riding the Whirlwind*. Film, n.d. Courtesy of Bill Carry.

———. *Taming the Tornado*. Film, n.d. Courtesy of Bill Carry.

Chrysler Corporation Press Information Service. "Biographical Data on George J. Huebner, Jr." Press release, n.d.

———. "CHICAGO, October 29—A 25-year-old computer systems engineer . . ." Press release, October 29, 1963.

———. "Chrysler Corporation Turbine Car Exhibition Round-Up Story." Press release, n.d.

———. "Chrysler Gas Turbine Combines Economy and Performance." Press release, March 25, 1954. Courtesy of Tom Golec.

———. "Compact Chrysler Gas Turbine in Plymouth Car." Press release, March 25, 1954.

———. "Family passenger cars powered by the gas turbine engine moved a step closer to reality today . . ." Press release, December 27, 1961.

———. "George J. Huebner, Jr. Executive Engineer—Research Engineering Division—Chrysler Corporation." Press release, n.d.

———. "NEWEST MODEL of Chrysler Corporation's gas turbine engine . . ." Press release accompanying press photo of the 1962 Plymouth Turbo Fury, n.d. Courtesy of Tom Golec.

———. "Strive to Perfect Turbine Engine." Press release, n.d. Courtesy of the Detroit Public Library, Automotive History Collection.

Chrysler Corporation Public Relations. "The Turbine automobile engine has the potential to become the dominant vehicle power source . . ." Press release, May 21, 1973. Courtesy of the Detroit Public Library, National Automotive History Collection.

Crellin, Jack. "Chrysler's Turbine-Powered Cars Have Smooth Unveiling." *Detroit News*, May 14, 1963.

———. "Chrysler Turbine Car Stalls, Causes Manhattan Traffic Jam." *Detroit News*, May 15, 1963.

———. "Royal Oak Banker Tests Chrysler's Turbine Car." *Detroit News*, December 4, 1963.

DeMoss, Jeff. "Michigan-Based Jet Engine Firm to Lay Off 3 Percent of Ogden, Utah, Workforce." *Standard-Examiner*, November 11, 2003.

Design News. "Fewest Parts = Lightest Turbofan." September 4, 2000.

Detroit Free Press. "Chrysler Corp. Will Chop." April 15, 1966.

———. "Turbine Cars Due in 1963." December 28, 1961.

Detroit Historical Museum. Accession document no. 67.142. January 1967.

Courtesy of the Detroit Historical Museum.

Detroit News. "New Engines in Action." March 26, 1954.

———. "Turbine Test Ride Offered by Chrysler." May 6, 1963.

Dinkel, John. "Turbine Drive." *Road & Track*, December 1972.

Dixon, Leon. "Yesterday's Cars of the Future." *Special Interest Autos*, June 1980.

Donovan, Leo. "Turbine Car Heads West." *Detroit Free Press*, March 27, 1956.

———. "Turbine Test Stepped Up." *Detroit Free Press*, February 13, 1957.

Dunn, Jim. "Will You Commute in GM's New Turbine-Powered Bus?" *Popular Science*, July 1969.

Energy Information Administration. *Annual Energy Review 2003.* Washington, DC: U.S. Department of Energy, 2004.

Farmer, Robert C. "The Automotive Gas Turbine: How Far Down the Road?" *Gas Turbine International*, July–August 1971.

Fendell, Bob. "Why Chrysler Nixed Turbine Car in '67." *Automotive News*, November 19, 1973.

Flint, Jerry. "Corporate Jets for the Masses." *Forbes*, July 6, 1992.

Francis, Devon. "Is There a Steam Car in Your Future?" *Popular Science*, September 1968.

Friedlander, Paul J. C. "Gas Turbines: Present and Future." *New York Times*, April 1973. Huebner Papers, courtesy of the Bentley Historical Library, Ann Arbor, MI.

Gammage, Jeff. "20 Died. The Government Took Heed: In 1948, a Killer Fog Spurred Air Cleanup." *Philadelphia Enquirer*, October 28, 1998.

Globe and Mail (Toronto). "Still Undecided on Turbine Car, Chrysler Plans Further Tests." April 13, 1966.

Gunnell, John. "Carrozzeria Ghia/Chrysler Turbine." *Car Exchange*, March 1980.

Henny, Willi, and Giovanni F. Savonuzzi. "Outer Shroud for Gas Turbine Engine." U.S. Patent 3,078,071, filed September 28, 1960, and issued February 19, 1963.

Horowitz, Joel. *Would Declaring Federal Smog Days Reduce Automobile Travel in the Washington, D.C. Area?* Washington, DC: Environmental Protection Agency, 1976.

Huebner, George J., Jr. "Alternative Powerplants." Presentation to U.S. Department of Transportation Secretary John A. Volpe and group, February 12, 1970. Huebner Papers, courtesy of the Bentley Historical Library, Ann Arbor, MI.

———. "An Article Written by George Huebner in 1976 to the Wife of the First Turbine Car User." Courtesy of www.turbinecar.com and Mark Olson.

———. "The Automobile—Pollution or Propaganda?" Speech to the University of Michigan Graduate School of Business Administration, April 5, 1971. Huebner Papers, courtesy of the Bentley Historical Library, Ann Arbor, MI.

———. "The Automotive Gas Turbine—Today and Tomorrow." *SAE Transactions*

65 (1957).

———. "The Chrysler Regenerative Turbine-Powered Passenger Car." Paper presented at the Society of Automotive Engineers, Automotive Engineering Congress and Exposition, Detroit, MI, January 13–17, 1964. Document 777A.

———. "A First in Automotive History: We Drove a Turbine Car Coast-to-Coast." *Popular Mechanics*, June 1956.

———. "50-Car Turbine Program—Technical Results." Remarks to the press, Detroit, April 12, 1966.

———. "Gas Turbine Paper Presented by George J. Huebner, Jr. at the S.A.E. Annual Meeting Detroit, Michigan, January 13, 1964." Draft copy with hand-written notes of "The Chrysler Regenerative Turbine-Powered Passenger Car" (see above). Huebner Papers, courtesy of the Bentley Historical Library, Ann Arbor, MI.

———. "Rehearsal for Space." *Boys' Life*, September 1959.

———. Remarks to members of the California Motor Vehicle Pollution Control Board, Chrysler Proving Grounds, Chelsea, MI, August 10, 1965. Huebner Papers, courtesy of the Bentley Historical Library, Ann Arbor, MI.

———. Remarks to the press on delivery of a turbine car to a Cleveland-area motorist, May 28, 1964. Huebner Papers, courtesy of the Bentley Historical Library, Ann Arbor, MI.

———. "Speech Given by G. J. Huebner, Jr., Dealer Enterprise." Speech to unknown audience, Sheraton-Cadillac Hotel, Detroit, MI, December 9, 1963. Huebner Papers, courtesy of the Bentley Historical Library, Ann Arbor, MI.

———. Statement before the Senate Committee on the Judiciary, Subcommittee on Antitrust and Monopoly. 90th Cong., 1st sess., September 26, 1967. Hueb-ner Papers, courtesy of the Bentley Historical Library, Ann Arbor, MI.

Huebner, George J., Jr., Samuel B. Williams, and David Borden. "Arrangement of Component Elements of a Gas Turbine Powerplant." U.S. Patent 2,795,928, filed October 29, 1953, and issued June 18, 1957.

Hyde, Charles K. *Riding the Roller Coaster: A History of the Chrysler Corporation* Detroit: Wayne State University Press, 2003.

Industry Week. "Other Engines Favored, but Turbines Have Not Been Forgotten." January 8, 1973.

Iron Age. "The Detroit Engine Debate Isn't Small Talk to Suppliers." August 5, 1974.

Irvin, Robert W. "Chrysler Reports Break in Auto Turbine Development." *Detroit News*, May 5, 1972.

———. "Chrysler Turbine's Happy Drivers Near Test's End." *Detroit News*, October 10, 1965.

———. "Turbines Please Test Drivers." *Detroit News*, April 12, 1966.

Lamm, Michael. "Driving Chrysler's Bronze Blowtorch!" *Special Interest Autos*, January/February 1992.

Landers, Ann, letter to George Huebner Jr., October 27, 1975. Huebner Papers, courtesy of the Bentley Historical Library, Ann Arbor, MI.

Lawlor, John. "Testing the Turbine." In *Petersen's Complete Book of Plymouth, Dodge, Chrysler*. Los Angeles: Petersen, 1973, 86–91.

Mayfield, Dan. "From Cruise Missiles to Commuter Jet, Eclipse Partner Enjoys the Challenges." *Albuquerque Tribune*, July 10, 2000.

———. "Getting Off the Ground." *Albuquerque Tribune*, July 10, 2000.

McCahill, Tom. "Chrysler's Gas Turbine Car." *Mechanix Illustrated*, September 1963.

McNeely, Mark. "Cast Components Increasing in Industrial Gas Turbines." *Diesel & Gas Turbine Worldwide*, June 2004.

Melley, Brian. "GM Pulling Plug on Electric Cars." Associated Press, April 8, 2003.

Metalworking News. "Chrysler Will Test Gas Turbine Engine, Reportedly 138 HP with Reduced Whine." April 25, 1966. Courtesy of the Detroit Public Library, National Automotive History Collection.

Middleton, John T. "The Automobile Internal-Combustion Engine and the Interests of the American People Are on a Collision Course." *Popular Science*, May 1967.

Miller, David F. "Remarks by Dr. David F. Miller, Manager of Marketing and Consumer Research." Press release, April 12, 1966. Courtesy of the Detroit Historical Museum.

National Academy of Engineering. "Candidate: George J. Huebner, Jr." Nomination form, n.d., ca. 1973. Huebner Papers. Courtesy of the Bentley Historical Library, Ann Arbor, MI.

Norbye, Jan P. *The Gas Turbine Engine*. Radnor, PA: Chilton Book Company, 1975.

———. "Tiny 80-HP Gas Turbine to Power Compact Car." *Popular Science*. March 1971.

Norbye, Jan P., and Jim Dunn. "For the Gas Turbine Car, It's Now or Never." *Popular Science*, September 1973.

———. "GM Takes the Wraps off Its STEAM CARS . . ." *Popular Science*, July 1969.

O'Keefe, Brian, letter to George Huebner Jr., September 30, 1975. Huebner Papers, courtesy of the Bentley Historical Library, Ann Arbor, MI.

Olmstead, Fred. "Public Sees Turbine Cars." *Detroit Free Press*, February 2, 1962.

———. "Third Chrysler Turbine Due for Auto Test Soon." *Detroit Free Press*, May 11, 1960.

Organization of the Petroleum Exporting Countries. "About Us." www.opec.org/opec_web/en/17.htm.

Pontiac Press. "Jet Auto Age Fired by Engine." December 27, 1961. Courtesy of the

Detroit Public Library—Automotive History Collection.

Pool, Bob. "Drivers Find Outlet for Grief Over EV1s." *Los Angeles Times*, July 25, 2003.

Rothenberg, Al. "America's First Turbine Car." *Look*, June 4, 1963.

Roy, Amedee, Frederick A. Hagen, and Claude Belleau. "Chrysler's Gas Turbine Car: Materials Requirements." Paper presented at the Society of Automotive Engineers, Automotive Engineering Congress and Exposition, Detroit, MI, January 13–17, 1964. Document 777C.

Roy, Amedee, Frederick A. Hagen, and John M. Corwin. "Development of New Iron-Based Superalloys for 1500 Degrees Fahrenheit Applications." Paper presented at the annual meeting of the Metallurgical Society of the American Institute of Mining, Metallurgical, and Petroleum Engineers, February 15, 1965.

Rubin, Neal. "Jay Leno Gets Rare Chrysler, Author Gets Plug for Book." *Detroit News*, August 3, 2009, www.detnews.com/article/20090803/OPINION03/908030315/Jay-Leno-gets-rare-Chrysler--author-gets-plug-for-book.

Ryan, Richard A. "Chrysler Blames U.S. for Gas Turbine Delay." *Detroit News*, March 14, 1973.

Savonuzzi, Giovanni F. "Gas Turbine Engine Housing." U.S. Patent 3,167,914, filed July 3, 1961, and issued February 2, 1965.

Schonfeld, Erick. "The Little (Jet) Engine That Could." *Fortune*, July 24, 2000.

Simpson, Roger A. "Gas Turbine Car Is Great, But . . ." *Detroit Free Press*, April 13, 1966.

Staley, Allen C., and Samuel B. Williams. "Gas Turbine Power Plant Having Coaxially Arranged Combustors and Regenerator." U.S. Patent 2,631,430," filed December 12, 1946, and issued March 17, 1953.

Stoddard, Burt. "How to Win Friends—Test Drive a Turbine." *Detroit News*, December 11, 1963.

Stone, Brad. "A Taxicab at 30,000 Feet: Aviation Mavericks Are Trying to Mint a New Class of Airplane—and Air Travel." *Newsweek*, October 6, 2003.

Sunday Times (London). "The Battle to Power the Car of Tomorrow." May 27, 1973.

Swett, Clint. "If Idea Flies, Jet Travel Could Enter New Era." *Sacramento Bee*, July 14, 2002.

Thornton, Gary, ed. "Headline History: Los Angeles County 1946 to 1962." *Los Angeles Almanac*, www.laalmanac.com/history/hi01h.htm.

Time. "The Big Test." May 10, 1963.

———. "Lynn Townsend and Chrysler's Comeback." December 28, 1962.

Urbinato, David. "London's Historic 'Pea-Soupers.'" *EPA Journal*, Summer 1994.

U.S. Department of Energy. "The Gas Turbine: A Future Automotive Engine."

Trifold booklet, n.d. Contains detached sheets describing "Ceramic Applications in Turbine Engines (CATE) Project," "Advanced Gas Turbine (AGT) Powertrain System Development Project," and "AGT 101: Advanced Gas Turbine Powertrain System Development Project." Courtesy of Tom Golec.

U.S. Environmental Protection Agency. *Smog, Health, and You.* Washington, DC: Environmental Protection Agency, 1977. Courtesy of the Library of Michigan, Lansing.

Vance, Bill. "When Turbines Came to Indy." *Times Colonist,* November 12, 2004.

Ward's Automotive World. "Those Tantalizing Turbines." November 1973.

Watts, Ralph R. "Auto Turbines Display Worth." *Detroit News,* June 17, 1954.

———. "Chrysler Stresses Turbine Research." *Detroit News,* February 13, 1957.

———. "19 Miles a Gallon Reported by Chrysler in Gas Turbine." *Detroit News,* January 11, 1959.

———. "Public Test of Turbine Car Starts." *Detroit News,* October 29, 1963.

———. "Turbine Car Stirs Public." *Detroit News,* February 2, 1962.

———. "Turbine Car to Get Test of 3,000 Mi." *Detroit News,* March 23, 1956.

———. "Turbine Test Ends Rumors." *Detroit News,* December 27, 1961.

Wegmann, Earl F. "Chrysler's Diplomat in Coveralls." *Michigan Alumnus,* February 15, 1958.

Williams, Sam B. Written testimony before the House Committee on Transportation and Infrastructure, Subcommittee on Aviation. 106th Cong., 2nd sess., May 16, 2000.

Wrigley, Al. "Gas Turbine Findings Lift Hopes." *Metalworking News,* April 18, 1966. Courtesy of the Detroit Public Library, National Automotive History Collection.

Yergin, Daniel. *The Prize: The Epic Quest for Oil, Money, and Power.* New York: Simon & Schuster, 1992.

Young, Gordon, and James P. Blair. "Pollution: Threat to Man's Only Home." *National Geographic,* December 1970.

The author also conducted numerous interviews; information from those interviews is so noted within the text. Among those interviewed were Camilla Bicknell, Al Bradshaw, Charlie Bicknell, Stuart Bicknell, Bill Carry, Ray and Doris Fenstermacher, Edwin Fox, Tom Golec, Jerry Gross, Bill Hamer, Shirley Herman, Bruce Jolivette, Frank Kleptz, Jay Leno, Bonnie Lippman, Bud Mann, Dean Musgrave, Mark Olson, Amedee Roy, Dick, Patricia, and Rick Vlaha, and Jerry Wenk.

Index